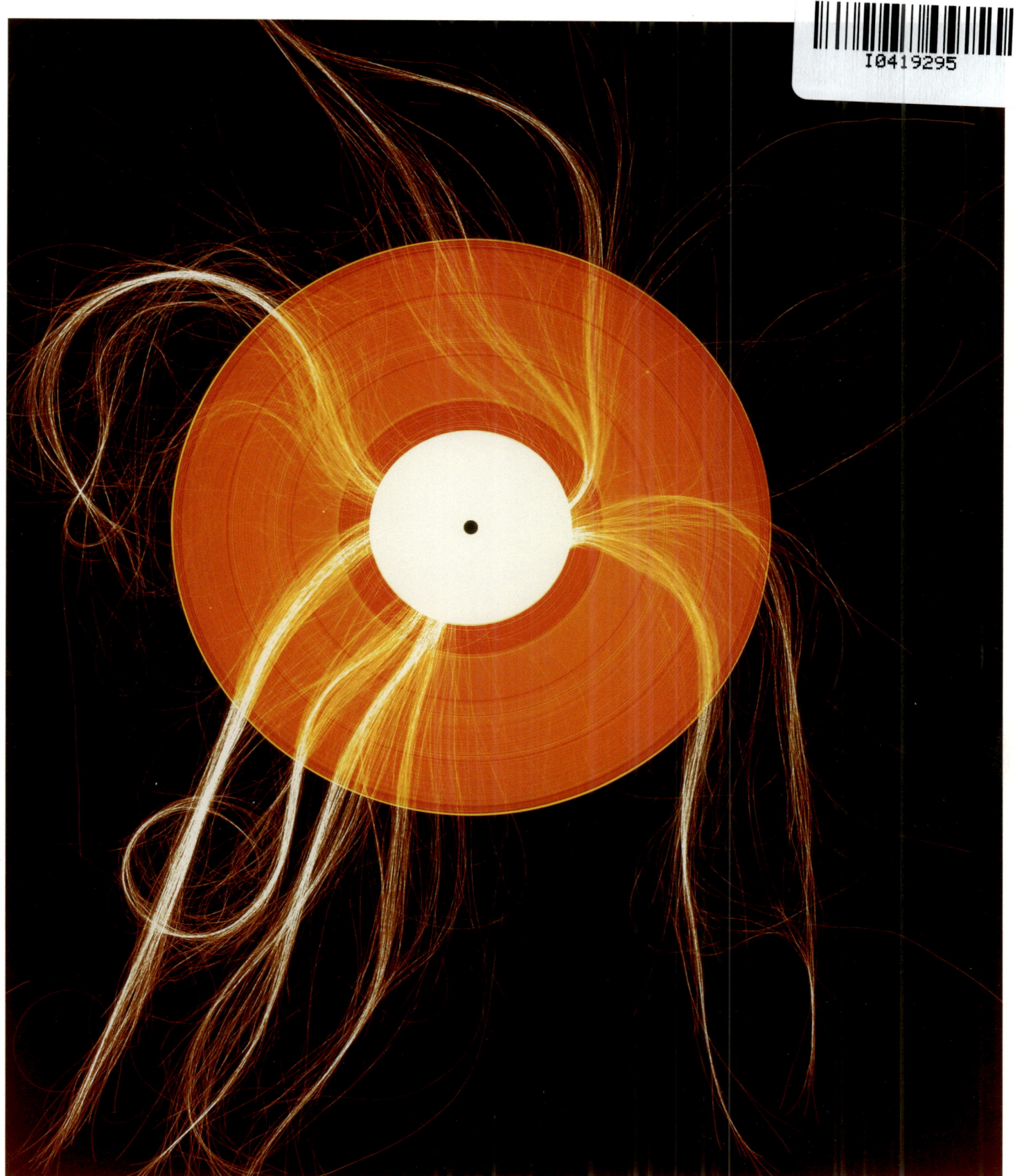

Christian Marclay, *untitled*, 2004; photogram on c-print paper, mounted on cintra board; 19 3/4 × 23 3/4 in. © Christian Marclay

CHRISTIAN MARCLAY

PAULA COOPER GALLERY

534 W 21ST STREET NEW YORK   212 255 1105   WWW.PAULACOOPERGALLERY.COM

PHOTOGRAPHY

FROM CHICAGO

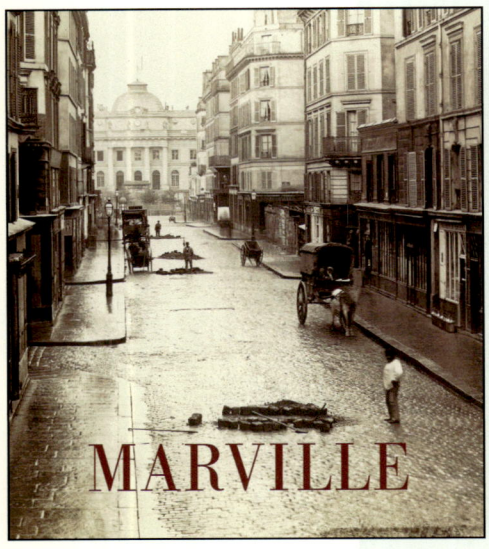

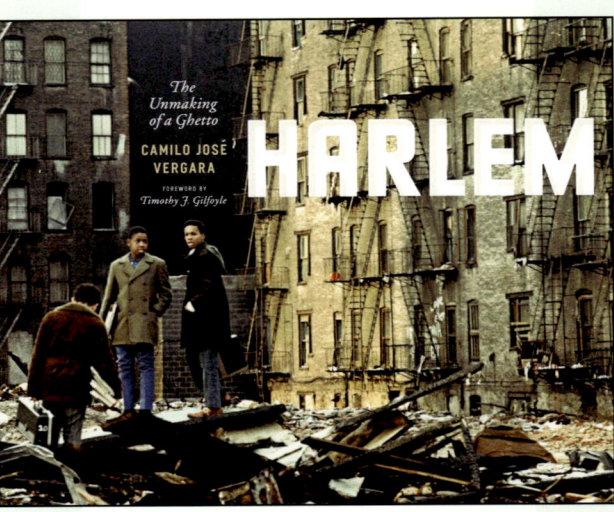

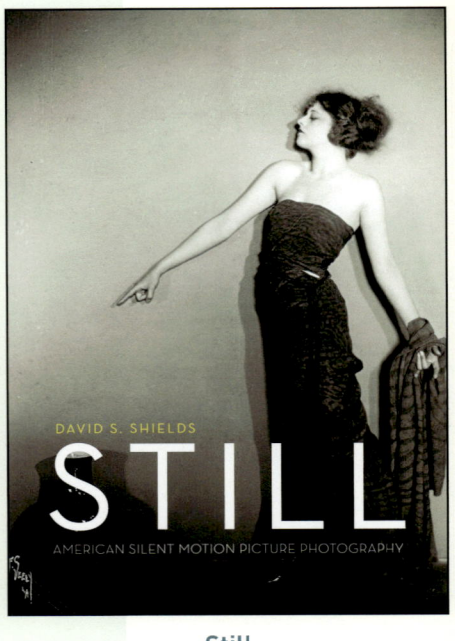

Charles Marville
Photographer of Paris
Sarah Kennel

This beautiful volume begins with the city scenes and architectural studies Charles Marville made throughout France and Germany in the 1850s and explores his landscapes and portraits, as well as his most famous photographs of Paris.

Copublished with the National Gallery of Art, Washington D.C.
256 P., 110 TRITONES, 20 DUOTONES
CLOTH $60.00

Harlem
The Unmaking of a Ghetto
Camilo José Vergara
With a Foreword by Timothy J. Gilfoyle

"Camilo Jose Vergara has watched—and photographed—Harlem as it fell apart and then rose back up as something else. He chronicles the passage from poverty to selective luxury, from segregation to selective integration, from street life to tourism. He asks the unanswerable question: which is preferable?"—Luc Sante, author of *Low Life*

312 P., 268 COLOR PLATES
CLOTH $55.00

Still
American Silent Motion Picture Photography
David S. Shields

"*Still* is not just a labor of love or the fruit of a personal passion. It's not just an astonishing album of 'beauty' and beauty. In the process it amounts to one of the most radical reappreciations of the origins of film we have ever had."
—David Thomson, author of *The New Biographical Dictionary of Film*

416 P., 164 HALFTONES
CLOTH $50.00

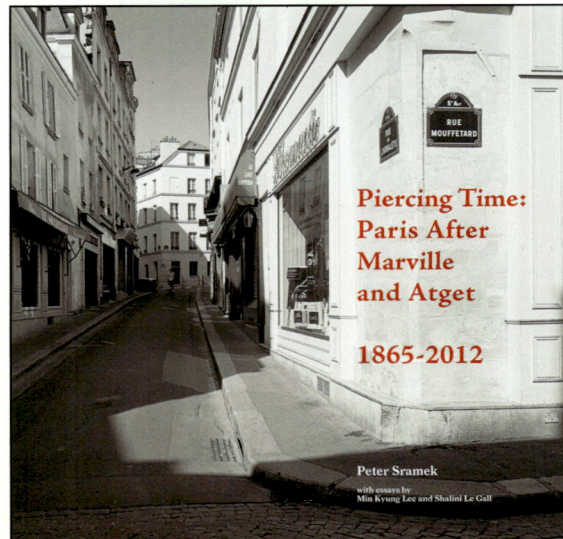

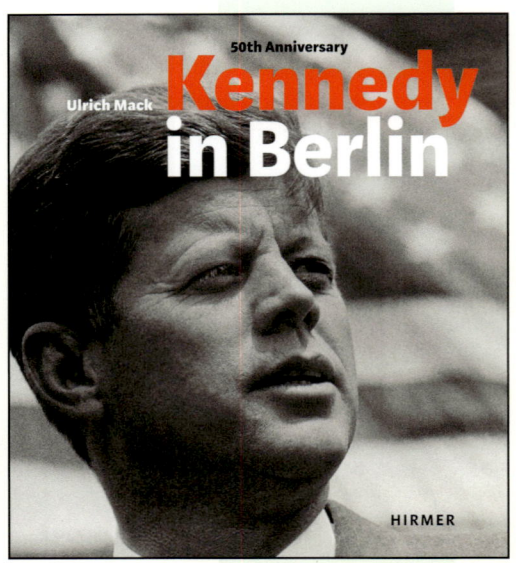

From INTELLECT BOOKS

Piercing Time
Paris after Marville and Atget 1865–2012
Peter Sramek
With Essays by Min Kyung Lee and Shalini Le Gall

Piercing Time juxtaposes contemporary "rephotographs" taken by the author with images of nineteenth-century Paris taken by Charles Marville and corresponding photographs by Eugène Atget taken in the early twentieth century.

576 P., 300 COLOR PLATES, 210 HALFTONES, 22 MAPS
PAPER $60.00

From HIRMER PUBLISHERS

HIRMER

Kennedy in Berlin
Photographs by Ulrich Mack
Edited by Hans-Michael Koetzle

This book presents more than one hundred never-before-published photographs of Kennedy's historic visit to Berlin.

144 P., 120 HALFTONES
CLOTH $24.9

The University of Chicago Press • www.press.uchicago.edu

Art | Basel
Miami Beach | Dec | 5–8 | 2013

Vernissage | Wednesday, December 4, 2013 | By invitation only
artbasel.com | facebook.com/artbasel | twitter.com/artbasel

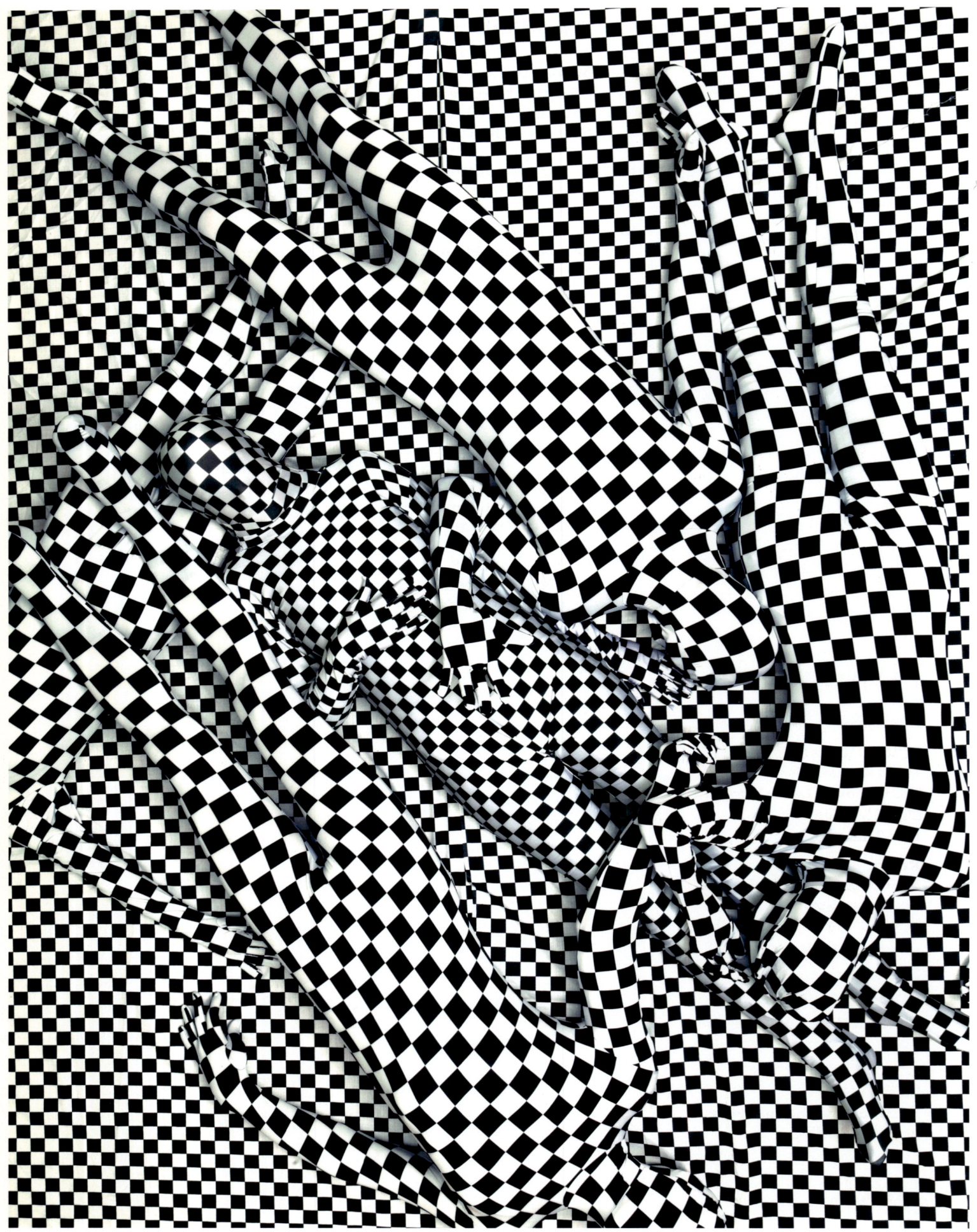

Fall 2013

Front cover and opposite:
Olaf Breuning,
Pattern People, 2013
(see Ceschel, page 100)
Courtesy the artist and
Metro Pictures, New York

Editor
Michael Famighetti
Senior Editor
Diana C. Stoll
Associate Editor
Brian Sholis
Assistant Editor
Paula Kupfer
Production Manager
Matthew Harvey
Work Scholars
Martina Caruso, Luke Chase, Elli Trier

Art Direction, Design & Typefaces
A2/SW/HK, London

Editor-at-Large
Melissa Harris

Publisher
Dana Triwush
magazine@aperture.org
Advertising Representative
Bill Besch
631-665-0467
bbesch1@verizon.net
**Executive Director,
Aperture Foundation**
Chris Boot

Minor White, Editor (1952–1971)

Michael E. Hoffman, Publisher and Executive Director
(1964–2001)

Aperture, a not-for-profit foundation, connects the photo community and its audiences with the most inspiring work, the sharpest ideas, and with each other —in print, in person, and online.

Help maintain Aperture's publishing, education, and community activities by becoming one of our Philanthropists ($5,000), Benefactors ($2,500), Patrons ($1,000), or New Collectors ($500). Donors are acknowledged in *Aperture* magazine and invited to private salon events with artists, receive complimentary publications and special discounts, and enjoy many other benefits. Aperture Foundation welcomes support at all levels of giving, and all gifts are tax-deductible to the fullest extent of the law. For more information about supporting Aperture please visit aperture.org/donate or contact the Development Department at 212-946-7108.

Aperture (ISSN 0003-6420) is published quarterly, in spring, summer, fall, and winter, at 547 West 27th Street, 4th Floor, New York, N.Y. 10001. In the United States, a one-year subscription (four issues) is $75; a two-year subscription (eight issues) is $124. In Canada, a one-year subscription is $95. All other international subscriptions are $105 per year. Visit aperture.org to subscribe. Single copies may be purchased at $24.95 for most issues. Periodicals postage paid at New York and additional offices. Postmaster: Send address changes to *Aperture*, P.O. Box 3000, Denville, N.J. 07834. Address queries regarding subscriptions, renewals, or gifts to: *Aperture* Subscription Service, 866-457-4603 (U.S. and Canada) or e-mail custsvc_aperture@fulcoinc.com.

Newsstand distribution in the U.S. is handled by Curtis Circulation Company, 201-634-7400. For international distribution, contact Central Books, centralbooks.com.

Library of Congress Catalog Card No: 58-30845.

Printed in Germany by optimal media.

aperture.org

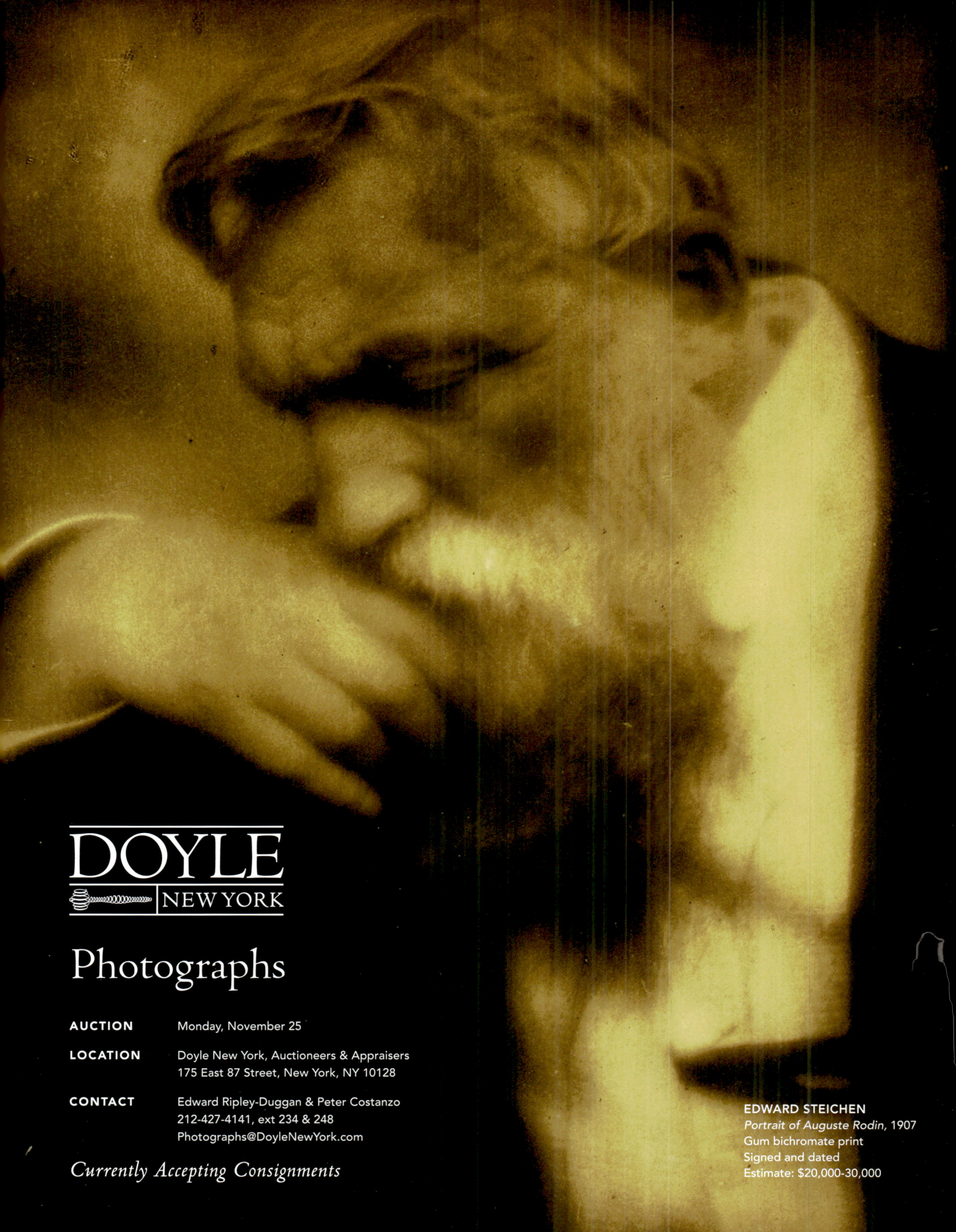

DOYLE
NEW YORK

Photographs

AUCTION Monday, November 25

LOCATION Doyle New York, Auctioneers & Appraisers
175 East 87 Street, New York, NY 10128

CONTACT Edward Ripley-Duggan & Peter Costanzo
212-427-4141, ext 234 & 248
Photographs@DoyleNewYork.com

Currently Accepting Consignments

EDWARD STEICHEN
Portrait of Auguste Rodin, 1907
Gum bichromate print
Signed and dated
Estimate: $20,000-30,000

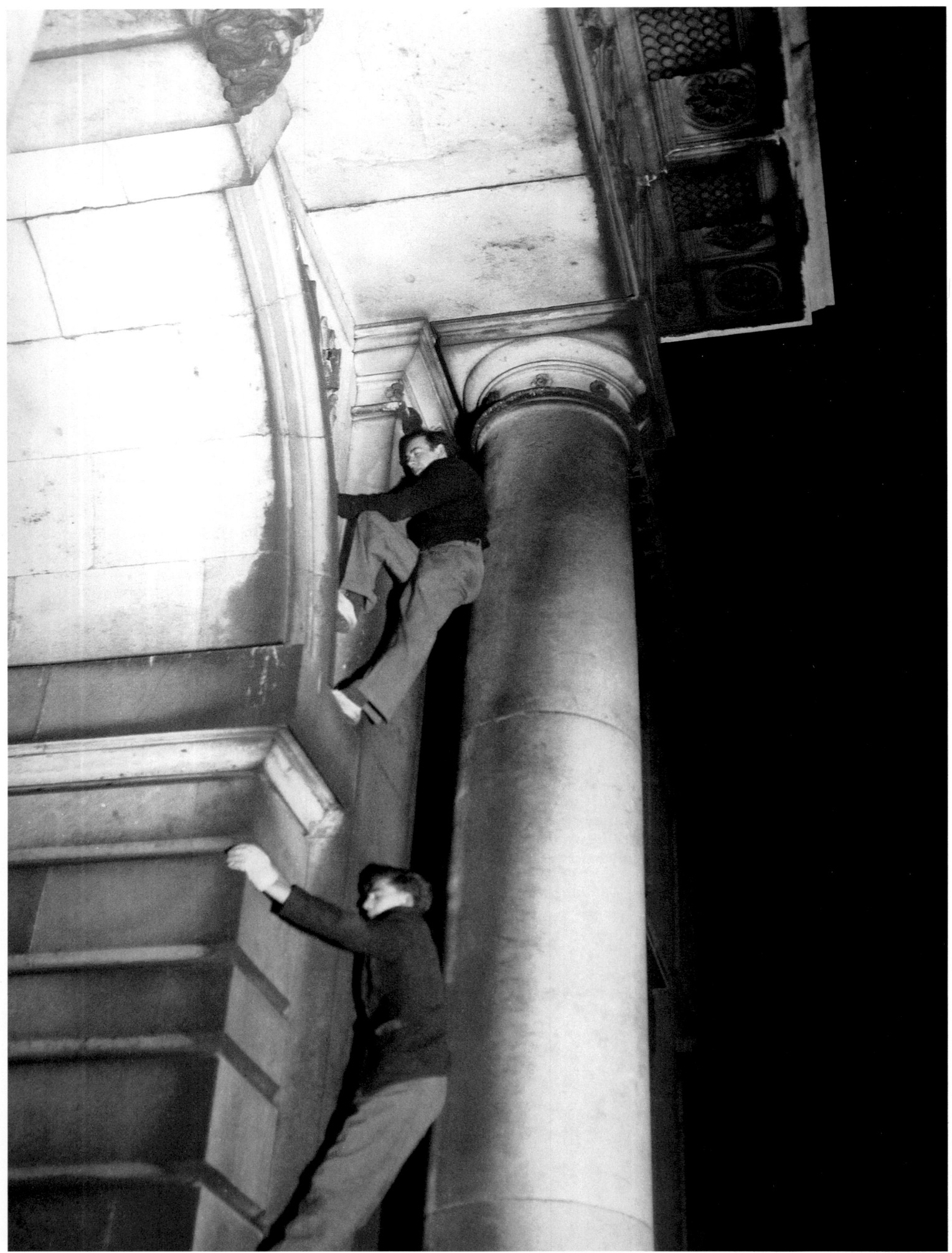

Opposite:
**Central Archway
Gibbs building,
King's College, ca. 1937**
© Noël Howard Symington,
*The Night Climbers of
Cambridge* / Collection
Thomas Mailaender
(see page 74)

Playtime

Over the course of her career Helen Levitt found no shortage of off-the-cuff comedy playing out in New York's streets. It's fitting then that Tim Davis shared Levitt's images with his photography students as examples of both levity and joy in the medium. Davis, in a diagnosis in these pages of "photogeliophobia"—fear of funny photographs—observes that photographers have tended to downplay their sense of humor while responding to a world full of unexpected hilarity. Famously laconic, Levitt didn't comment much on her work—maybe explanation took the fun away—but she did once admit to "looking for comedy more and more," a quality she often found by surreptitiously photographing children at play.

This issue is loosely organized around the title *Playtime*, a nod to French filmmaker Jacques Tati's brilliant 1967 send-up of the absurdities of modern living. Tati's signature poker-faced slapstick is felt across these pages. Erwin Wurm, speaking of his jarringly illogical *One-Minute Sculptures* and other works, remarks that he views humor as a vehicle to arrive at other meanings, including pathos. With her *Drape* series, Eva Stenram digitally rewires vintage pinup pictures, performing a kind of *détournement* that takes the wind out of the original images' erotic charge. Italian polymath Bruno Munari—who began his artistic career as a Futurist painter in the 1920s—also worked as an illustrator, designer, and inventor, and brought all these talents to bear upon his photographs, which are performative, inventive, and unabashedly fun.

What are games and play without rules? Invented, often arbitrary rules governed the work of the Conceptual artists of the 1960s and '70s discussed by Robin Kelsey: figures such as John Baldessari and Eleanor Antin, who responded to a tumultuous, uncertain era—and to the machismo and self-importance of "serious" art—by making games and clever gags a purposeful artistic strategy. More recently, Maya Rochat, one of the artists in the portfolio of young Swiss photographers assembled by Bruno Ceschel, suggests that "non-seriousness is a refusal to fall asleep." This group of artists exchange austerity and formality for absurdity and humor, freely mixing media to create brash and messy images fueled by a curiosity about how the medium can be stretched and explored. A number of these figures are associated, as instructors or one-time students, with two of Switzerland's major art academies.

Schools, clearly, can serve as incubators for experimentation, playful thinking, and productive distraction. Over the last few years, James Mollison has photographed the anarchic theater that unfolds each afternoon across the globe's schoolyards. Campus antics are of course nothing new, as we see in a portfolio from the 1930s showing a group of daredevil students at the University of Cambridge performing a precursor to parkour: scaling the walls and turrets of King's and Trinity Colleges as though they were alpine slopes. Their dizzying images are reminders of how vertigo can remove us from the everyday, that play is often purposeless—sometimes undertaken primarily for the benefit of a spectator. Jo Ann Callis's darkly physical images, published here for the first time, suggest a game of *what-does-this-feel-like?* enacted for the photographer.

In his 1961 book *Man, Play, Games*, philosopher Roger Callois noted that "secrecy, mystery, and even travesty can be transformed into play activity." Sophie Calle, an artist celebrated for her clever, mischievous projects, discusses her new series revisiting the brazen theft of artworks from Boston's Isabella Stewart Gardner Museum. In her conversation with Melissa Harris, Calle teasingly suggests of her "documentary" project: "Maybe everything is invented.... Who knows?" Inversely, Japanese photographer Kazuyoshi Usui offers us admittedly fictional images that appear to be real, spinning Japan's bygone Showa era into a pink-tinged future that never really happened. Poet Frances Richard speaks with Christian Marclay about his snapshots of found musical notation, repurposed and then literally played by musicians. Marclay notes that his approach to photography "includes a sense of playfulness because you're not sure what the consequences are going to be." This inquisitive spirit unites the many guises of play found in this issue—play as games, as fictions, as digital simulations; role-playing, playing music, and so on. The beauty of play, it seems, is that you never quite know where the game will take you.

After this issue, Diana C. Stoll, *Aperture*'s longtime senior editor, will be moving on to pursue personal projects. We will greatly miss Diana's endless wisdom, brilliant editing, and impeccable eye. We wish Diana the best of luck in her new endeavors, but we don't consider this a good-bye as we look forward to having her as a writer in our pages.   —The Editors

What Matters Now?
Photography, Technology, and the World

Left:
Detail view of *Interference*, a room-sized game by Nathalie Pozzi and Eric Zimmerman
Photograph © Cameron Sterling

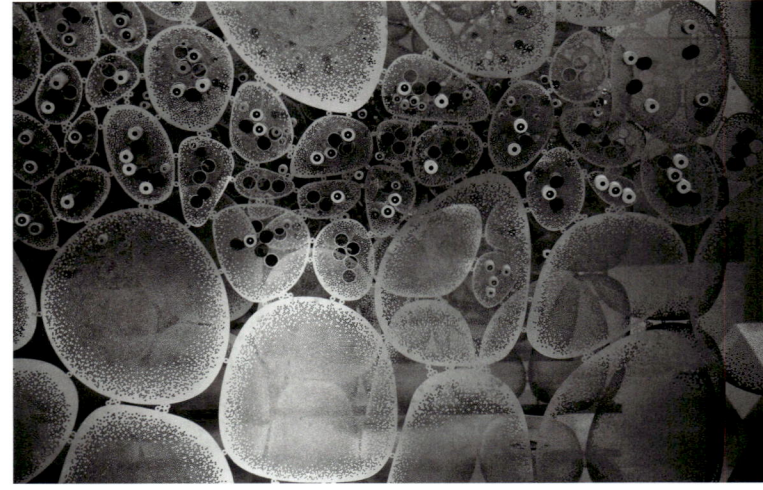

A Century of Play

We live today in a world of systems. The way that we work and learn, communicate and socialize, conduct our finances and engage with our governments—all these fundamental aspects of our lives are increasingly mediated through digital networks of information. We no longer research by consulting experts in encyclopedias or libraries. In the age of Wikipedia, we are the experts. This blurring of boundaries between producers and consumers, professionals and the public, has happened in photography too: who today is not in some way a photographer?

For the past one hundred years, the still and moving image embodied personal storytelling, news reporting, and epic narrative. But in our present age of digital interactive systems, games are ascendant. Every game, from chess and tennis to Tomb Raider and Angry Birds, is a lesson in how to interact with systems, a laboratory for exploring and expanding creativity and innovation.

If the twentieth century was the age of the image, the twenty-first century will be a *ludic* century—a century of play. The question for the next hundred years is: how can photography play? Can images shift and change in response to our choices or desires? Can they be collaboratively authored and systemically structured? What happens to photography in an age of games?

Only one way to find out: let's play.

—**Eric Zimmerman, game designer and arts professor at the New York University Game Center, and co-author of the game design textbook *Rules of Play* (MIT Press, 2003)**

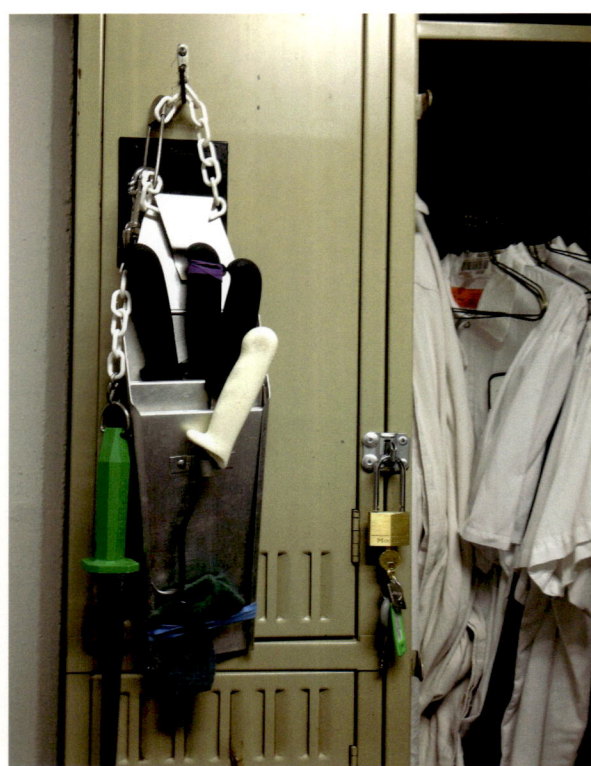

Buttonhole Cameras

Inside the Cargill Meat Solutions slaughterhouse in Schuyler, Nebraska, is an area reserved by law for federal meat inspectors. Inside that area are a break room, two offices for veterinarian-supervisors, and locker rooms. Inside the men's locker room was my locker.

I took this photograph, showing my scabbard with its knives and meat hook, with my iPhone. I was often tempted to bring the iPhone onto the kill floor with me, as the room is a visual extravaganza, and I am a journalist; I had taken a job as an inspector because I thought it would be interesting to write about. But that would have gotten me in trouble.

Animal-rights activists, of course, have overcome that challenge by using buttonhole cameras, to great effect. Their web videos of animal abuse are so potent that six states have recently passed so-called "ag-gag" laws making it a felony to take photographs or video of an agricultural facility without permission. Rather than curing the abuse, the industry would like to shoot the messenger.

—**Ted Conover, author of "The Way of All Flesh" (*Harper's*, May 2013) and *Newjack: Guarding Sing Sing* (Random House, 2000)**

Above:
Locker at Cargill beef-processing plant, Schuyler, Nebraska, 2012
© Ted Conover

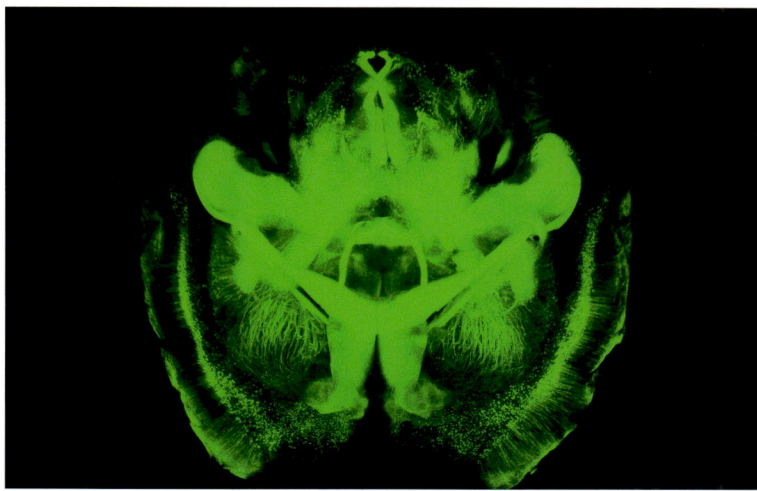

Clarity

Scientists in Karl Deisseroth's bioengineering lab at Stanford recently announced Clarity, an imaging technique rendering thick animal tissues transparent, along with a visually stunning image of a mouse brain turned clear. Clarity unmasks the camouflage of dense surrounding tissue. The image of the mouse's brain received tremendous publicity. I asked applied mathematician Chris Wiggins to explain why. "When I read about the 'clear brain,' made transparent optically, I was struck by how it captured the imagination of neuroscientists hoping that it will make the brain more transparent in the sense of understood." Wiggins described collaborating with molecular biologists "whose walls were covered not in blackboards of equations, but in pictures like [neuroscientist Santiago] Ramón y Cajal's drawings of neurons. For centuries this has been how we understand in biology: by seeing."

Vision is often described as a way of knowing the world, or even as constructing knowledge of the world, but it also provides abundant data. "Microscopes are now seen as devices for generating numbers, not pictures," adds Wiggins.

As Deisseroth says: "We're talking about terabytes of data being created. And it's not just the size of the data, but the nature of it."

Tissue image data complement data recorded from active neurons and whole brains while exhibiting memory, movement, emotion, and vision—all the things that make us human. The clear brain is both image and data simultaneously.

—**Laura Kurgan, author of** *Close Up at a Distance: Mapping, Technology, and Politics* (**Zone Books, 2013**)

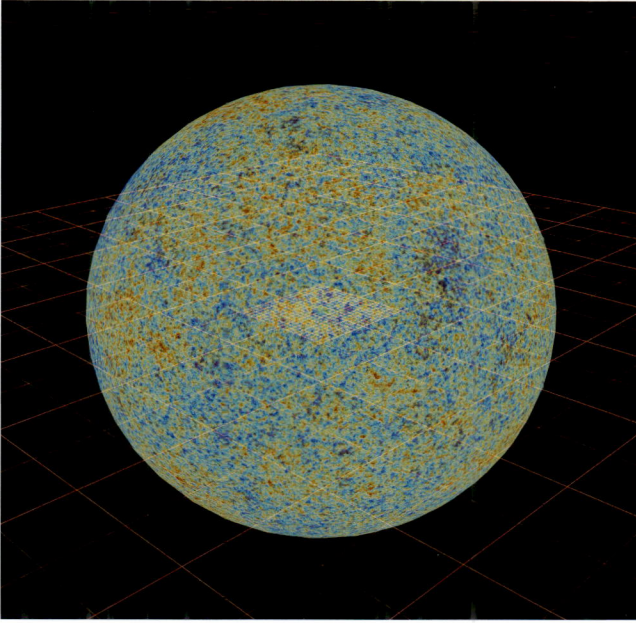

Mapping Radiation Patterns

Imaging technologies enable detection of frequencies far beyond the visible range of the electromagnetic spectrum. These have radically extended human perception, allowing us to peer deep into our cosmic environment. This photograph of the cosmic microwave background, or CMB, visualizes our primeval origins, what is believed to be radiation shortly after the birth of the universe. It's a cosmic baby picture, whose patterns represent slight energetic variations that eventually gave rise to quasars, galaxies, stars, planets, and us.

This image appears spherical because it's a panorama of humanity's cosmic horizon, taken from the Planck satellite. Because of the limited speed of light, it's centered on what astronomers call our *observational center*, or the point from which it was photographed. But it's also a profound reminder that Earth is our *ecological center*, the only place we've found where life has emerged after billions of years of cosmic evolution. Its increasing complexity has yielded our own self-awareness, and this photograph is a product of our inquiry into the origins of existence. By attempting to map our finite perceptions within an infinite 3-D virtual world, we have once again encountered a perennial paradox known as *squaring the circle*. As we've attempted to map an "external" universe, we've discovered that, in the truest sense, it has always been inside us. The universe matters because we are the universe mattering.

—**David McConville, president of the Buckminster Fuller Institute**

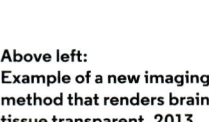

HERITAGE®

PHOTOGRAPHS &
MODERN & CONTEMPORARY
— AUCTION —
NOVEMBER 2, 2013

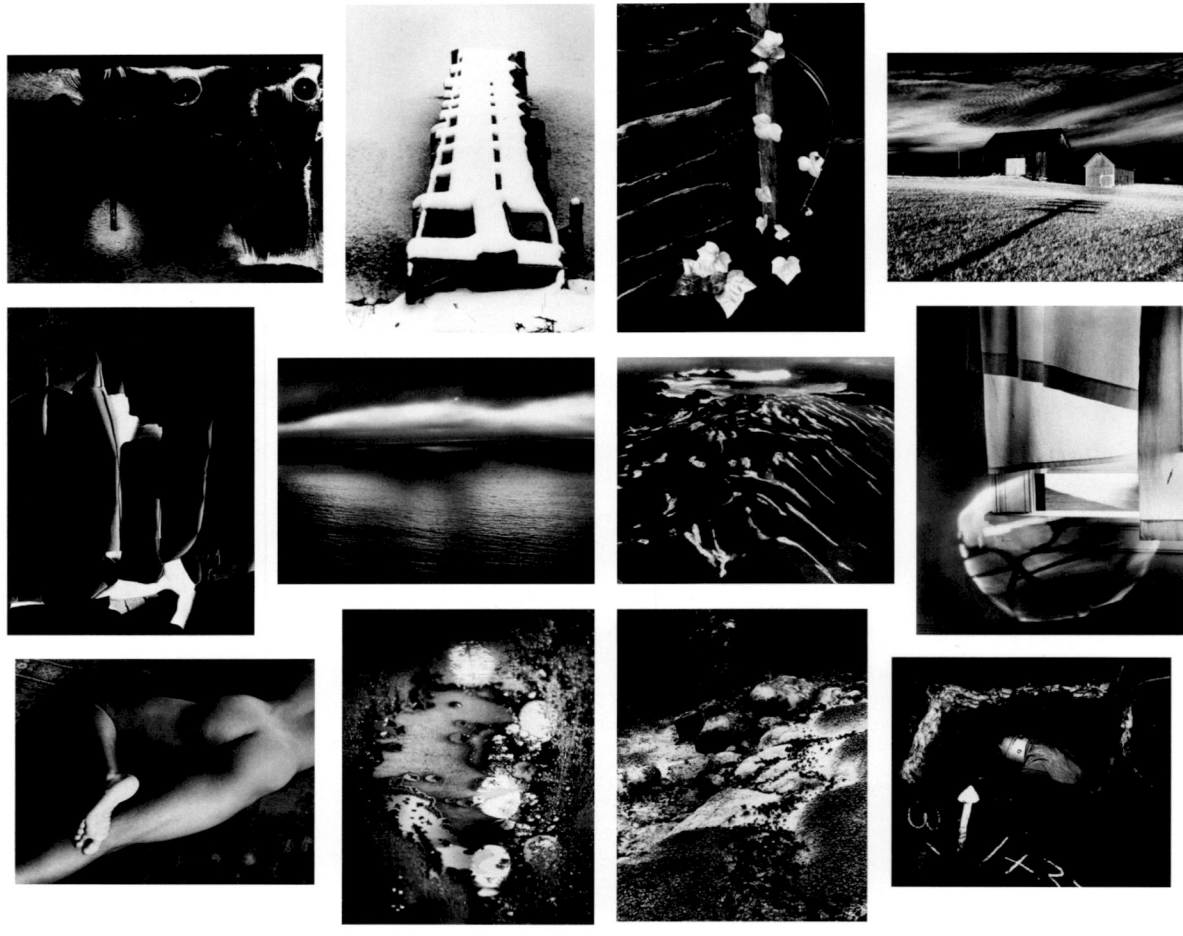

MINOR WHITE
Jupiter Portfolio (Twelve Photographs), 1947-1971
Gelatin silver, 1975
Estimate: $15,000-$25,000

INVITING CONSIGNMENTS.

INQUIRIES | RACHEL PEART | 800-872-6467 - EXT 1625 | RPEART@HA.COM

FRANK HETTIG | 800-872-6467 - EXT 1157 | FRANKH@HA.COM

DALLAS | NEW YORK | BEVERLY HILLS | SAN FRANCISCO | PARIS | GENEVA

TX & NY Auctioneer license: Samuel Foose 11727 & 0952360. Heritage Auction Galleries CA Bond #RSB2004175; CA Auctioneer Bond: Carolyn Mani #RSB2005661. HERITAGE Reg. U.S. Pat & TM Off. | Buyer's Premium 12% - 25%. See HA.com for details.   28319

Redux
Rediscovered Books and Writings

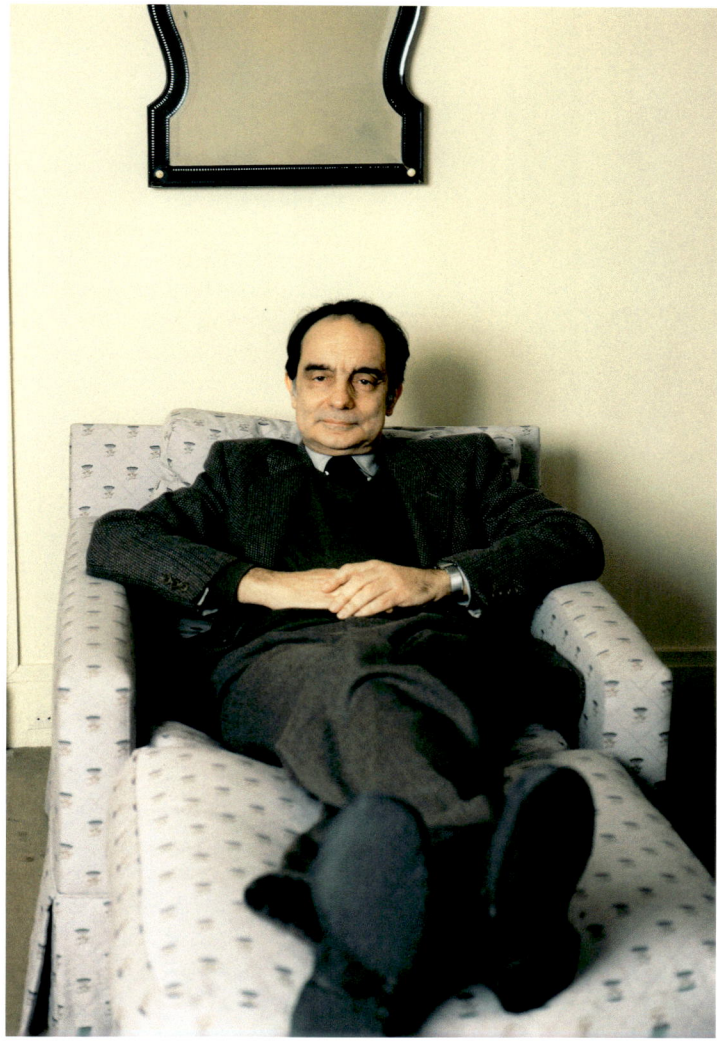

Italo Calvino's
"The Adventure of a Photographer"
Aveek Sen

Italo Calvino, Paris,
January 1984
Photograph by Ulf Andersen/
Getty Images

Italo Calvino, the Italian writer, began his tribute to Roland Barthes in *La Repubblica* with a horrific image of defacement. Barthes, Calvino noted, had been disfigured beyond recognition by the accident that had killed him on February 25, 1980, lying unidentified for hours in the hospital. This reminded Calvino of the book that he was reading only a few weeks before its author's death: *La Chambre Claire*, or *Camera Lucida*, as it is better known today. Sitting down to write the tribute in April 1980, Calvino was struck by how *Camera Lucida* was more a book about love and death than about photography. It made him think of Barthes lying dead, "name unknown," in Salpêtrière, "the frail and anguished link with his own features … suddenly torn as one tears up a photograph."

Most of us find it strangely difficult to tear up a photograph, even when it is of an inanimate object, a landscape, or someone we do not know. We find ourselves stopping short of the imagined violence of the act, finding it much easier to tear up, say, a letter. The flea markets of Europe, as Tacita Dean discovered while making *Floh* (2001), are full of photographs that have been abandoned rather than destroyed. Yet, the tearing up of photographs as an extreme gesture that fuses madness and violence forms the climax of a story written by Calvino in the mid-1950s. It is called "The Adventure of a Photographer" and became part of *Difficult Loves*, a collection of finely reflective short stories, or "adventures," each involving a different figure: a poet, a reader, a traveler, a soldier. Written more than two decades before *Camera Lucida* and Susan Sontag's *On Photography*, Calvino's "The Adventure of a Photographer" reads, to me, like a far more contemporary parable about the medium than those canonical texts by the Sontag-Barthes-Benjamin trinity that remain mandatory for serious photographers or writers on photography today.

Calvino's photographer, Antonino, is a "hunter of the unattainable." Initially reluctant to pick up the camera his friends use so avidly, Antonino's relationship with photography starts as a pursuit of "life as it flees," but soon turns into a "passion difficult to put up with"—a state of isolation caught between obsessiveness and a pervasive sense of loss; everything that is not photographed is lost. Antonino realizes very quickly that what lurks in his "black instrument" is nothing but a kind

Italo Calvino, *Gli amori difficili* (*Difficult Loves*) (Einaudi, 1970)
Courtesy Fondazione Luigi Einaudi, Turin

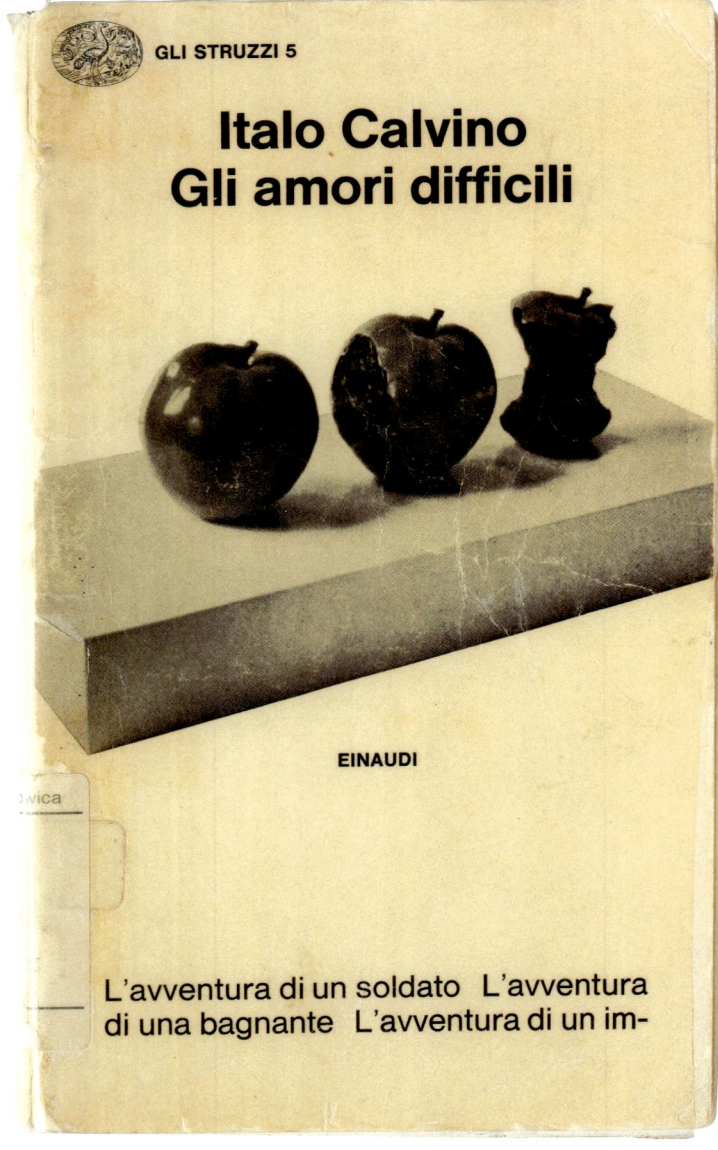

transformed into something unexpected, something that even before the transformation is already frightening, because there's no telling what it might be transformed into." "Did he want to photograph dreams?" the half-mad photographer asks himself, and the suspicion strikes him dumb.

In recording Antonino's descent into a psycho-pathology of everyday life driven by the camera, Calvino shows how photography could lead, *through* an obsession with capturing the real, toward the unhinging of the mind from that very reality. It is, paradoxically, the compulsion to document that dooms photography to transgress the limits of the visible, opening up a terrain that belongs to the imagination rather than to empirical certitude. In his tribute to Barthes, Calvino described the capacity of language to speak about things "that are not": this was its fundamental difference from photography. Yet, in this story, Antonino takes photography close to the inwardness of the imagination unshackled from the real, and to the irreducible logic of memory, dream, and fantasy. This is also the domain of fiction and, dare one say, of art. It is the rigorous unruliness of fiction— rather than the discursiveness of theory, or the objectivity of history—that becomes the mode in which Calvino fathoms the meaning and possibilities of photography. It is fiction that rescues photography from the risk-averse middle path of empiricism by toppling the eye, and the eye's mind, into the abyss of the invisible. As he lets go of the hope of capturing with his camera the "essence" of the woman he desires, Antonino stumbles upon his art's most difficult secret: "Photography has a meaning only if it exhausts all possible images."

In recording Antonino's descent into a psycho-pathology of everyday life driven by the camera, Calvino shows how photography could lead toward the unhinging of the mind from reality.

of madness. This madness is a forking path. One path beckons outward, toward the doomed and impossible desire to document everything that exists and happens before it is lost forever. The camera must record *all* reality, all history; only then would it begin making some sort of crazy sense. The other one leads inexorably within, into the labyrinths from which the eyes, windows of the soul, look at the world outside. Yet, in his studio, as the photographer focuses the camera on his model, her body forced into a sequence of grotesque poses, the two roads, inner and outer, seem to cross again "in the glass rectangle." It is "like a dream, when a presence coming from the depth of memory advances, is recognized, and then suddenly is

Aveek Sen writes usually from Calcutta. In 2009, he was awarded the Infinity Award for Writing on Photography from New York's International Center of Photography.

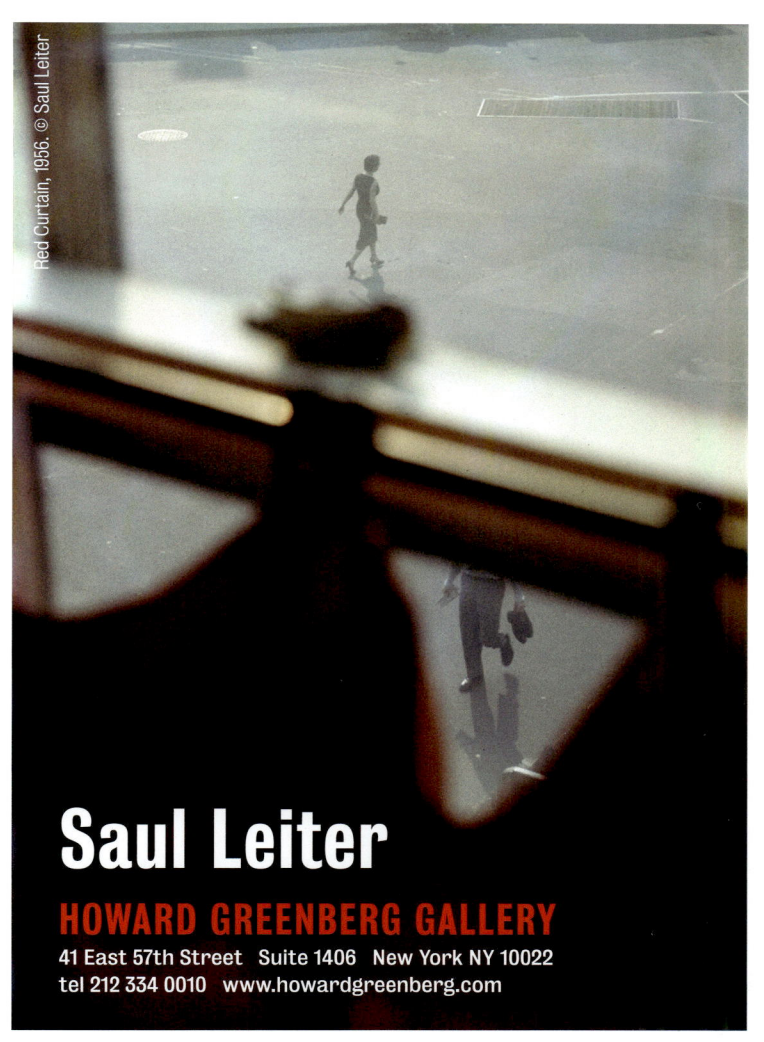

Red Curtain, 1956. © Saul Leiter

Saul Leiter
HOWARD GREENBERG GALLERY
41 East 57th Street Suite 1406 New York NY 10022
tel 212 334 0010 www.howardgreenberg.com

aperture

Benefit & Auction

October 2013
aperture.org/benefit

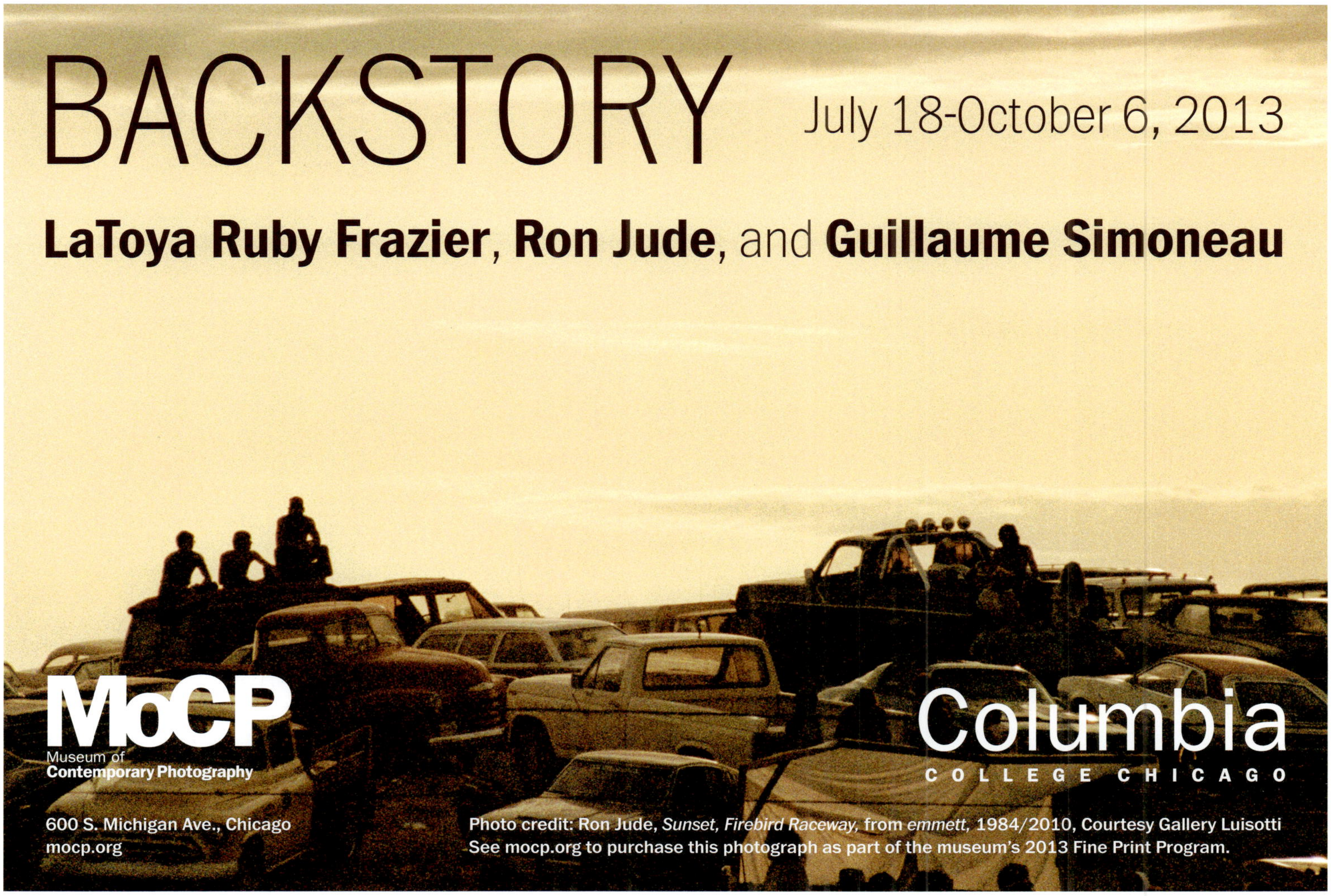

BACKSTORY July 18-October 6, 2013

LaToya Ruby Frazier, Ron Jude, and Guillaume Simoneau

MoCP
Museum of
Contemporary Photography

Columbia
COLLEGE CHICAGO

600 S. Michigan Ave., Chicago
mocp.org

Photo credit: Ron Jude, *Sunset, Firebird Raceway*, from *emmett*, 1984/2010, Courtesy Gallery Luisotti
See mocp.org to purchase this photograph as part of the museum's 2013 Fine Print Program.

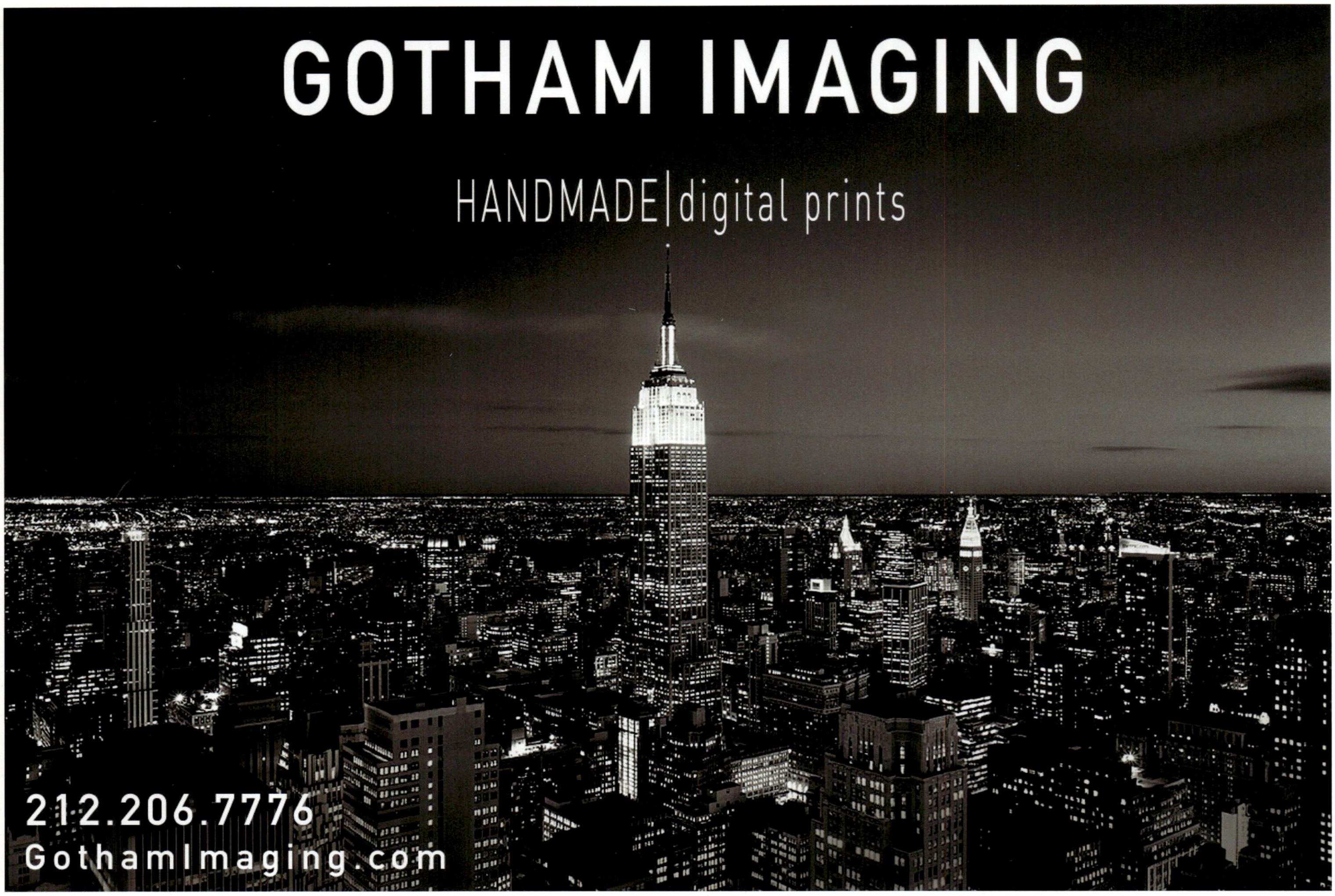

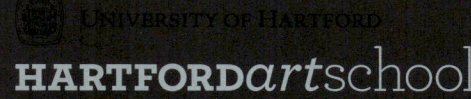
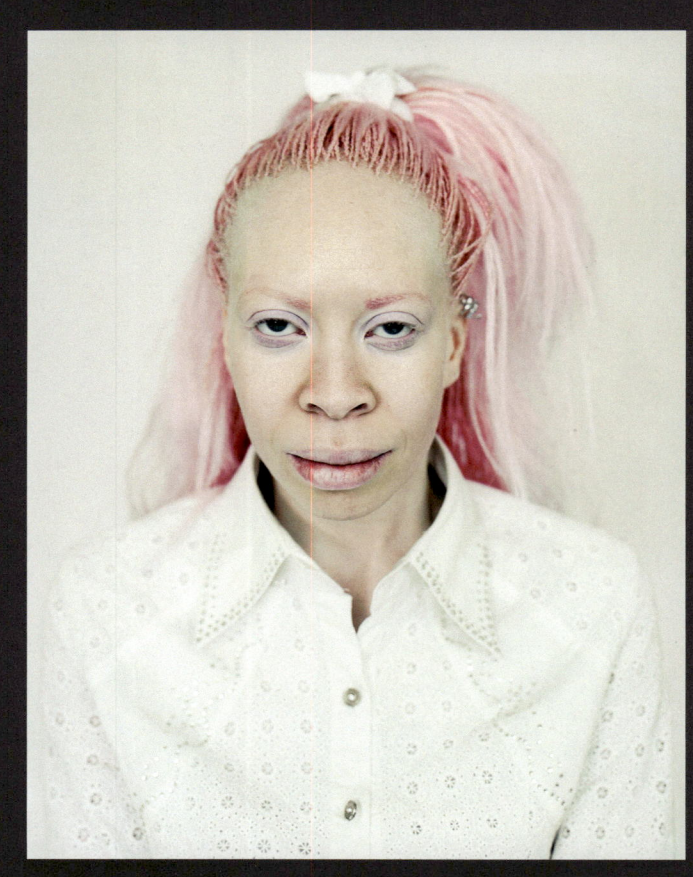

Dispatches
Photography Scenes Worldwide

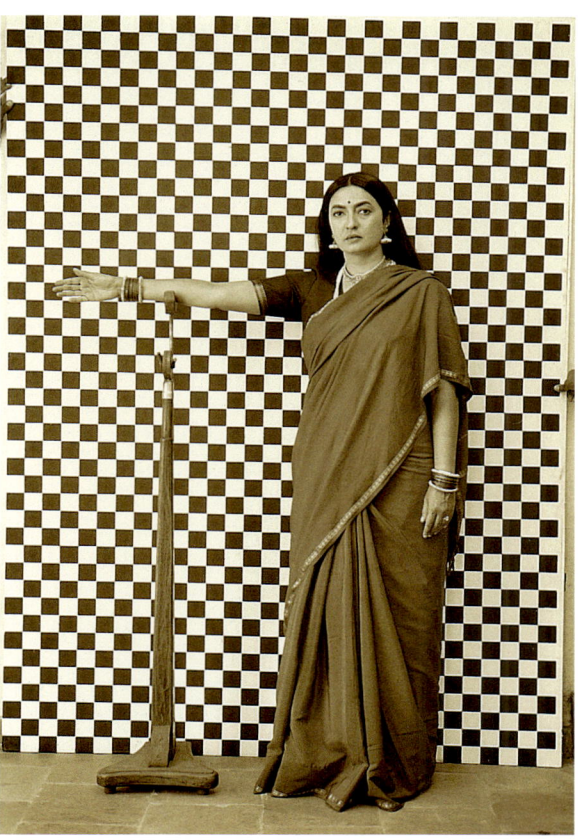

Prajna Desai on Mumbai

Photography is working its mojo on Mumbai. Proving this is Focus, the city's first photography festival, which ran for two weeks last March. Tapping into citizen pride, the event peppered the conceit of "the city" across a multi-site program that encouraged people to engage with photography's pivotal role in modern life and contemporary art discourse. Ranging from nineteenth-century vignettes of Mumbai to images of the city's distinctive Zoroastrian community to slices of urban architecture from the world over, Focus optimistically claimed a place for photography as one of the most stimulating cultural expressions of this maximum city.

From the country's independence in 1947, documentary necessity drove Indian photography. Rural life, statesmen, social campaigns and protests, dams, the architectural icons of an emerging, modern nation—these were the principal photographic subjects of mid-twentieth-century India. Strongly graphic and formally sophisticated, this photography's forte was not conceptual but narrative. Almost exclusively shown in print media, not art galleries, its inventory engaged viewers otherwise separated by ethnicity, language, and class.

The mid-1990s, in contrast, witnessed the arrival of photo-based art. Earlier practitioners such as Raqs

Media Collective, Pushpamala N, and Dayanita Singh are now joined by a powerful younger set, Shilpa Gupta and Tejal Shah among them. Playing discursively with photographic realism and truth, these artists tackle subject matter drawn from philosophy, or from consumer and media culture—but rarely from current affairs. Implicitly built with a scaffolding of Western art theory, their work offers pointed arguments that are tailored to rarefied international gallery culture, but exhibits indifference to the larger Indian social milieu.

Some photographers wish things were different. Mumbai-based Chirodeep Chaudhuri notes: "My interest in photography is usually not the variety done by 'artists' who also shoot pictures, but pictures produced by 'photographers.' Today, few photographers whose primary practice is photography seem to be finding favor in galleries. This has varied implications in how photography gets disseminated, seen, and perceived here in the long run."

Art photography has been building a considerable head of steam. Older institutions include Piramal Gallery, the city's only photo-specific non-commercial space for photojournalism, and the nonprofit Goethe-Institute Mumbai, an established venue for photographic collaborations between German artists and young Indian aspirants. Newer is Tasveer, a multi-gallery network founded in 2006 by three art collectors to promote contemporary photography. It presents traveling exhibitions and catalogs produced in conjunction with Seagull Books, a leading Indian publisher of avant-garde art and literature. Tasveer's strength is showcasing Indian and international photographers to cultivate understandings of photography as an art of rigorous formal standards and critical acumen. With an impressive list of over one hundred shows to date, its program's aim is to rethink familiar genres—portraiture, still-life, street photography—and to reactivate photography's storytelling potential.

Also key has been Matthieu Foss. In 2010 he opened an eponymous gallery, the city's only commercial venue dedicated solely to photography. An early group show, *Light Drifts*, organized by French curator Eve Lemesle, demonstrated photography's impact on artists who work in drawing, graphic design, and sound. A 2011 exhibition presented photographs by Montreal-based artist Alain Paiement, who shoots hundreds of like items,

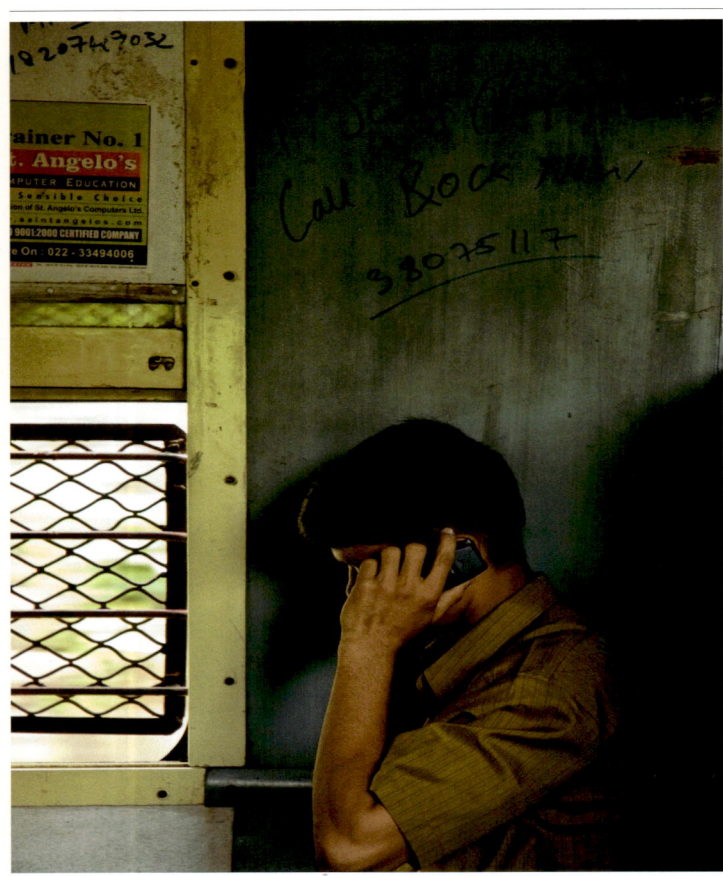

Previous page:
Pushpamala N and
Clare Arni, *Lady in
Moonlight I-25*, from
the ethnographic series
*Native Women of South
India: Manners and
Customs, Bangalore
2000–2004*
Courtesy the artists and
Bose Pacia, New York

Above:
Chirodeep Chaudhuri,
from *XXX—Mumbai's
Suburban Train Graffiti*,
2006–7
Courtesy the artist

Right:
Jyotti Bhatt,
Black Light, 1971
Courtesy Tasveer Gallery,
Bangalore

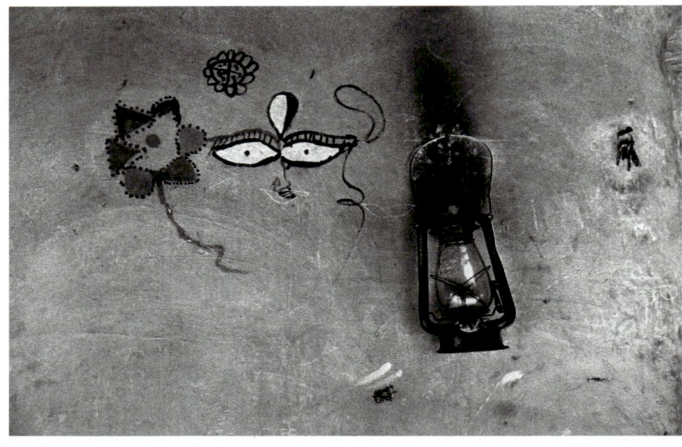

Blue Book, a suite of pictures of industrial spaces displayed in 2009 at Galerie Mirchandani + Steinruecke, was promoted as a meditation on still-life and Color Field painting.

In addition to distancing itself from photojournalism and straight photography, the art photography paradigm also provides an easy way to avoid dealing with the language of mainstream photography. It is said that there are almost as many cellphones in India as people. Social media are also widely used, and strongly shape public conceptions of photography, especially among the young. The democratizing effects of this ubiquity can be seen driving social opinion and major news stories. One spectacular instance took place in August 2012. Incensed by YouTube videos and images on Facebook of Muslims killed by Bodo tribespeople in India's northeastern state of Assam, a Muslim group in Mumbai organized a protest rally that soon turned violent. Cellphone pictures and footage of the Mumbai protesters setting fire to television news vehicles and police cars reached online platforms in real time, before the channels themselves were able to cover the story. No gallery exhibitions in Mumbai reflect this important stream of photography.

The separation is arguably tactical. Art photography thrives on ostensibly high craft and intellectual gestation. What makes it desirable is precisely that it does not record, like democratized photography, but obliquely proposes ideas that are meant to be politically, socially, or philosophically galvanizing. Undoubtedly, these are good times for art photography in the city. But in order to connect with the cultures of photography outside the art world, only a willingness to kick away the crutch of contemporary art, and greater mettle in exhibiting what many galleries currently prefer not to show, will help the photographic community, as Chaudhuri says, "figure out what finds an audience here in Mumbai."

such as various stuffed animal heads or different pieces of furniture, from overhead vantage points, then stitches them together into seamless panoramas. The result is hyper realistic, like fastidiously painted still lifes by seventeenth-century masters. Unfortunately, Foss was forced to close the space in 2012, but remains active as a curator in the city, including serving as one of the organizers of Focus. "Not having a gallery space," he says, "has given me the opportunity to work on projects like Focus Festival Mumbai, which is more about creating awareness than concentrating on building a market."

Otherwise, photo-based art enjoys limited exposure vis-à-vis painting, installation, video, or collage. While some city galleries are increasing their photography programming, it is presented in tandem with video and installations and framed in the terms of contemporary art theory. Take multimedia artist Hetain Patel's photographic series *Eva* (2012), shown at Chatterjee & Lal in the neighborhood of Colaba, where Mumbai's galleries are concentrated. The works feature his wife's naked back marked with henna tattoos of nontraditional patterns, such as Spider-Man imagery or a botched love letter, paired with his video *First Dance* (2012). Installation artist Shilpa Gupta's exhibition *Someone Else* (2012), at Gallery Chemould Prescott Road, presented a supersize set of blurred photographs of a moving figure alongside installations that included an enormous sculpture of microphones emitting sound. Dayanita Singh's

Prajna Desai is a writer
of fiction and nonfiction
currently based in Mumbai.

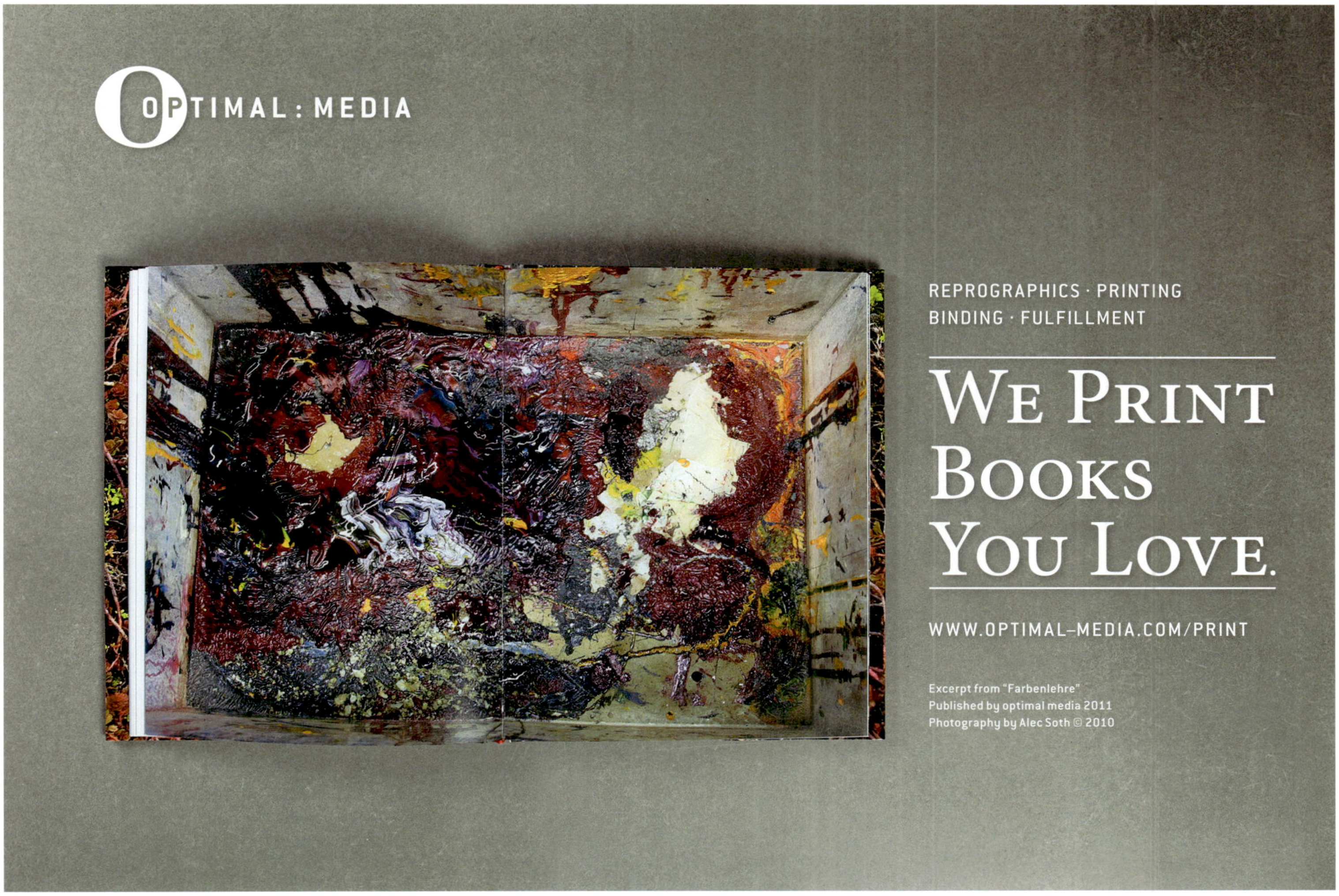

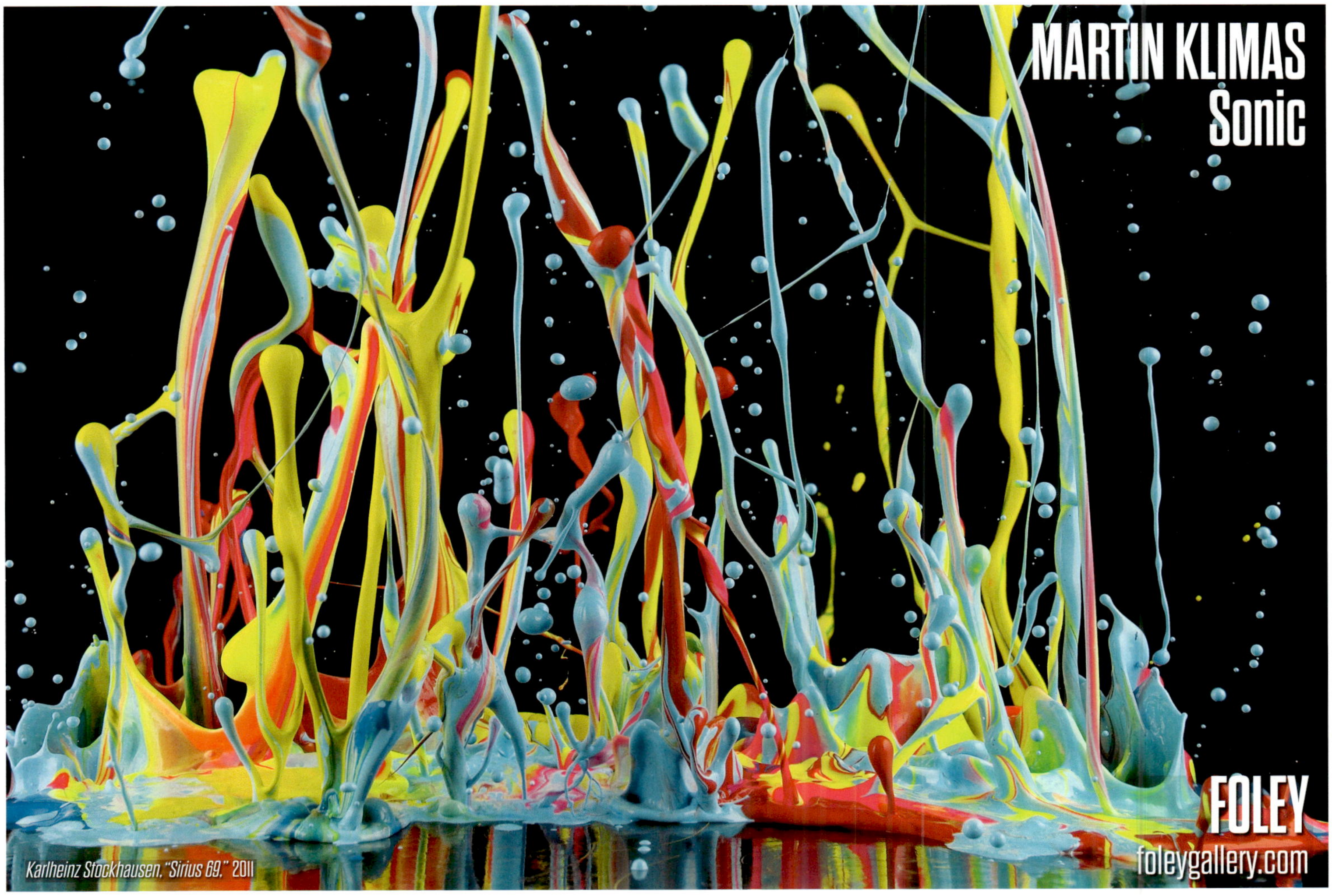

Collectors
The Filmmakers
On Recent Acquisitions

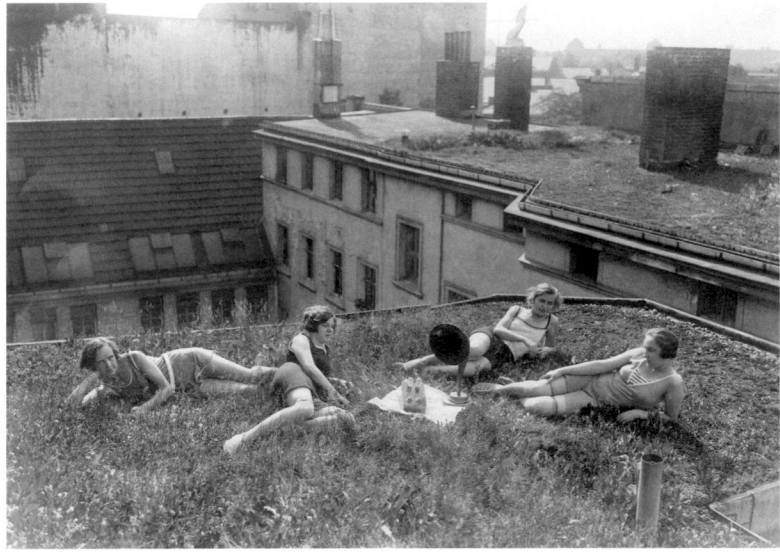

Sommertag auf einer Berliner Dachwiese—das Radio sorgt für Unterhaltung (Summer day on a rooftop lawn, with a radio for entertainment), Berlin, 1926. Photographer unknown
bpk, Berlin / Art Resource, New York

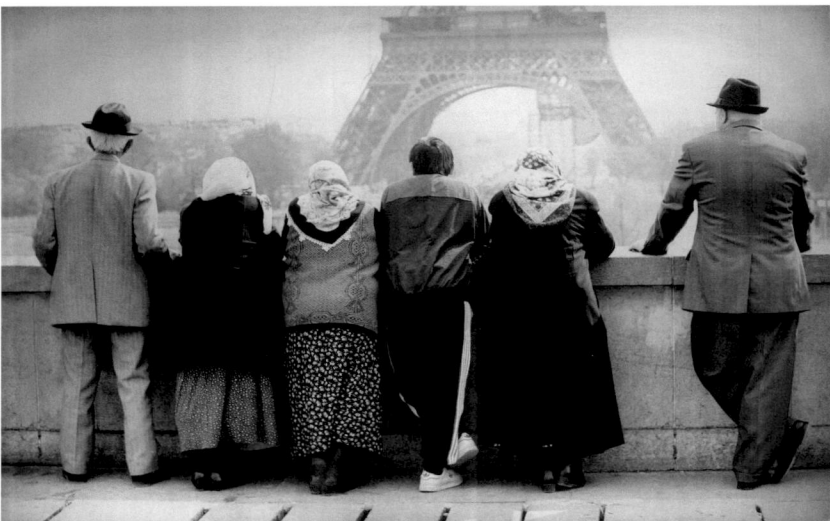

Paris, ca. 1970–71. Photographer unknown

Abbas Kiarostami

This photograph was made by an unknown photographer in 1970 or 1971. The title could be *A Dream Fulfilled*. It is not a new acquisition: I have kept this photograph—it is large, at forty-seven by seventy inches—in my office for the past two decades. I don't know why the photograph was taken; I cannot exactly explain where I found it or where it found me. And I don't think it really matters. What matters to me is that I have had it on my wall for the past twenty-two years. It is a frozen moment of unknown viewers looking at the Eiffel Tower (the Montparnasse Tower, built in 1973, was not yet keeping it company) with such infatuation, reveling in their spectatorship. This photograph highlights a distinctive characteristic of spectatorship, the very experience I attempt to create for the viewers in most of my films: in *Shirin*, watching women watching an old epic movie; in *Close-Up*, witnessing witnesses; and in *Certified Copy*, observing a couple observing the city.

(*As told to Ava Ansari*)

Abbas Kiarostami is an Iranian director and photographer. His film *Close-Up* was made in 1990; *Shirin* in 2008. His most recent films are *Certified Copy* (2010) and *Like Someone in Love* (2012).

Matt Wolf

I've always been obsessed with images of women listening to records. My favorites are scenes from Fassbinder films. At the conclusion of his first feature, *Love Is Colder Than Death* (*Liebe ist kälter als der Tod*, 1969), a female gangster lies on the floor in a stark white bedroom in front of a turntable. The motif repeats in his 1975 television movie *Fear of Fear* (*Angst vor der Angst*). A housewife named Margot suffers from inconsolable postpartum depression. In the film's climax, she locks her oldest daughter out of the apartment, lies on the floor, and blares a pop record.

I recently finished making a film called *Teenage* about the birth of youth culture. In that process, I saw thousands of archival images, including this remarkable photograph of 1920s German teenagers listening to the radio on a green roof. The photographer is unknown, but I found the image in an incredible book called *Wir wollen eine andere Welt* (We want another world) by Fred Grimm. When Fred learned about my film last year, he sent me his book, and it hugely inspired me.

In the early twentieth century, young people endured incredible oppression from their parents, governments, and the police. Pop culture and friends were their refuge, and teenagers struggled to create their own private world. This image is like a dream, and it conveys the transporting, hypnotic power of music.

Matt Wolf is the director of *Wild Combination* (2008), about the avant-garde cellist and disco music producer Arthur Russell, and *Teenage*, which premiered at this year's Tribeca Film Festival. He is a 2010 Guggenheim Fellow.

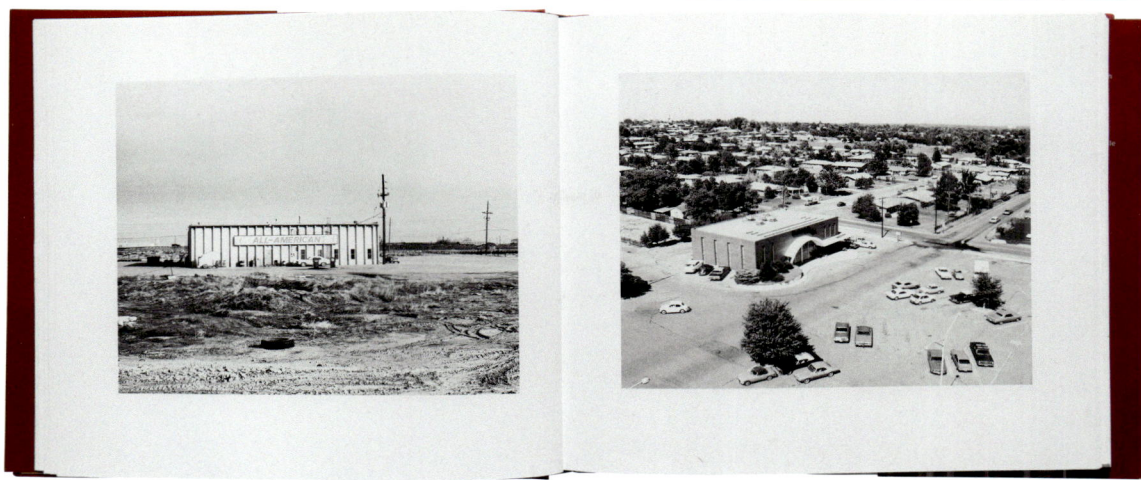

Pages from Robert Adams's *What We Bought: The New World* (Yale University Press, 2009, first published 1995)

Mike Mills

I've loved Robert Adams's work for a long time, but I kind of just discovered him again—his understanding of the West, and all the processes, plans, and things that have been done to its landscape. I think his work jumps out at me now because it's so deeply political, in such a concrete, unspoken way; especially his book *What We Bought: The New World*, which, to me, documents the long tail of manifest destiny. I had to not look at Adams's pictures for a few years before I could come back to them and have that spontaneous reaction of sadness and surprise at how our dreams can lead us so far astray.

Mike Mills's films include *Thumbsucker* (2005) and *Beginners* (2010).

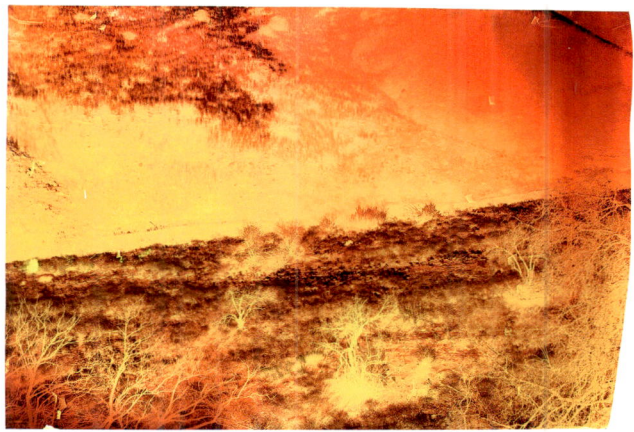

John Chiara, *Agua Dulce at Route 14*, 2012
Courtesy the artist, Von Lintel Gallery, New York, and ROSEGALLERY, Santa Monica

Jan de Bont

These images by John Chiara and Matthew Brandt are the most recent additions to our collection. I was drawn to them by their common sense of urgent exploration of the principles of photography. These young artists have both found their inspiration in the very origins of the medium—the use of lenses, light-sensitive material, and the different chemicals that make latent images visible.

Looking at the two photographs, I feel like there is a battle between the artists and the different photographic processes they use. Chiara built his own (very rudimentary) camera, a camera so large that he has to crawl inside it to manipulate the lens and thus its projected image on the photographic paper. The way he must then develop and treat these images is equally innovative. Brandt often experiments with interaction between the environment and his images. The picture shown here, *West Lake CA 9*, was soaked for many days in water from that same California lake. This process alters his C-prints in such a way that it creates hallucinogenic effects unique to each image.

Although these artists use very different techniques, their images seem to live in a similar, undiscovered world. Their photographs are unpredictable and utterly fascinating unique pieces of art. No multiple prints here.

As a collector of photography, you always fall in love with each new picture you acquire, no matter the price or size. These were no exceptions; my wife and I certainly fell in love with these new explorations in the history of photography.

Jan de Bont directed *Speed* (1994) and *Twister* (1996) and was the cinematographer on many films, including *Die Hard* (1988), *The Hunt for Red October* (1990), and *Basic Instinct* (1992). His collection of photography is extensive.

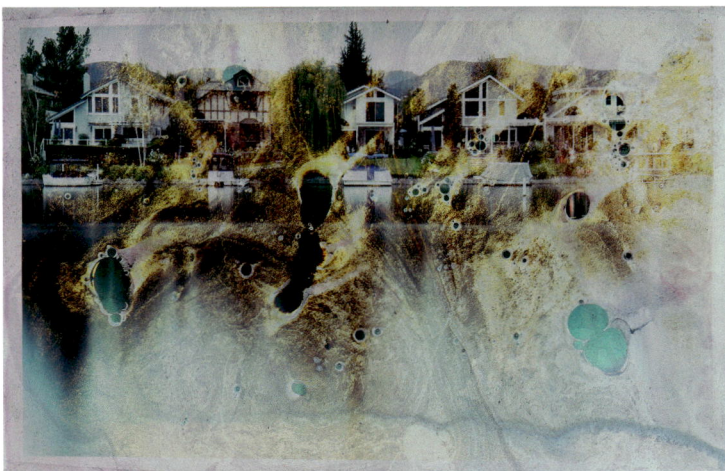

Matthew Brandt, *West Lake CA 9*, 2013
© Matthew Brandt; courtesy M+B Gallery, Los Angeles, and Yossi Milo, New York

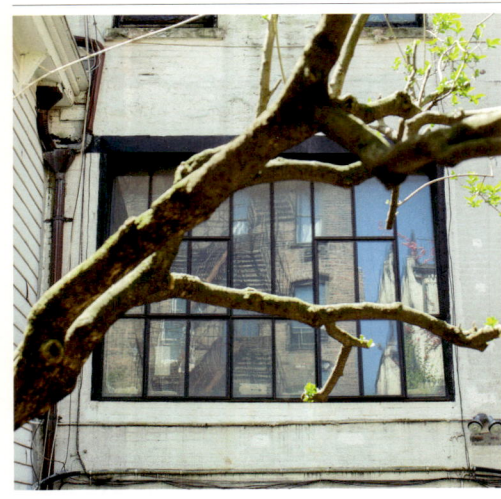
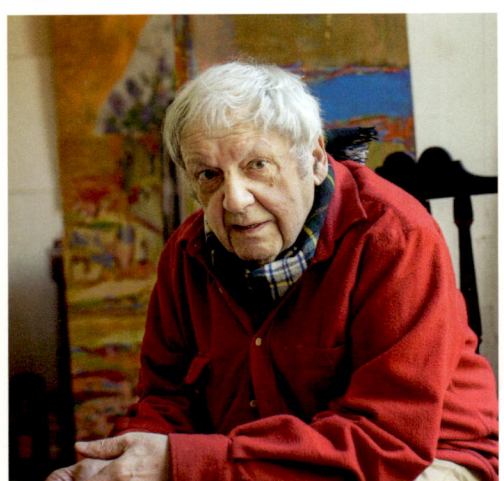
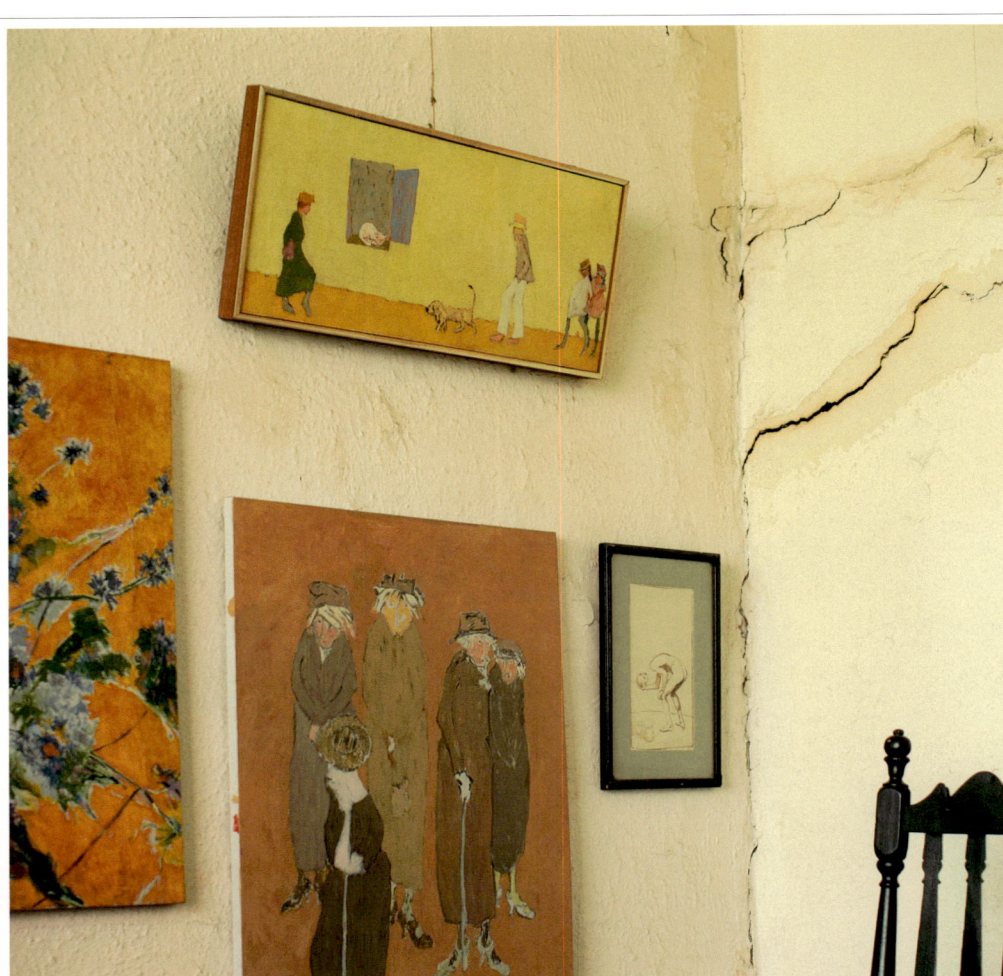
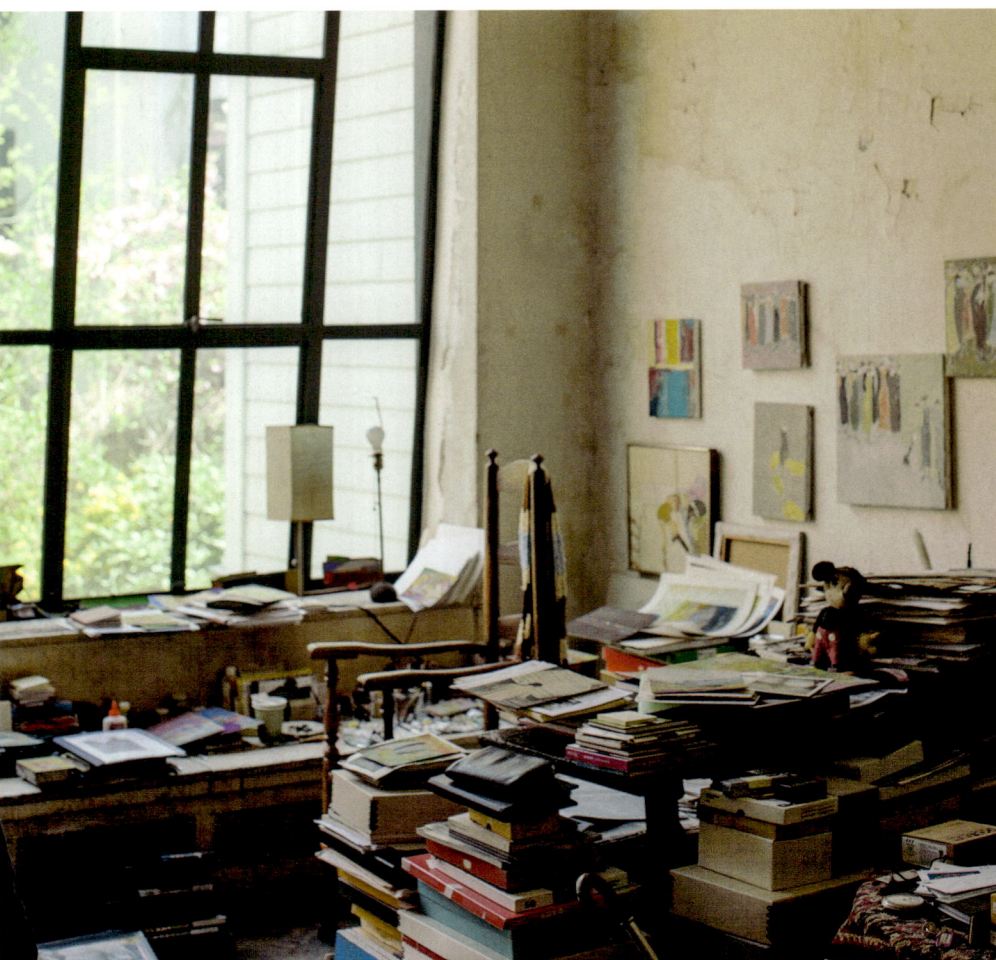
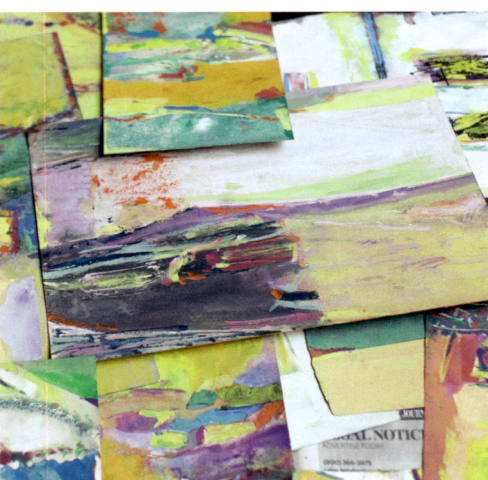
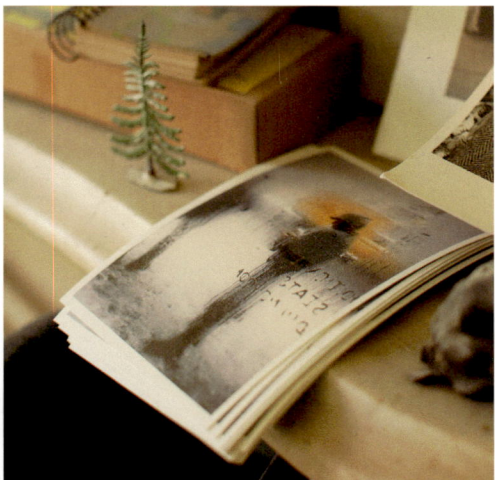

Studio Visit
Photographers at Work

With Saul Leiter in the East Village
Eric Banks

The East Village block where Saul Leiter lives and works is a short walk from any number of reminders of what the neighborhood used to look like—the Strand Bookstore, the pierogi emporium Veselka. In mythic times this was a landscape hopping with artists who frequented the Cedar Tavern and the Club, among them Richard Pousette-Dart, who early on encouraged Leiter to continue his explorations with a camera. That is a distant memory in this stretch of the East Village, along the streets that Leiter famously photographed during that Ab-Ex decade, today in the shadow of the gleaming new towers that are monuments to Michael Bloomberg's Gotham.

Once you've crossed the threshold of Leiter's floor-through apartment, the dislocation between the now and the then is intensified. It's a solidly New York space that gets a muted dose of sunlight on either end, but of a type that's rarely so well preserved. It's filled with a life's work—paintings, stacks of books, knickknacks, odds and ends —but it seems more robustly lived in than cluttered. The hearsay about Leiter's studio leads you to expect a hovel that would make the Collyer Brothers envious. Instead, there's a kind of graceful accumulation that feels more like a painter's garret than a packrat's digs. Leiter does most of his work in the large room framed by a wall-size bay of windows overlooking a lovely little courtyard filled with cherry trees, yellow jonquils, and a gurgling fountain. If you forgot for the moment that you were in New York, you might believe you'd been transported to Paris.

Leiter has had ample time to accumulate. He moved into the building in 1952, six years after he arrived in New York via Cleveland from Pittsburgh, the son of a rabbi who didn't approve of his ambition to be an artist. He took over the second-floor space in 2002, after the death of his longtime friend and partner, Soames Bantry, who had been there since 1960. (He now uses his original upstairs apartment as a second and more private studio as well as a storage space.) A number of Bantry's quiet figurative canvases hang on the wall alongside a couple of Leiter's own small-scale painted abstractions. His photographs, which belatedly won him recognition as a colorist far ahead of his time, are notably absent from the wall.

"Sometimes I think I love painting more than I do photography. But I love photography," Leiter says, as we look through a small pile of brightly painted slabs of cardboard at his feet. "I wonder sometimes if I would have been a better painter if I had just been a painter. Would I have explored certain areas of painting? But what's the point of thinking about it—if you do both, you do both. And sometimes I think you're lucky if you do both."

Painting remains Leiter's touchstone, and our talk is filled with anecdotes about two of his great loves, Pierre Bonnard and Édouard Vuillard, as much as with stories of the New York School photographers he knew. A self-deprecating figure at eighty-nine, he is impatient with the story that has long been told about him: how the printing of the astonishing, lyrical color street scenes he shot mostly in the 1950s and early '60s led to his rediscovery over the past two decades as a landmark figure in the history of New York photography. Leiter seems more bemused than angry over the opportunities he let pass by and ends most anecdotes with a rolling laugh that oddly reminds me of Buddy Hackett's at the end of his jokes. His work was included in a group show at the Museum of Modern Art in 1953, but when he was invited to show in Edward Steichen's 1955 *Family of Man* exhibition, he skipped it. He famously let other invitations pass by. "Some people have said to me: 'I've never known anyone who has taken less advantage of so many opportunities.' Someone wrote a letter to me in the '70s inviting me to show in some exhibition in France, but I never opened the letter until this year. That's not good. That's not the way to advance a career."

Saul Leiter, *Saturday
Morning, The Cloisters*, 1947
Courtesy Howard Greenberg
Gallery, New York

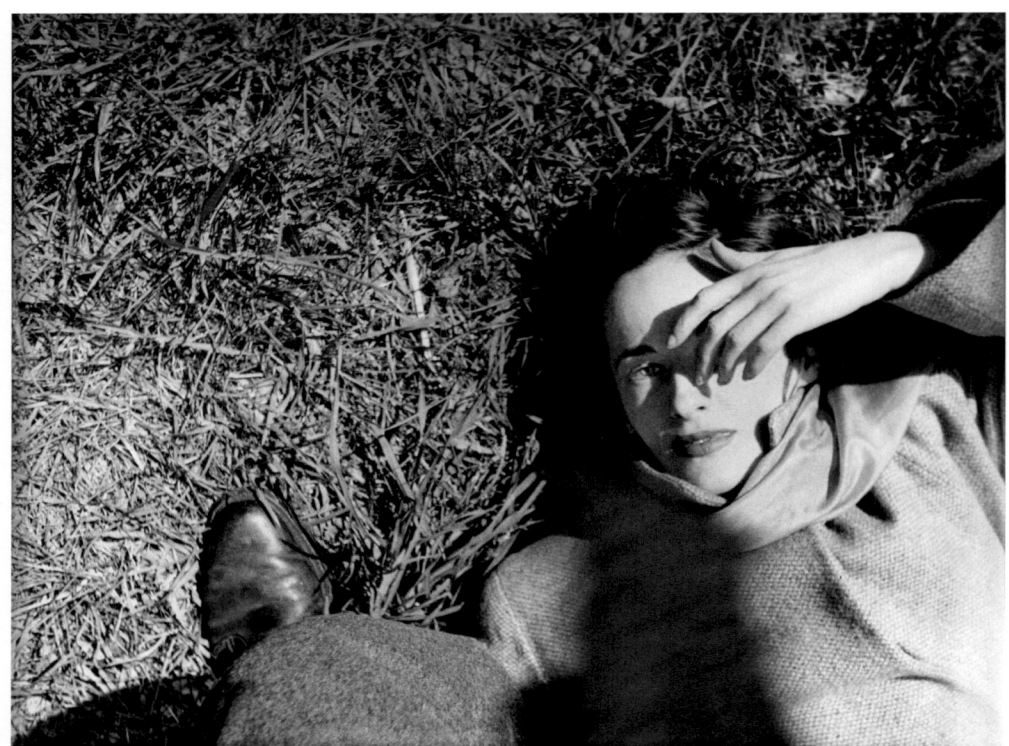

The newly printed works are the perfect analogue of the uncanny sense of spatial and temporal dislocation in Leiter's studio. In one of the photographs, I recognize the very skylight we're looking through, though now much less clean, from 1960. His talent for capturing a little explosion of color through the reduced light of a smeary shop window or a sudden downpour is a constant. ("I do seem to have a weakness for red umbrellas," he laughs.) In others, the humorously cropped bits of signage that Leiter captured while shooting from behind a storefront seem almost like a Conceptual photography joke *avant la lettre*. The scenes of street life are at once locally familiar but utterly foreign. I wonder if they strike him in the same way. "Sometimes I do something and I don't take it too seriously, and then years later I look at it and it may be more interesting than I thought it was. If you take a picture of a row of cars in 1950, it's a boring picture of a row of cars. But in 2013, you're looking at antiques and objects that have a certain kind of something or other."

Without missing a beat, he adds: "Sometimes I say time is on the side of the photographer."

If it has not been an exemplary career trajectory, Leiter's own path has led to the attention he is receiving now. An exhibition of his black-and-white and color work, as well as some of his paintings, organized by the Deichtorhallen in Hamburg, Germany, just toured the Kunsthaus Hundertwasser in Vienna, while an exhibition of his black-and-white work opened last month at Galerie 51 in Antwerp, Belgium. And in September, Steidl and Howard Greenberg Gallery —which hosted breakthrough shows of his early color work in 1995 and 2007— are co-publishing *Early Black and White*, a lavish two-volume monograph of work from the 1950s.

"People say now that I'm a pioneer. I don't know how true that is. Kertész used color, Moholy-Nagy used color. There have always been artists who questioned the extreme use of color— Mary Cassatt thought Matisse was a complete faker. There has always been the thought that color is not as profound as the search for form. Maybe my work lacks structure, I don't know?" And he laughs that Buddy Hackett laugh. "I'm mystified that anyone thinks liking color is a bad thing."

As we look through a set of recently printed work in hushed tones, part of a series from 1948 to 1960 that Leiter is working on, I ask if he ever tired of shooting the area around the Village. He grins: "People think I made this story up, but I used to go the same breakfast place as Robert Frank, and he came in one day and said he was going back to Switzerland. I said, Why? He said there was nothing to photograph here. Then of course he did *The Americans*.

"I'd see something lying on the ground and take a picture of it, maybe because I was lazy." When he was invited in the 1950s to project a group of his slides—images from what he calls his "garbage" series of "things flying in the street"—at the Club, he recalls that "someone vaguely thought that I had rearranged the stuff. He meant it as a kind of compliment, because they thought the arrangements were too good."

Eric Banks is a writer based in New York.

Words

Erwin Wurm,
The Magnate
(Hermès), **2008**
Courtesy Lehmann Maupin,
New York
(see page 46)

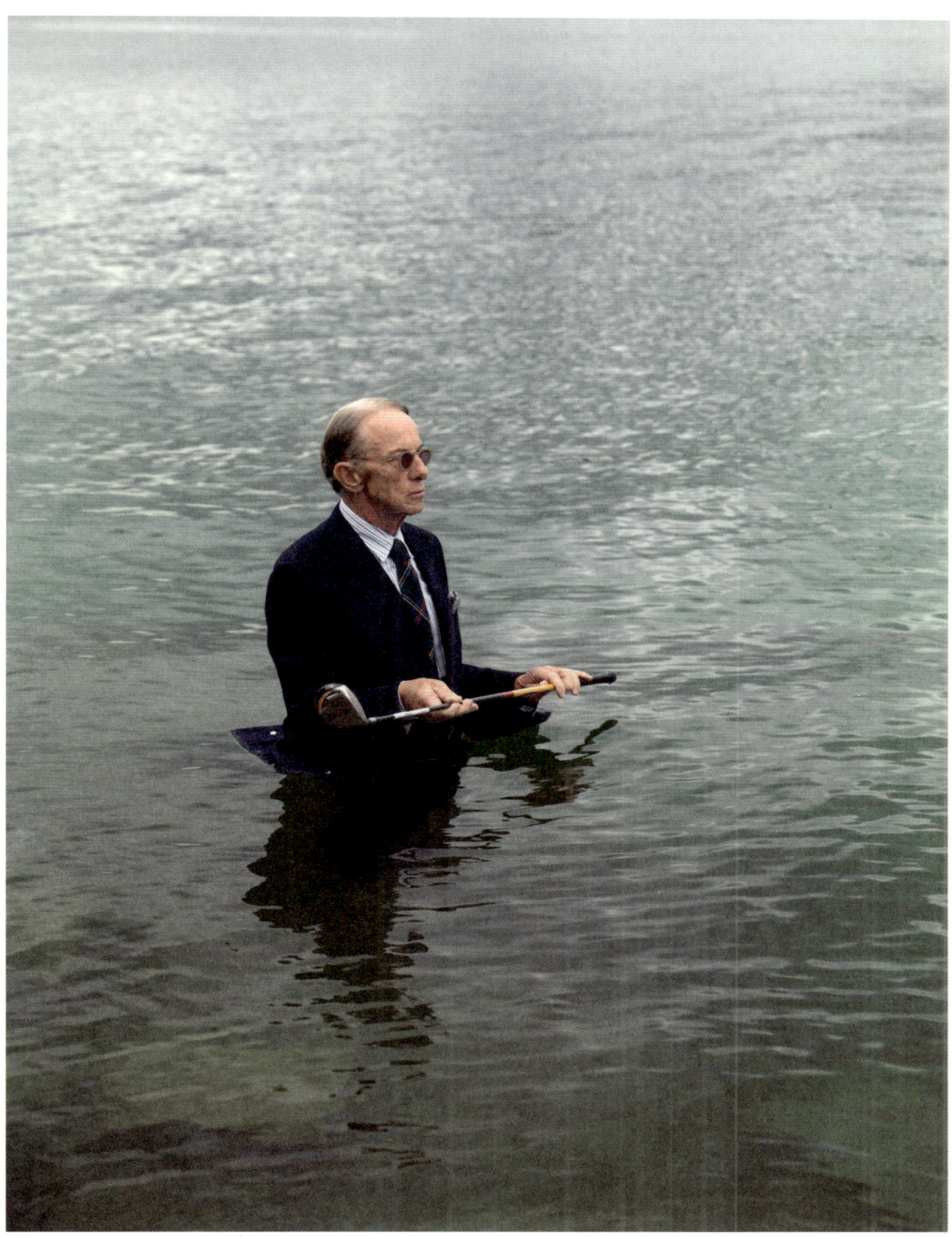

Music I've Seen

Christian Marclay in conversation
with Frances Richard

We tend to think of photography as a silent medium, but visual artist and composer Christian Marclay, known for his projects that explore the interplay of image and sound, reveals the sonic dimension of images. For his project *Shuffle* (2007), Marclay photographed musical notation found in everyday miscellany —on signage, clothing, and objects—eventually publishing the photographs as a deck of cards. The photo-cards are intended to literally be played; when performed, the photographic scores are selected at random by musicians who create improvised compositions. *Zoom Zoom* (2007–9) similarly employs visual sounds—onomatopoeias photographed by Marclay—that he projects during performances as a prompt for performance artist Shelley Hirsch's vocal improvisations. Marclay's other projects with photography include his series of elegant cyanotypes made from the guts of audiocassettes, bringing together two archaic analog technologies. Last April, Marclay spoke with poet Frances Richard at San Francisco's Fraenkel Gallery. Marclay, who divides his residence between New York and London, was in the Bay Area for an exhibition of his photographs, titled *Things I've Heard*, at the gallery and to open his celebrated video work *The Clock* (2011), a monumental twenty-four-hour piece comprised of collaged film clips featuring each minute of the day, at the San Francisco Museum of Modern Art.   —**The Editors**

Frances Richard: **You laminate so many layers of meaning into a simple gesture. In the *Zoom Zoom* and *Shuffle* photographs, for instance, we get a direct depiction of packaging and signage. That brings along references to various visual regimes—street photography, Pop art, Flickr. Then, if we read the images as transcriptions of sounds instead of as representations of objects, we can choose to imagine that sound as abstract. Or as sound that communicates a specific message. We can conjure up audible sound—"Pop pop puff"—or just think about sound-ness: "Ah, onomatopoeia." So many interpretive options are in play.**

Christian Marclay: That's when things are interesting and successful, when there are many possibilities for entering the work and interpreting it. In *Shuffle*, the pictures are far from being interesting in themselves. It's about documenting quickly, and not about composing a perfect image that would stand alone. I was interested in how musical notation is used every day by nonmusicians—by graphic designers, by decorators—to signify "music," but without any intention of generating real music. Yet, because of the symbols, if I put these pictures in the hands of musicians, they're potentially playable. They made me think of graphic scores in experimental music. I have to mention that I can't read or write music.

FR: **I was going to ask you about that.**

CM: So these, to me, are very abstract. But if you give them to musicians, something can happen, and that's what interests me: how they get translated. There's also an element of randomness, because the cards get shuffled and the responses are improvised. So there's definitely a notion of play. *Zoom Zoom* is also very playful. In the performance of *Zoom Zoom*, I select on the fly

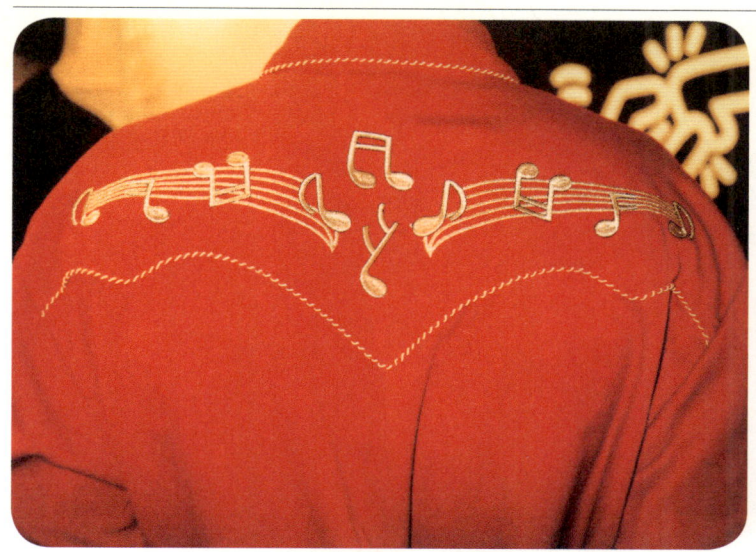
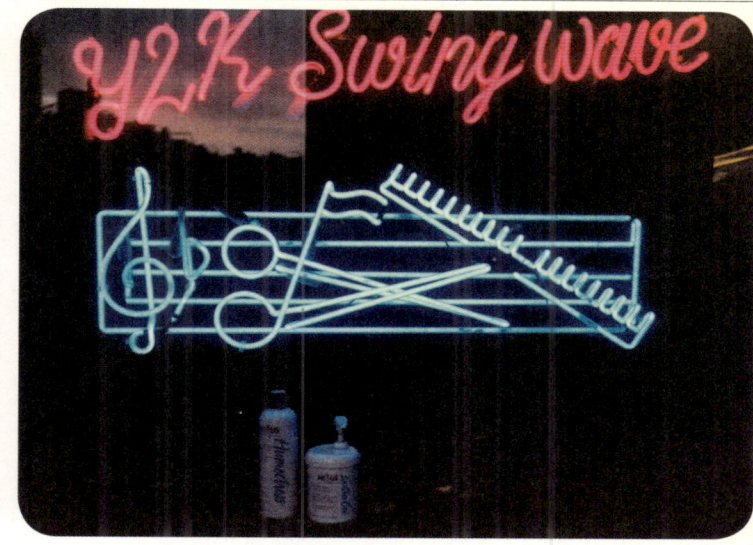
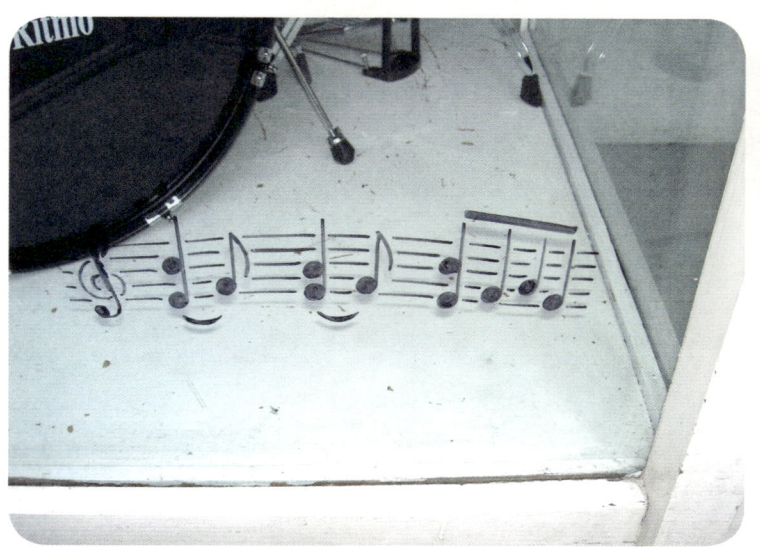
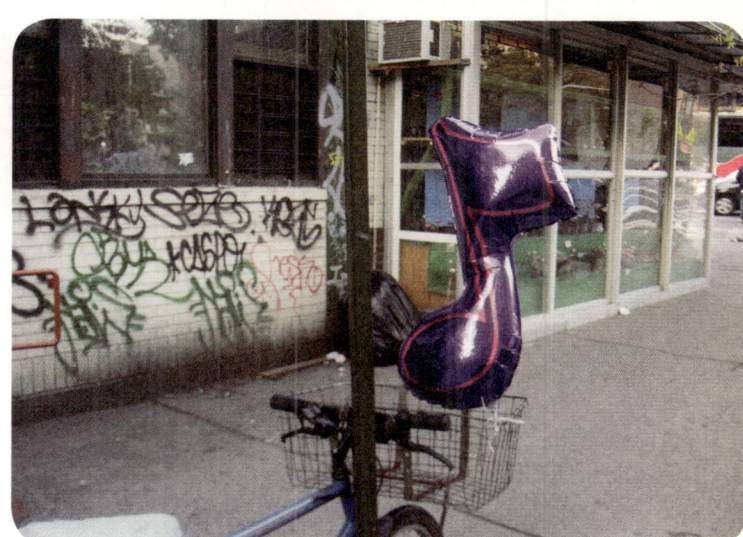
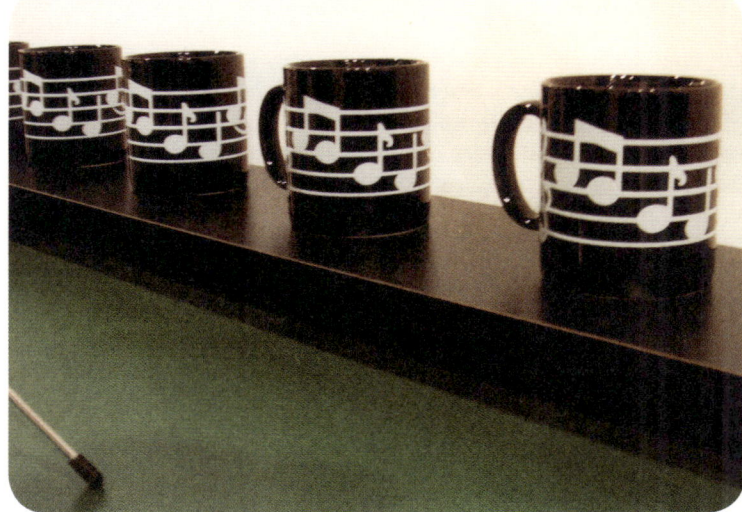
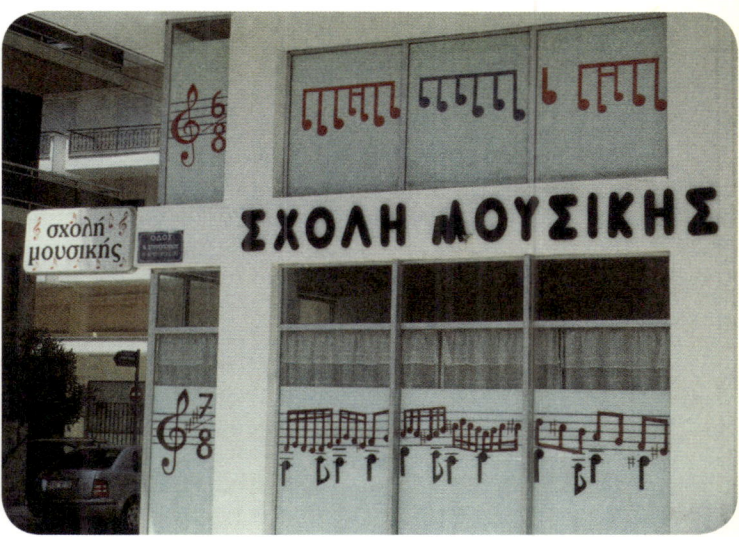

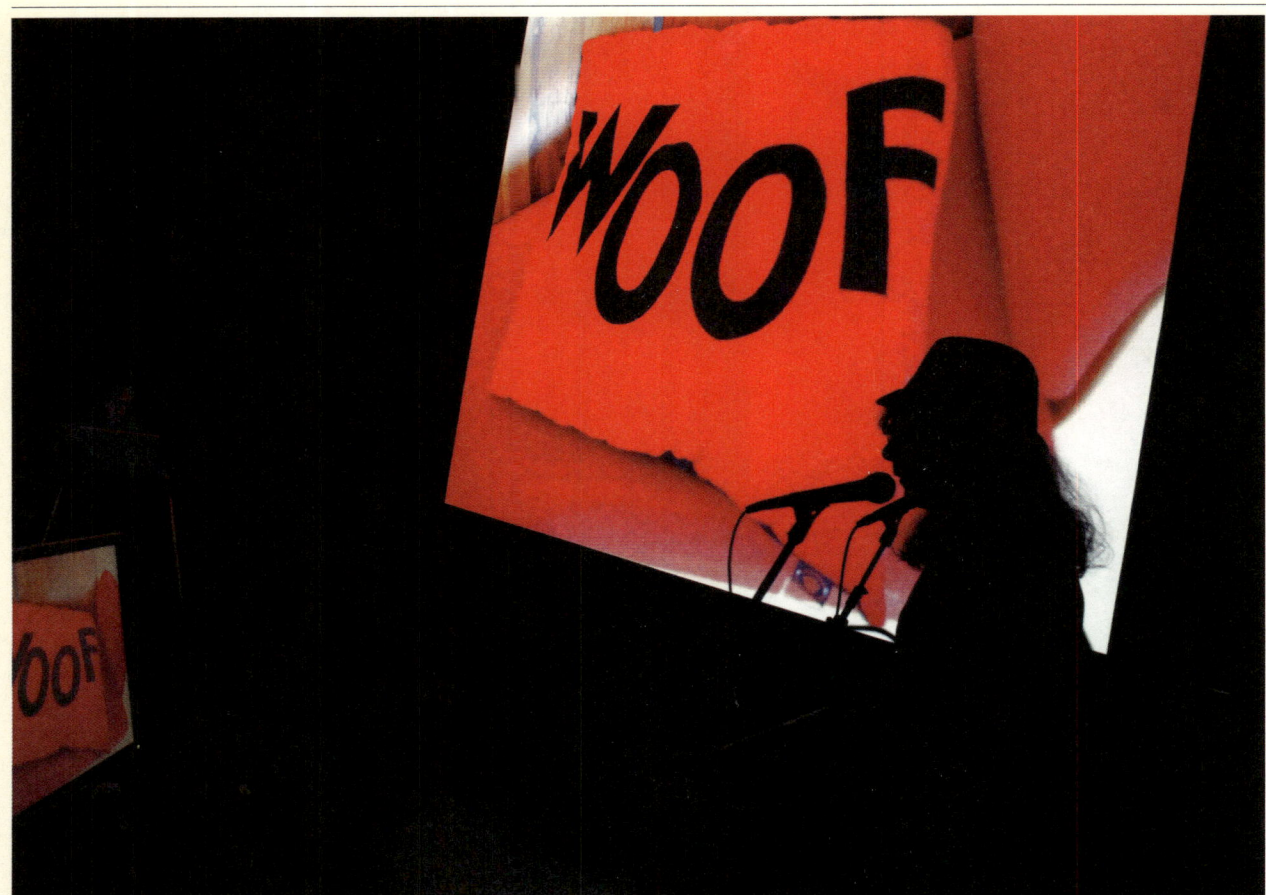

Shelley Hirsch and
Christian Marclay,
Zoom Zoom, performance
at the Whitney Museum
of American Art, New York,
July 17, 2010

from a pool of images on my computer while Shelley Hirsch improvises in response. I trigger her, and I react to what she does. I have all these thumbnail images in a grid onscreen, and I click on what I want. So no two performances are alike. Shelley has this incredible ability to tell stories and pick up on details in the image that extend beyond the onomatopoeia. She might comment on a person's haircut or whatever.

FR: **You're deejaying images, and Shelley Hirsch is the "dancer"—her voice is responding to the visual "music" you play, in the way that bodies on a dance floor might respond to aural music. You make these complex transpositions from image to music to text, and onomatopoeia seems like a perfect vehicle for that. Was it intentional, to build up a library of images that could be performed this way?**

These images become "live" again. They offer cues for action. As with the way I use records, they don't document as much as offer material for new sounds.

CM: These pictures were taken over more than a decade. I wouldn't have been able to accumulate so many in a short amount of time, and this project started without my having in mind the idea of a score. It became a score later on, as I realized that I was accumulating these images and that Shelley would be the perfect interpreter. I always have a camera. It's like a sketchbook, a way to quickly remember. These days the pictures are digital, so I put them on my laptop; I look at them once in a while…. But I don't take a picture with a strong intention. What I like about taking pictures is that it's instantaneous—

FR: **—and in that way playful. Do you record sound in the same wanting-to-remember way?**

CM: I don't do it with sound. I'm thinking of doing it with video, because my phone makes good videos. I don't even print most of my images. They exist only as digital files. Photography-as-photography is kind of dying. As soon as photography became portable, you could take it on the street. Now cameras are so small, it is even easier. But making a print as a way to share an image is not what is popular now. We're constantly e-mailing pictures to people, and they have a different nature: more ephemeral, less tangible.

FR: Although here we are in a gallery full of framed prints. And *Shuffle* presents a box of prints—mass-produced, yes, but still made to be handled, dealt out, toyed with.

CM: There are so many ways to think about photography. It can be tiny, on your phone, or it can be a billboard, or a film-sized projection, or printed in a magazine. I don't think we've been in a time before when so much photography is available in so many formats, when everybody is a photographer.

FR: Isn't that something people have said about photography since the very beginning, from Charles Baudelaire to Walter Benjamin to Susan Sontag?

CM: Yes, but if you were Baudelaire being a *flâneur* on the street, it was complicated to take a picture. I used to take pictures with a 35-millimeter camera. It was a small point-and-shoot, always in my pocket. But I had thirty-six shots, and it cost money to process, so I made different decisions. Now, I shoot-shoot-shoot. I don't think about it.

FR: Both *Zoom Zoom* and *Shuffle* center on performance, collaboration, the real-time interaction of live bodies. Even so, do you think that in some deep way these are digital projects, in that the images depend on that dematerialized, shoot-shoot-shoot attitude?

CM: Yes, in a way, because these images become "live" again. They offer cues for action. As with the way I use records, they don't document as much as offer material for new sounds. If you put a unique print behind glass, it becomes a precious thing, while the *Shuffle* images are cheaply available and made to be handled. A digital picture can be sent to a friend with your phone, and you lose control over it—it can be sent around, even go viral. These are new ways to communicate that didn't exist before.

FR: I read a comment somewhere about your video *Telephones* (1995)—a compilation of film clips of people using telephones —remarking that many of the movie vignettes stitched together in this piece would never happen now, simply because the phone no longer has a cord. Drama is attached to the fact that we used to have to sit by the phone and wait. And if we wanted to know who was calling, we had to answer.

CM: Right. It is interesting how objects affect our state of mind.

FR: Vinyl albums, even CDs, are moribund formats. Turntablism has revived vinyl for the cognoscenti, but it's not a universal form the way it was for decades. Even decks of cards are a sunsetting technology. We play solitaire on our phones; we play video poker.

CM: Social game-playing still exists. But it also has an old-fashioned quality because it forces people to sit physically together in one room instead of virtually.

FR: Here's something you said more than a decade ago: "I've always had this theory that recorded sound is dead sound, in the sense that it's not live anymore. Old records have this

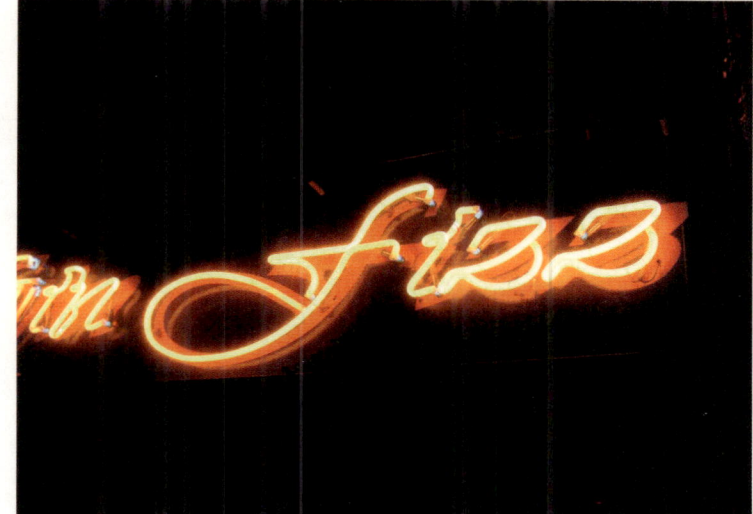

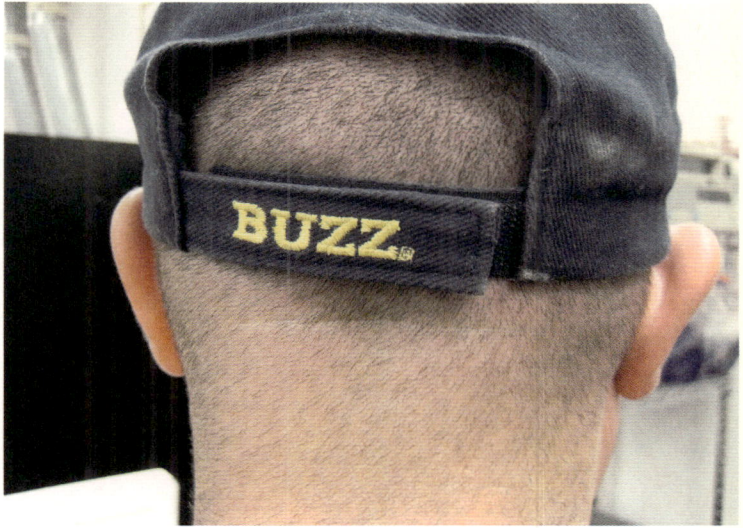

Slides from *Zoom Zoom*, 2007–9 (slide projection of 150 digital color photographs accompanying performance)

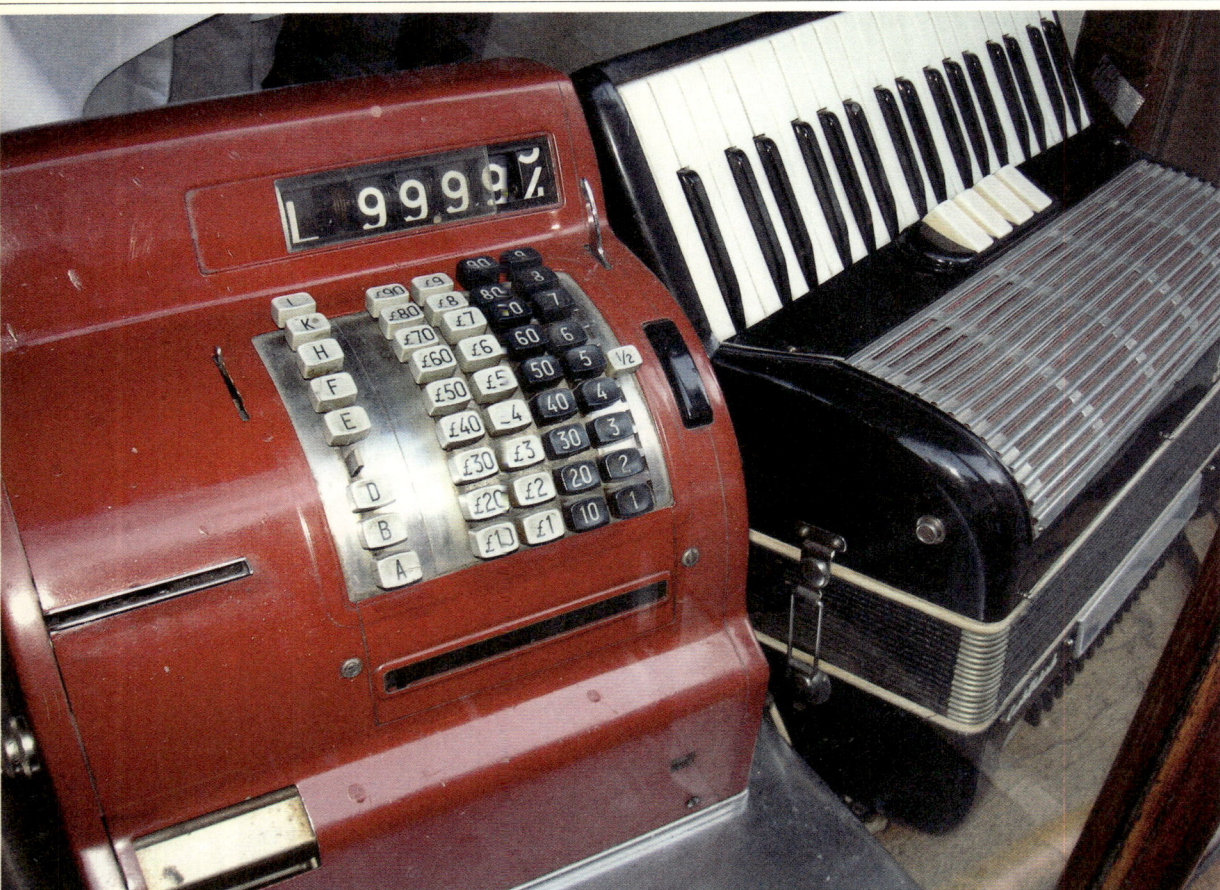

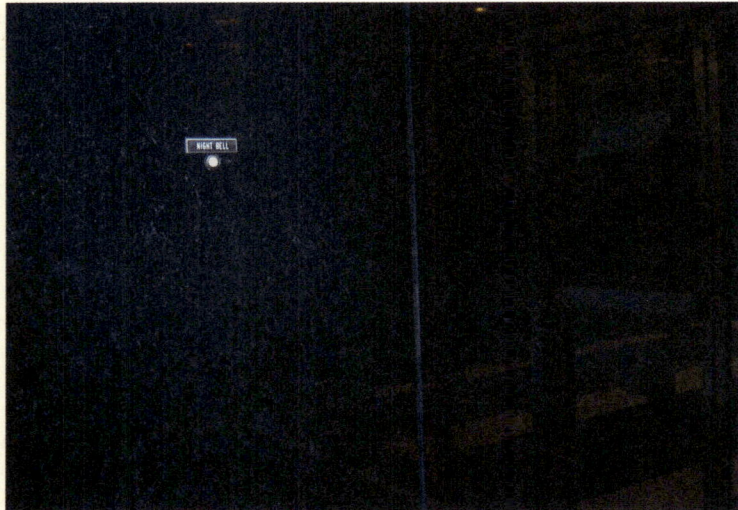

New York, 2003

quality of time past, this sense of loss. The music is embalmed. I'm trying to bring it back to life through my art." That's what we're talking about, no? Something embalmed by reproduction and obsolescence, that gets re-enlivened by being noticed in new ways.

CM: Technology has a short lifespan. It's almost as if you need that sunset to be aware of a technology as itself. As in a sunset, there's this extraordinary view that you don't get during the day; suddenly it gets very colorful; there's a sense of, "Oh, it's almost over; let's have a better look at it." You can be more critical, and more appreciative, because it's on the way out.

FR: So criticality and nostalgia sort of sit in the same spot? Maybe *nostalgia* isn't exactly the right word. *Retro*?

CM: Nostalgia and criticality do seem to be opposites. But there's always a sense of nostalgia in something that records the passing of time. You can't escape that. But you can have a critical look at things that seem nostalgic. We assume, because we're able to capture sounds or images, that they will exist forever—when, in fact, obsolescence makes you feel the limit of those assumptions. There's a nice tension there. Life is short, and all we have that's certain is the past.

FR: I slip from thinking about these traces of time past to thinking about realizations that come from seeing repetitions to thinking about, as it were, a score imprinted on the world by accident. This is something I return to as a poet. The medieval trope of the Book of Nature—which is there to be decoded by the initiated—speaks to this idea. The scores in *Shuffle* and *Zoom Zoom* are like this; they're inscribed on the world by the world's own self-perpetuating logic, hiding in plain sight, waiting to be noticed and interpreted by those who have the eyes to see and ears to hear. Except—and this

is a giant difference!—these signs are made not by nature, but by culture. Specifically late-capitalist, consumerist, more-or-less-trashy advertising culture.

CM: I relate this "writing" to the idea of an open score, where there are no rules, really, but a potential for events. You have to interpret it. You have to decipher it in whatever way you can, and everybody has different abilities, makes different connections. I think my work is about showing the multiplicity of interpretations rather than creating a strict, closed structure which is only understandable in a unique way.

FR: **I see these images as poised on a threshold, lighthearted but not overly affirmative**—

CM: Right.

FR: **Not negative. Not positive. Formal, but not intensely so. Curious, maybe**—

CM: Hesitant, maybe. There's a hesitance.

FR: **About?**

CM: The picture-taking happens quickly, and I don't know what I'm looking for. I tend to frame things in a fairly classical way. We all have this baggage of compositional devices that are so ingrained in our ways of seeing; we can't help using them. I still frame things straight-on, try to square the horizon line with the camera. These conventions are reflexes. I'm making the images recognizable for the viewer. But, then, I might pair things within the frame to trigger a possible narrative or critical point of view.

[CM and FR page through his catalog *Things I've Heard*]

For example, here's an image of a night bell [*New York*, 2003, opposite]. The fact that the sign is posted on a black wall, and there's nothing else—if it was on a white wall, the picture would be very different. Or, another example: Here are two things side by side. One is a cash register, the other is an accordion [*London*, 2006, opposite]. They are different objects, yet formally similar, and money and music go hand in hand.

FR: **Do you think about pseudomorphism a lot?**

CM: What do you mean?

FR: **Well, you make this proposition, in effect, that *Zoom Zoom*, or *Shuffle*, or the group of images in *Things I've Heard* make up a set, that these things—which are so disparate— rhyme somehow, or belong in a series. Take the accordion and the cash register. They both have a vaguely Deco curved silhouette. They're red and gold and black and white. They have keys. They have numbers. They have a grille or slot where something comes out or goes in.**

CM: They also both make a sound. *Ka-ching*!

FR: **But one could argue that's all pseudomorphism, superficial accident. They don't really have anything to do with one another.**

CM: Yes. But the reason they are together is to offer a third reading, totally disconnected from their initial usage. They tell

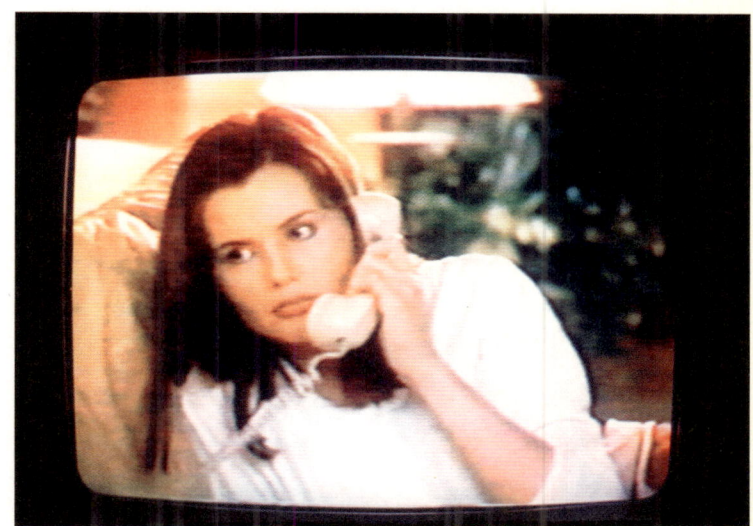

Photography is solitary and there are lags between seeing with your eyes and seeing through the lens, and then seeing the image on your computer…. I often see things after the fact. This revelatory quality includes a sense of playfulness, because you're not sure what the consequences are going to be.

There's always a sense of nostalgia in something that records the passing of time. You can't escape that. But you can have a critical look at things that seem nostalgic.

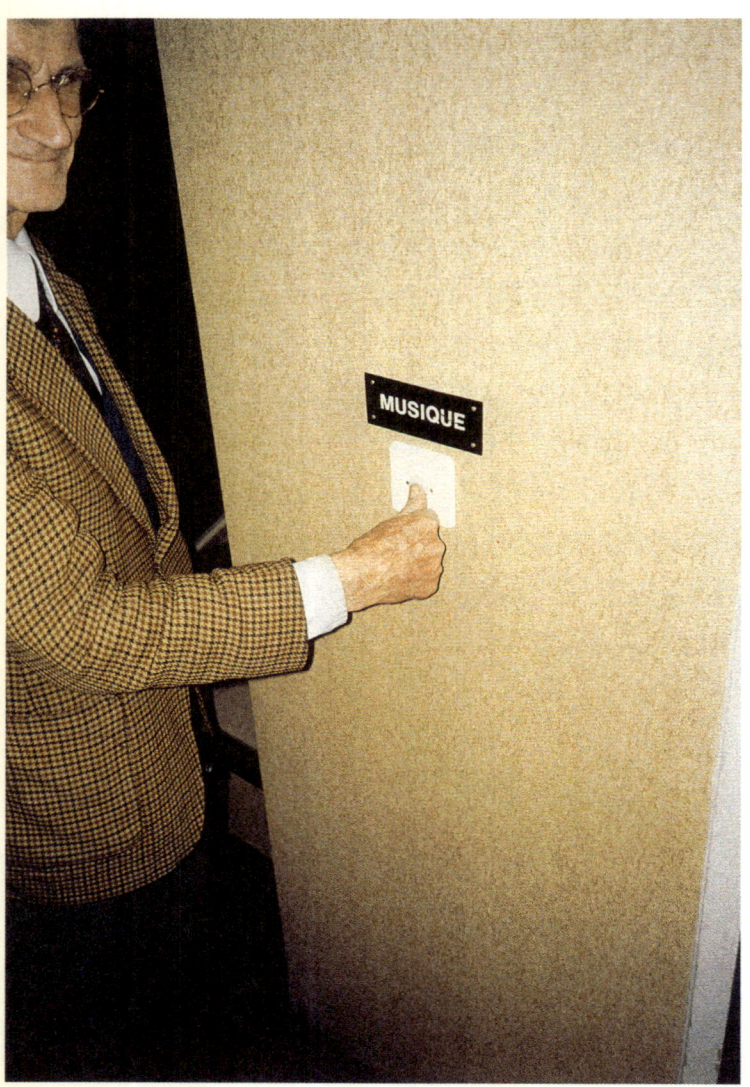

a beautiful story together. Like if you're writing poetry, you put together two words that rhyme or off-rhyme, and even though they may be unrelated, that rhyme is going to give the phrase a different weight. It kind of forces them together.

FR: **That's true. This is like a game structure, where the game is about accumulation yielding a meaning that couldn't emerge in any other way. Like in *Telephones*, where it becomes about the pathos and repetitiveness of trying to communicate, the relentless similarity in unlike situations. "Hello." "Hello?" "Hello." "Hello?" "Good-bye." "Good-bye." "Good-bye."**

CM: That's why I said "hesitant." When I snap a photograph, I'm just seeing something, and I capture it. It's very different than, let's say, if I were to create a set and stage a situation to be photographed, or if I went out of my way to document specific things.

FR: **You would never arrange a photograph.**

CM: No. I might adjust something, the way I scraped the snow off the Yamaha box on the street [*New York*, 2003, opposite]. I'm not a purist in that sense. I wanted the viewer to know there was a picture of a guitar on the box. At first I thought you could see it through the snow, which was a nice kind of veil. But it didn't come through. So I brushed some snow off. There's something between the silencing of the snow and this guitar that is not in the box anymore. It's winter; the box is on the curb with the trash; maybe a kid received that guitar for Christmas. There's a potential for narrative. For me, there's always this moment of hesitation when I take the photograph. Is it worth stopping for? At the same time, it's never a big statement. Most of my pictures are really small statements. There's a banality to them.

FR: **How would you compare that moment, that split-second intuitive decision, with an improvisatory decision in performance?**

CM: It's a nice way to think about it, in terms of improvisation and playing music. It's not the "decisive moment" of classic street photography. Because my images rarely involve people, the notion of speed is less an issue. But still, there's that decision to pull the camera out of the pocket and use it. In playing improvised music, you are constantly making decisions; you are reacting to others, and you never know where the hell it's going to lead. Photography is solitary and there are lags between seeing with your eyes and seeing through the lens, and then seeing the image on your computer, or as a print, and seeing things that you hadn't noticed. I often see things after the fact. So there's a revelatory quality. And this definitely includes a sense of playfulness, because you're not sure what the consequences are going to be.

FR: **I'm thinking of John Zorn's game structures and the open work, the open score.**

CM: There are strict rules, but you are never going to play the same thing twice.

FR: **Maybe this is my bias as a poet. But, for me, both these projects have that sense of a script that isn't a script—a graphic meaning that's printed on the world just off the scale of language. Does that feel right?**

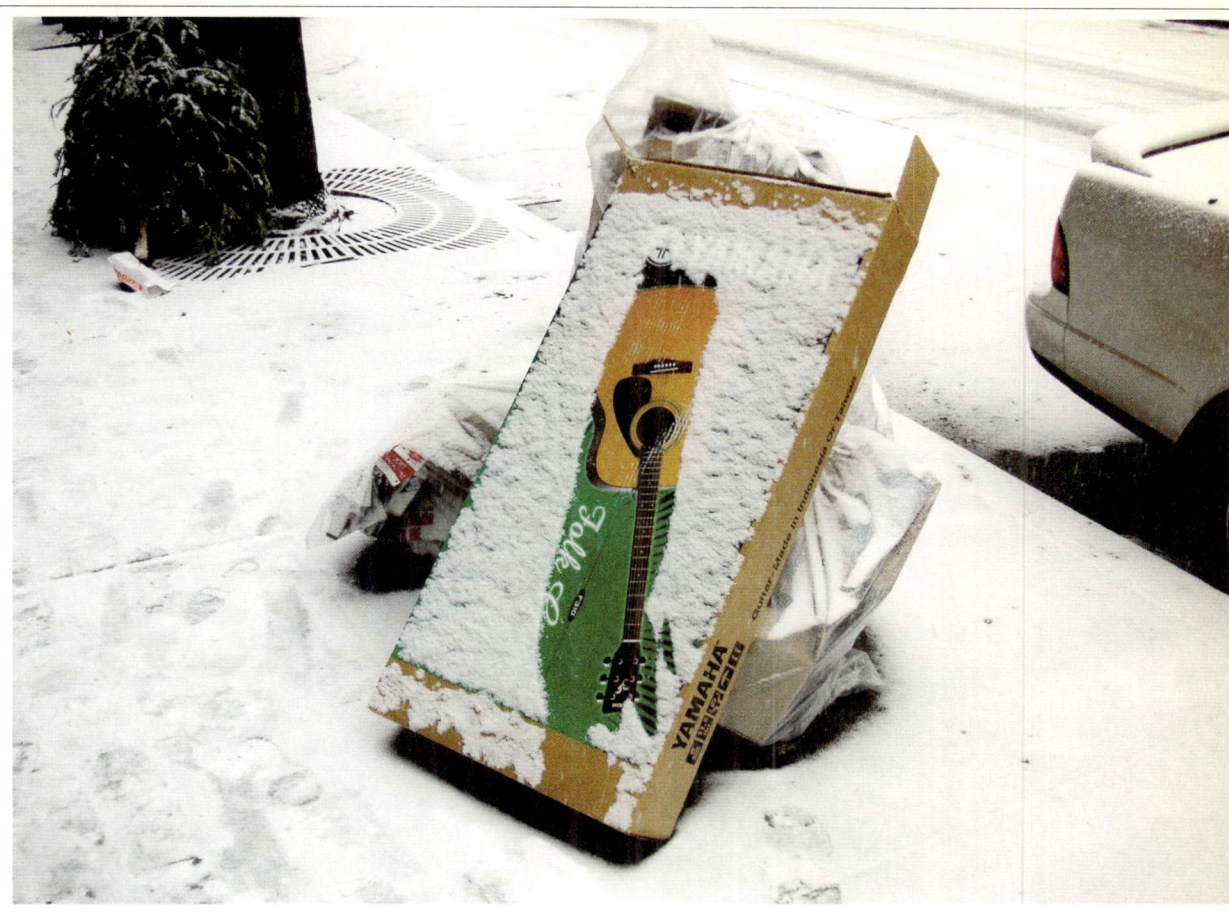

New York, 2003
All photographs © Christian
Marclay; courtesy Fraenkel
Gallery, San Francisco,
and Paula Cooper Gallery,
New York

CM: Yes, it does. I think of snapshots, often, in terms of poetry, just because they play with language. *Shuffle* also has to do with the different type of writing that is musical notation, a language I don't write or read. The project says something about my lack of musical knowledge and these shortcuts that allow me to generate music without knowing what the signs literally mean.

FR: Like the photograph of the night bell—the wit or resonance of the image depends on our being able to read English, to understand those two words. That's a different role for language than when we see some enigmatic sign that we know has meaning, but in a system in which we are illiterate. Take this image [from *Shuffle*, page 27, bottom-right—musical notation on a window, with lace curtain and other signage]. Is this Greek?

CM: Yes.

FR: So we have musical notation and Greek—two languages I don't read. That makes me ask myself about the filigree on the balcony railing or the laciness of the curtain. I'm ready to read those as a secret script too.

CM: Yes, definitely. This is what interests me, how everything in *Shuffle* is potentially music. You've got staff lines; you've got the reference to pitch, maybe, and to structure. You have rhythmic division.

FR: You could start playing the decorative metal musical notes attached to the metal gate, and then go on to play the holes in the bricks, the lines of the telephone wires, the lines of the siding on the house, the shapes of the trees….

CM: It invites you to look not just at music, but at the world around the music as its extension.

Christian Marclay's *The Clock* will be
on view at the Winnipeg Art Gallery
September 27, 2013–January 5, 2014.

Marclay's *Shuffle* was published
by Aperture in 2007.

Frances Richard is the author of *Anarch*,
(Futurepoem, 2012); *The Phonemes*
(Les Figues Press, 2012); and *See Through*
(Four Way Books, 2003). She writes
frequently about contemporary art and
teaches currently at the California College
of the Arts in San Francisco.

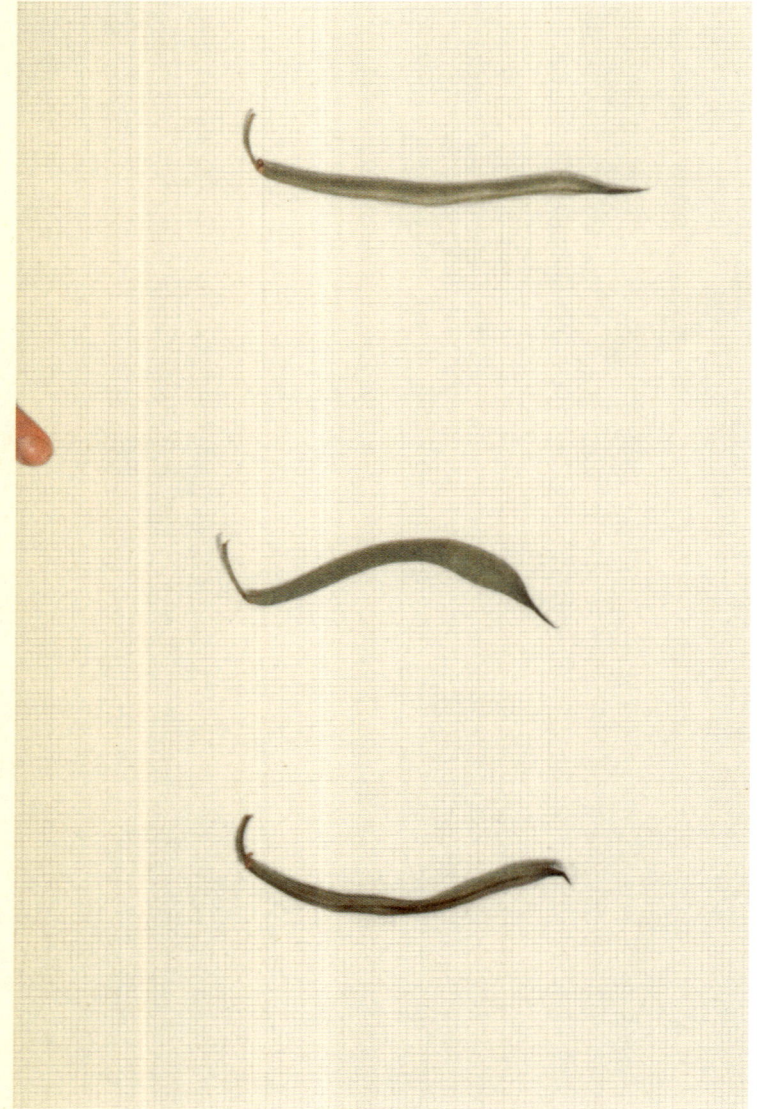
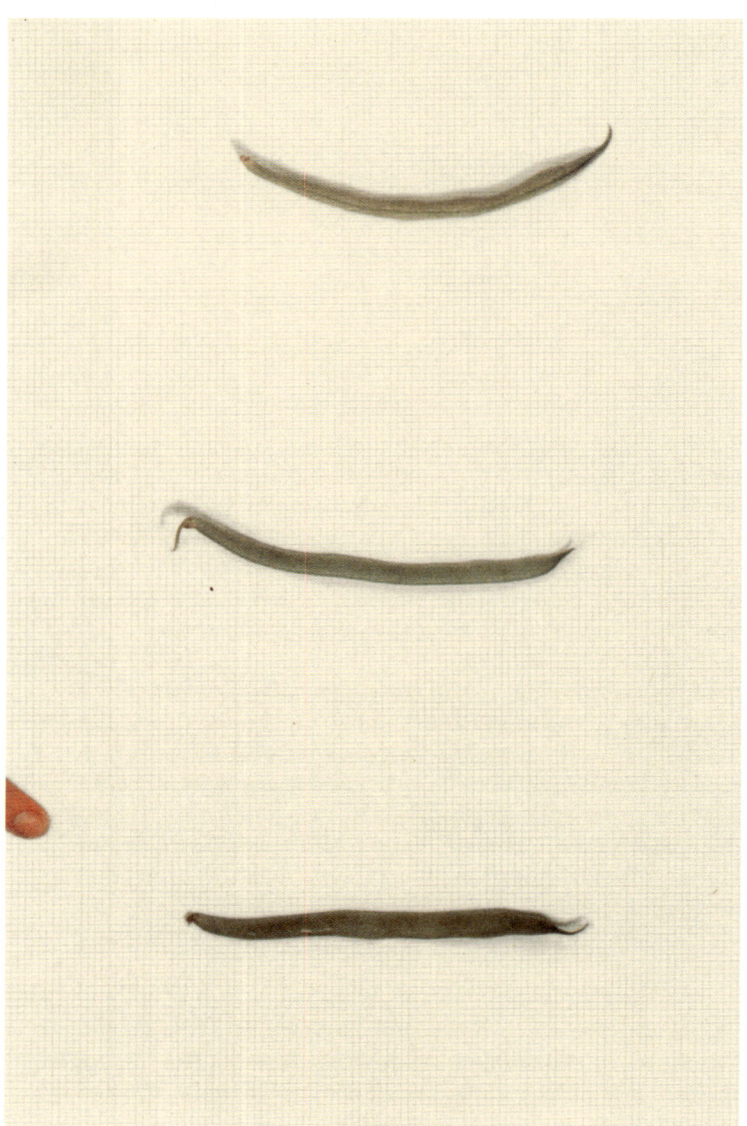

It was sometimes hard to take seriousness seriously in the 1960s and '70s. Robin Kelsey considers a group of artists who turned to games, whimsy, and clowning around as vehicles for their work.

Playing Around Photography
Robin Kelsey

In the 1960s and '70s, a bevy of artists experimented with photography as a means of making art from play. The rarified term commonly used to describe their work—*Conceptual art*—has tended to obscure its penchant for witty subterfuge. The approaches of these artists varied: some clowned around in front of the camera, others developed games that produced a series of photographs in compliance with absurd rules, while still others photographed constructed scenes featuring toy figures or other prosaic objects.

How might we understand this historical turn? One way to grapple with the emergence of such practices is to consider playful photography to be the opposite of serious painting. Although Abstract Expressionist painting of the postwar years looked like child's play to some, the art world treated it with great seriousness, finding in Jackson Pollock's dripped and clotted palimpsests the tortured cosmos of a distinctly masculine artistic selfhood. This exaltation of the solitary painter as the bearer of collective conscience in the atomic age struck a younger generation of artists as daft or unsustainable. Pop art arose as a rejoinder—with artists such as Andy Warhol and Roy Lichtenstein finding material for painting in popular subjects (e.g., Coke bottles, Donald Duck) and popular media (e.g., silkscreen, Ben-Day dots). Once this embrace of lowbrow pleasures deflated the momentousness of painterly angst, younger artists, led by Ed Ruscha, turned to photography—the popular form of picture making par excellence.

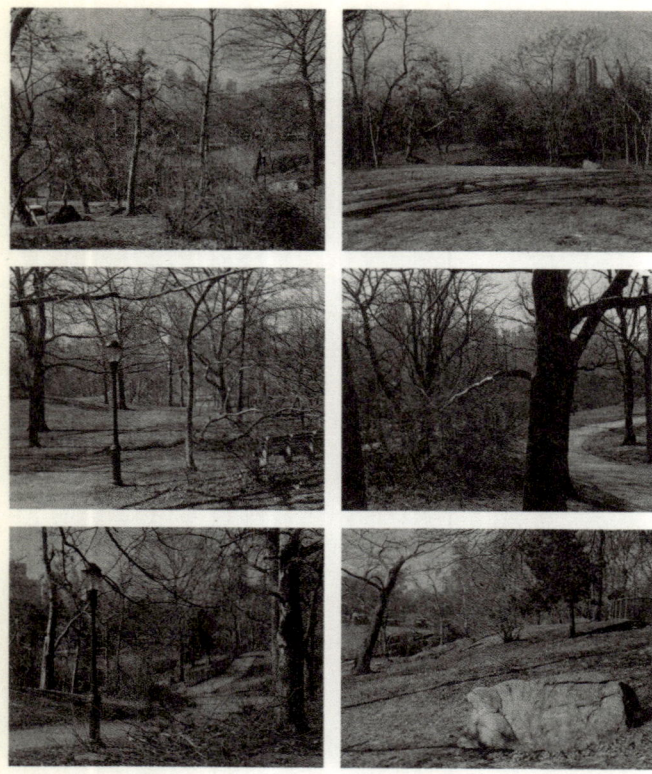
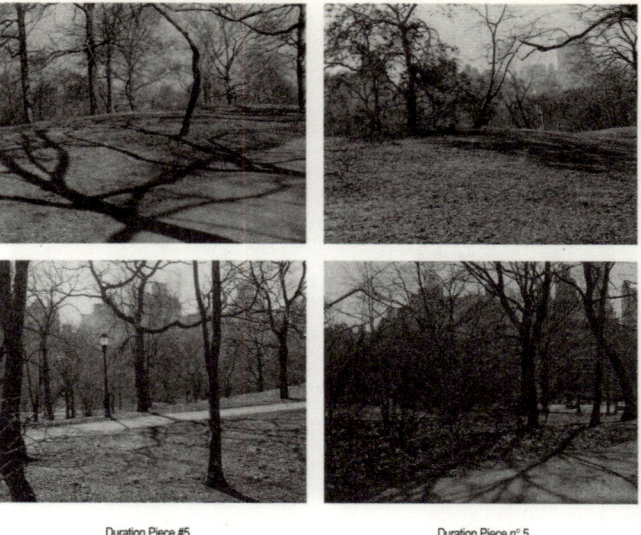

Duration Piece #5
New York

During a ten minute period of time on March 17, 1969 ten photographs were made, each documenting the location in Central Park where an individually distinguishable bird call was heard. Each photograph was made with the camera pointed in the direction of the sound. That direction was then walked toward by the auditor until the instant that the next call was heard, at which time the next photograph was made and the next direction taken.

The ten photographs join with this statement to constitute the form of this piece.

April, 1969

Duration Piece n° 5
New York

Pendant dix minutes, le 17 mars 1969, dix photos ont été prises, chacune ayant pour but de localiser, dans *Central Park*, l'endroit d'où provenait le chant très caractéristique d'un oiseau isolé. Chaque photographie était prise, l'appareil pointé vers la source du chant. Le chemin était ensuite parcouru dans cette direction jusqu'au moment où, d'un autre endroit, reprenait le gazouillis. Un cliché était alors aussitôt réalisé, et la nouvelle direction immédiatement suivie.

Les 10 photos, jointes à la présente déclaration, constituent la *forme* de cette oeuvre.

Avril 1969

Douglas Huebler, *Duration Piece #5, New York,* 1969
© 2013 Douglas Huebler; courtesy Paula Cooper Gallery, New York, and Darcy Huebler/Artists Rights Society (ARS), New York

Conceptual artists playfully critiqued photographic conventions to demystify *both* serious painting and serious photography.

By the 1960s, commercial interests were channeling photography in two main directions. One was toward public communication. Illustrated magazines of mass circulation, such as *Life, Look, National Geographic,* and *Sports Illustrated,* promoted the notion that photographs had a special capacity for communicating insights about modern experience. The other main direction was toward personal commemoration. Companies such as Kodak and Polaroid mass-marketed photography as an easy means of celebrating modern affluence and leisure. No vacation or family holiday was complete without a flattering record of its pleasures.

Photographers seeking to make art struggled to locate their efforts with respect to these commercial forces. Many of them regarded the illustrated magazines with ambivalence or outright disdain and denigrated popular photography as so much thoughtless button-pressing. These highbrow practitioners responded to the commercialization of photography by exalting the fastidiously composed and executed print.

But Ruscha and some other young artists took a contrary tack, adopting photography in a manner that sidled up to both journalistic and popular modes, often to satirical effect. Artists in Southern California were particularly active in this regard: consider Ruscha's deadpan 1963 book *Twentysix Gasoline Stations,* or John Baldessari's 1966–68 image of himself standing beneath a tree that appears to be growing out of his head, captioned succinctly: *Wrong.* Such works spurned the dictates of fine-art photography in favor of slipshod or outright "incorrect" compositions, banal subject matter, and dopey didacticism.

Conceptual artists playfully critiqued photographic conventions to demystify *both* serious painting and serious photography. For example, they debunked the notion of *expression,* which had been crucial for a preceding generation of artists in both media. When Bruce Nauman made his *Self-Portrait as a Fountain* (1966–67), not only did he stage sculpture as a photograph, acknowledging the photographic mediation of aesthetic experience, he also punctured the aura of artistic expression, depicting it as a literal stream of water emerging from the artist's mouth. The modern notion of artistic expression often confused the artist with the work; Nauman countered by confusing the work with the artist, by becoming his own sculpture.

Artists of the 1960s and '70s also lampooned the vaunted eye and transformative art of the modernist photographer. At the time, no modernist photograph had won more acclaim than Edward Weston's *Pepper No. 30*, of 1930. In his daybooks, Weston had pointedly distinguished his search for exquisite modernist subjects from the housewife's perusal of produce in the grocery store. He construed his process of selection, composition, and printing as a kind of transubstantiation of an everyday vegetable into an eternal form. Baldessari responded by making a silly game of selecting the best vegetable. In his 1971 *Choosing (A Game for Two Players): Green Beans*, for example, Baldessari proffered a series of photographs based on a simple set of rules. From an array of green beans, one player selects three. The other player then chooses one of the three by pointing to it, and a photograph of this pointing is made. The two unselected vegetables are then discarded and replaced with two others from the array. The process is repeated until the supply of beans is exhausted. This game took all the air out of the modernist search for ideal form, collapsing Weston's transubstantiation into the arbitrariness of sheer whim. It also cleverly suggested that all artistic production is a constrained social process, not a free and solitary creative act.

This mischievous group of artists also used photography to dissect pictorial genres and the myths attending them. Consider, for example, the way Douglas Huebler critiqued landscape in his *Duration Piece #5* (1969), which consists of ten photographs and the following typewritten text:

> *During a ten minute period of time on March 17, 1969 ten photographs were made, each documenting the location in Central Park where an individually distinguishable bird call was heard. Each photograph was made with the camera pointed in the direction of the sound. That direction was then walked toward by the auditor until the instant that the next call was heard, at which time the next photograph was made and the next direction taken.*
>
> *The ten photographs join with this statement to constitute the form of this piece.*

In abiding by these rules, Huebler surrendered his autonomy to the unpredictable scattering of birdsongs in Central Park. He followed each avian vocalist until he heard the next one, ricocheting from one random aural encounter to the next. His game playfully skewered a host of romantic ideals of landscape, including the notions of following a natural muse, of achieving a correspondence between landscape and music, and of rendering an experience of the invisible visible. It produced arbitrary pictures, drained of subjective aesthetic judgment and lacking composition or taste. Once again, photographic play had become a corrective for painterly pomposity.

Some artists combined pictorial mischief with inventive new ways of getting their art to a public. When her gallery closed in the winter of 1970–71, Eleanor Antin purchased one hundred rubber boots at an Army-Navy surplus store and began photographing them at various sites in Southern California and printing the pictures as postcards. The photographed boots (a readymade rejoinder to Vincent van Gogh's painted shoes) tramp their way through a series of overlapping cultural references from one postcard to the next. The play of absence established by the empty boots is provocative and ambiguous.

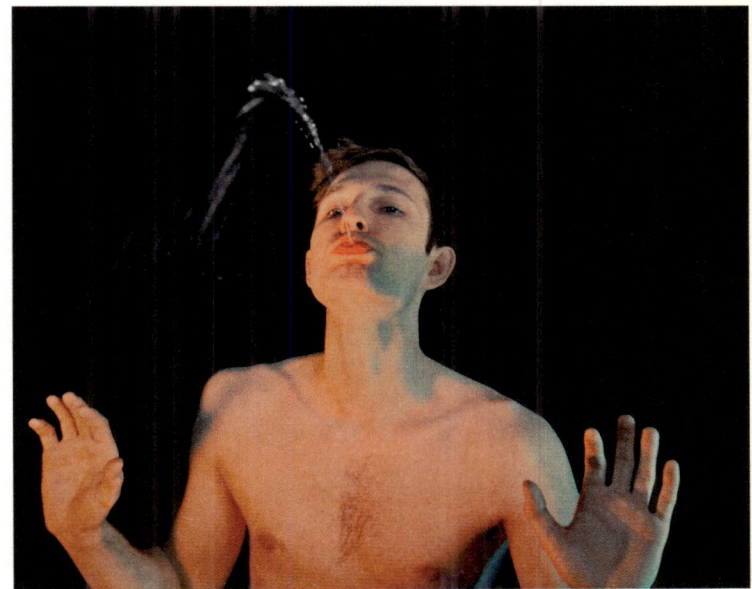

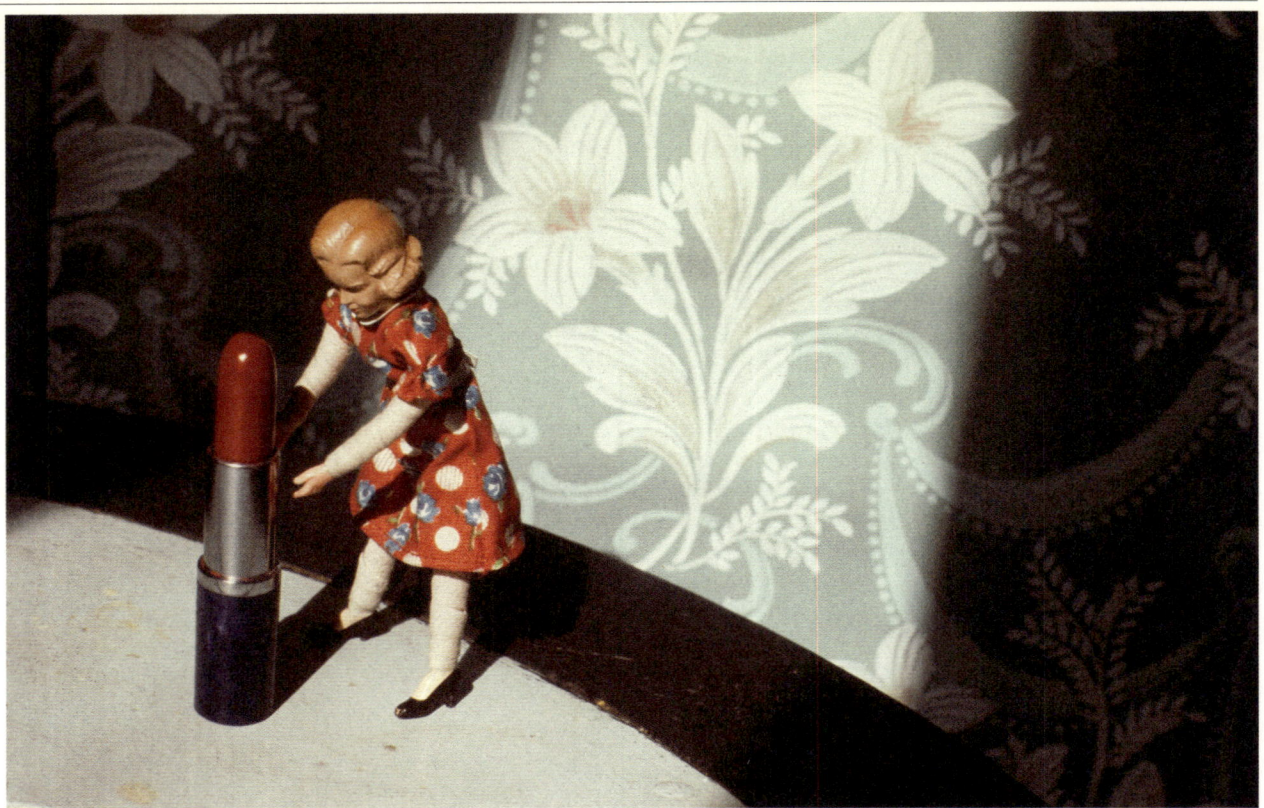

In one photograph, they cluster under a bridge, invoking a Jacob Riis–like depiction of the down and out. Whether we are to read the empty boots as a comment on the impossibility of representing one class to another, or on the vacuous conventionality of the composition, or on the suppressed-subject positions of women in representation, is left unresolved. Antin distributed the postcards through a mailing list of about a thousand people and institutions, sending them out in serial fashion over the course of more than two years. She thus harnessed a system built around the leisure industry to circumvent the gallery system.

In the 1970s, the artists Laurie Simmons and David Levinthal each began making photographs of miniature scenes featuring toy figures to explore the intersection of identity, mood, and the politics of representation. Simmons positioned toy figures in dollhouse-like spaces to question the formation of gender identity with the very materials that society uses to reproduce it. Her invocation of play as social preparation prompted critical reflection on how gender is regulated from the earliest stages of socialization. At the same time, she insisted that the spaces of femininity were valid sources for the imagery of ambitious art. Through the use of oblique lighting and stereotypical subject matter, she fashioned worlds haunted by the lifelessness and unreality of stereotype. In *Pushing Lipstick (Spotlight)* of 1979, Simmons played off the public scale of Pop—think of Claes Oldenburg's enormous *Lipstick Ascending on Caterpillar Tracks* (1969–74)—with the private scale of imaginative play.

A great aesthetic paradox of the 1960s and '70s was that to be serious was to risk not being artistically relevant, and some of the most playful artists were the most consequential. The conundrum for art historians is why at this historical juncture seriousness lost its secure grip on art.

Looking to the broader culture, two plausible explanations for this paradoxical state of affairs come to mind. The first is that by the 1960s, at least in the eyes of many young people, America was forfeiting the gravity and respect it had accrued through the defeat of fascism during World War II. The madness of the management of the Cold War and its atomic competition,

By playing around, young artists in the 1960s and '70s were both critically engaging with a new mode of knowledge production and also reclaiming play from a bureaucratic order bent on turning it to instrumental ends.

parodied in Stanley Kubrick's film *Doctor Strangelove* (1964), had made the solemnity of officialdom hard to take seriously. Pollock may indeed have been confronting Cold War madness in his own way, but he did so in a swaggering cowboy manner that seemed complicit in national hubris by the time America was riding west into Vietnam.

This hypothesis comports with the received notion of the 1960s as a time of Merry Prankster–style rebellion, but it explains both too much and too little. There are many ways to respond critically to corrupt or mad forms of seriousness besides play. Indeed, the interwar European avant-garde had largely responded to an earlier moment of madness with a perspicacious urgency, or an acerbic mode of absurdity. So why did many in the American neo-avant-garde insist on fooling around?

One answer is that American artists in the 1960s could afford it. Unemployment was low (3.8 percent during the Summer of Love), education was cheap, and productivity was soaring. Although the 1960s are routinely construed as a time of unrest and discontent, the background of the social foment was an unprecedented economic security, which fostered utopian aspirations and may have encouraged artists to mix levity with critique. For artists such as Ruscha, Baldessari, and Huebler, who were too old to be drafted for military service in Vietnam, it was evidently high time for hijinks.

An equally plausible and more interesting explanation for all this artistic tomfoolery is that play had *become* serious. By this I mean that the very military-industrial complex associated with the gray-suited judgment excoriated by Kubrick was giving forms of play a crucial instrumental role in its bureaucratic regime. In the wake of World War II, military specialists determined that handling the complexity of modern systems —from global military operations to nuclear fission—required moving beyond ordinary empiricism into games and simulations. John von Neumann and Oskar Morgenstern's landmark book *Theory of Games and Economic Behavior* (1944) provided the paradigm. As Peter Galison discusses in his 1997 book *Image & Logic: A Material Culture of Microphysics,* in the development of the hydrogen bomb, physicists and engineers used Monte Carlo methods to produce simulations of subatomic behavior, making the world of games and simulations an alternate reality in which otherwise unwieldy experiments could be conducted. The RAND corporation soon marketed the approaches it had developed for conducting military games and simulations to other social sectors, and specialists in the social sciences embraced gaming as a new means of modeling modern complexity.

By playing around, young artists in the 1960s and '70s were both critically engaging with a new mode of knowledge production and also reclaiming play from a bureaucratic order bent on turning it to instrumental ends. Play as an autonomous activity has for generations been under threat by bureaucratic managers wishing to instrumentalize it, and American social scientists during the Cold War were particularly concerned about the "durable benefits" and "yield" of leisure time. With games becoming a key instrument of social control, the threat to play as a sphere of autonomous pleasure was greater than ever. Herbert Marcuse, a thinker of importance to many artists, argued in his influential 1955 book *Eros and Civilization* that "play is unproductive and useless precisely because it cancels the repressive and exploitative traits of labor and leisure." In the 1960s and '70s, a young generation of artists sought to open a space between labor and leisure, between the overwrought rhetoric of painting as a kind of transcendental work and the stultifying conventionality of commercially packaged forms of recreation. They took up photography to free themselves from the straitjacketing legacy of Abstract Expressionism, and to free photography from its futile pursuit of a bankrupt respectability.

This history is interesting to recall today, when so many artists are constructing their photographic surfaces with meticulous care. The age of Chaos Theory is an age of resurgent determinism, when everything from images to weather patterns seems to be governed by computational algorithms and inexorable laws. The gap between video game and drone warfare seems thin indeed, and our anxious economic times contribute to a somber mood. Whether artists can once again find a dream of liberation in the play of photography remains to be seen.

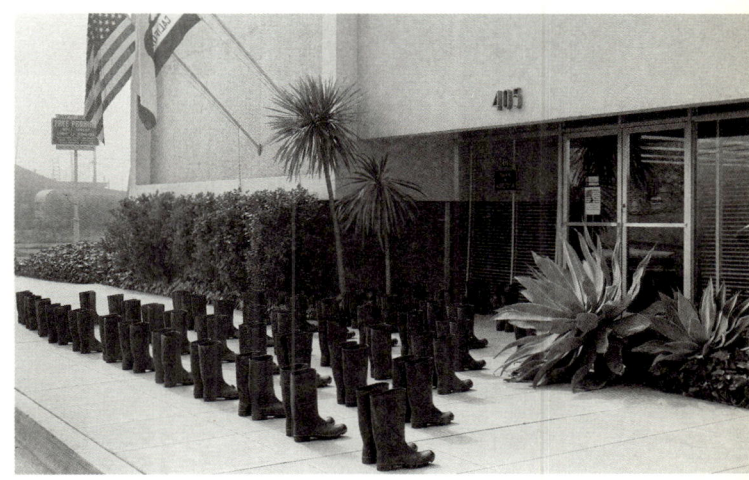

Eleanor Antin, *100 Boots at the Bank, Solana Beach, California, 10:00 am, February 9, 1971 (mailed: April 26, 1971)*, 1971
Courtesy Ronald Feldman
Fine Arts, New York

Robin Kelsey is the Shirley Carter Burden Professor of Photography and chair of the Department of History of Art and Architecture at Harvard University.

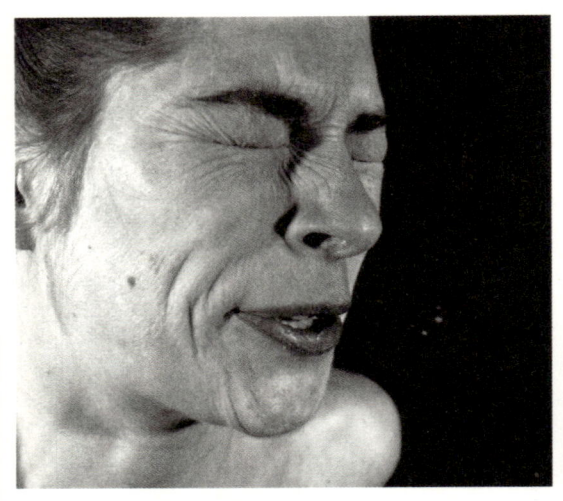

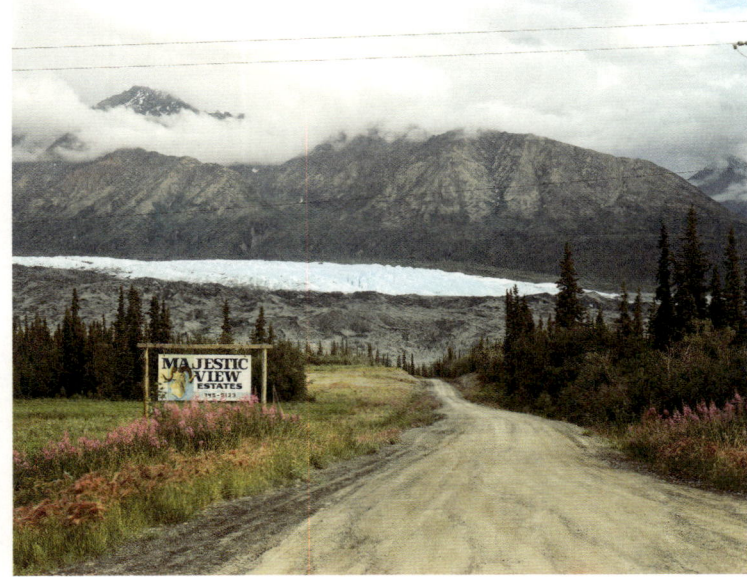

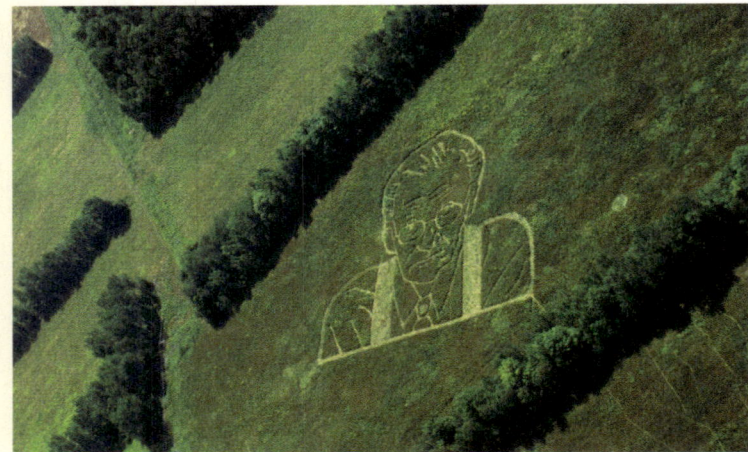

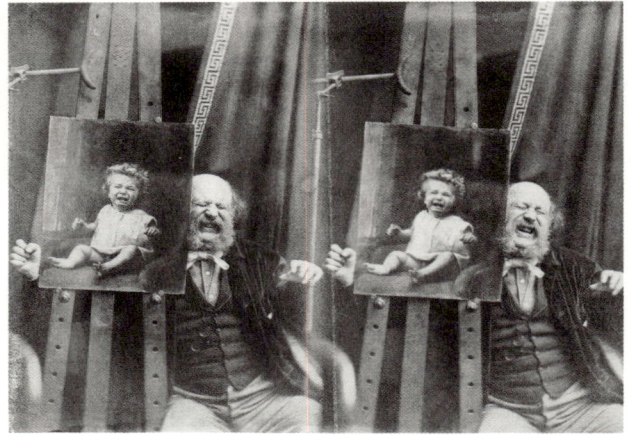

Clockwise from top left: Anna Gaskell, *Untitled (Sneeze) #3*, 1995; Joel Sternfeld, *Matanuska Glacier, Matanuska Valley, Alaska*, July 1984; Oscar Rejlander, *Laughing/ Crying* (Rejlander mimicking *Ginx's Baby*), 1871–72; Daniel Bozhkov, *Learn How to Fly Over a Very Large Larry*, 2002, 200-by-300-foot crop sign and flying lessons, East Madison, Maine

What is it about photography and its history that makes so many photographers suppress their sense of humor?

Xanthias: Master, should I tell the usual jokes which always make the audience laugh?...

Dionysus: Don't you dare, unless you want to make me sick.

—**Aristophanes,** *The Frogs*

Photogeliophobia: Fear of Funny Photography— A Diagnosis
Tim Davis

I taught my first photography class in the batty aftermath of 9/11. After muddling through a few sad-sack sessions, I decided the only way to deal with the utter upheaval was with humor. I showed slides of photographs that approached the world with levity and joy, starting with Helen Levitt and ending with Joel Sternfeld, and asked the students to go out and scan the world for some such thing. They were particularly roused by Sternfeld's *American Prospects* (1987), in all its grandiose lighthearted glory, giggling at the cycloramic puns of color, the sense that a photograph could be a great story your wiseacre uncle would tell, from a world radically more sane than the one outside. I got a call just as the class broke up. Cell phones were at the time still a novelty to me; I fumbled for mine like a man who's lost a live grenade in the lining of his coat, only to hear Joel Sternfeld on the other end. He asked if I could teach his class in a few weeks and before I could even agree, I told him I'd just showed his work to my students, and that the images had received—I overstated, quoting *A Thousand Clowns*, one of my favorite movie comedies —"outright prolonged laughter." There was a conspicuous silence on the other end. Not the silence of a dropped mobile network, even this novice knew, but the one Emily Dickinson described as "Wrecked, Solitary, Here." Joel rang off. I never taught his class.

(*Enter a blind old man with a violin*)

Mozart: Play us a little Mozart, would you?

(*The old man plays an aria from* Don Giovanni. *Mozart laughs loudly.*)

Salieri: And you can laugh at that?
Mozart: Oh come, Salieri, Don't you think it's funny?
Salieri: No, I don't. When Raphael's Madonnas are defiled by worthless daubers, I do not find it funny. When a contemptible buffoon dishonors Alighieri with his parodies, I do not find it funny.

—**Pushkin,** *Mozart and Salieri*

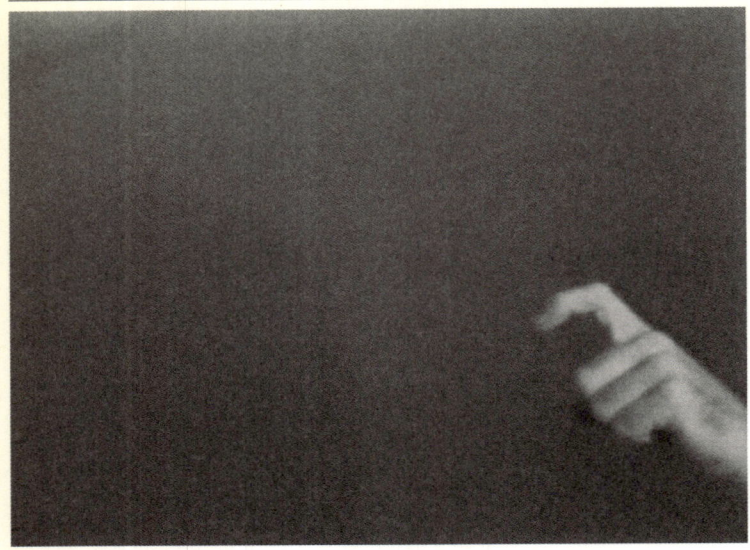

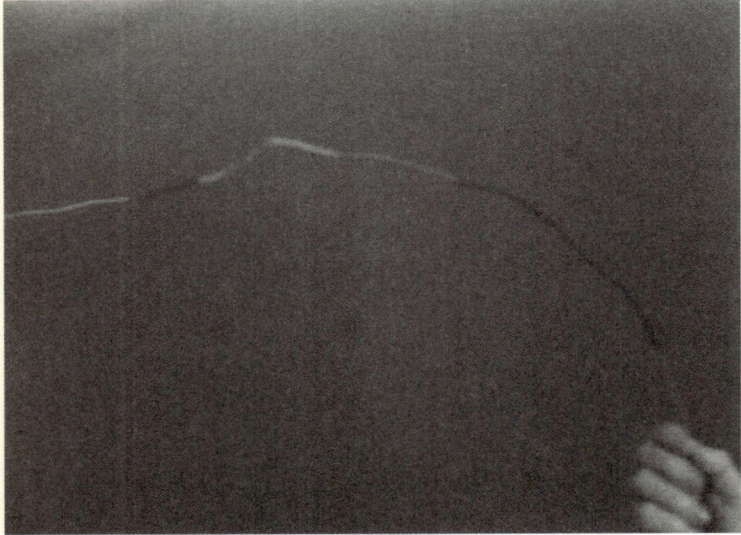

William Wegman,
stills from the video
*Crooked Finger,
Crooked Stick*, 1972–73
Courtesy the artist

There are no published case studies of *geliophobia*, the fear of laughter, but the history of visual art mostly is one. Despite how unbearable life would be without it, artists get anxious letting laughter leak into their work. I blame the advent of modernism —the period when novelty and restraint unseated art's social, communicative function—but the scarcity of laughter runs at least back to the Romans, the last people not to care if their art wasn't taken seriously. It was with modernism that cold, analytical, obscure art started to sneer at the warm, narrative, and direct. Photographers, whose works are in palpable, seductive contact with daily human stories, have felt the need to avoid appearing too *lite*.

At the Yale Art Gallery there are three large banks of study slides: "Painting," "Sculpture," and "Minor Arts." Professional photographers, condemned by Charles Baudelaire as a society of "poor madmen," who rush, "like Narcissus, to contemplate [the] trivial image on the metallic plate," feel the need to stay serious and avoid having too much Minor fun.

Even the funniest of photographers, such as Oscar Gustave Rejlander, the jaunty Swedish *artiste* who used a cat's dilating eyes as a light meter, felt the need to garnish his pie-in-the-face jokiness with a sprig of scientific inquiry. His 1872 double self-portrait with his own famous image *Ginx's Baby* was made to prove that laughter and tears can be indistinguishable in a still photograph. He sent a stereo card of the two images to Charles Darwin, who had hired him to make plates for *The Expression of the Emotions in Man and Animals*. Rejlander was a great clown, who loved to appear in his own constructed images in gaudy costumes, and whose cut-and-paste techniques would enable generations of amateurs who felt no anxiety at all about expressing silliness. But Rejlander, too, was concerned about not being taken seriously. His funniest pictures are *about* laughter, hiding the humor behind theoretical comedic masks. In fact, on February 12, 1863, he delivered a speech at the South London Photographic Society titled "An Apology for Art Photography," in which his obvious irony masks real humility in face of the debate about how seriously photography would be taken. "A funny thing it is that some people actually prefer the chalkings of a boy on the walls and shutter to the finest photographic pictures! Just think how superior are the mackerel and ship at sea we find drawn on the pavement in coloured chalks! I am ambitious, too—*I wish I was in Dixie! I do! I do!*"

"The secret source of Humor itself is not joy but sorrow. There is no humor in Heaven."
—**Mark Twain**

There are no published case studies of *geliophobia*, the fear of laughter, but the history of visual art mostly is one. Despite how unbearable life would be without it, artists get anxious letting laughter leak into their work.

I met Anna Gaskell at the opening of her 1995 MFA thesis show, and was so struck by her beauty and poise that I pirouetted away from our brief introduction and sidled up to the work on the wall. Here were images of this elegant Des Moinesian's face contorted like a Harold Edgerton apple, with fluids flowing from orifices, and the human body appearing anything but impermeable. With a fast strobe, Gaskell had photographed herself sneezing, yawning, and orgasming. These pictures were pure slapstick— the most uninflected form of humor—where the simple sanctity of the body must be defiled. The reason the Three Stooges were never as funny as Buster Keaton, say, or Harold Lloyd, was that there was nothing sacred being abused. I decided Gaskell was destined to become the Lucille Ball of contemporary photography, a bombshell about to explode into utter mayhem.

When I did begin to see her work on gallery walls, at her exhibition *Wonder*, in 1997, I kept looking around the room for Lucille Ball. These pictures, staged narratives using girl models, still contained a delirious obscurity, and a sense that something was askew in the world, but mystery had replaced buffoonery.

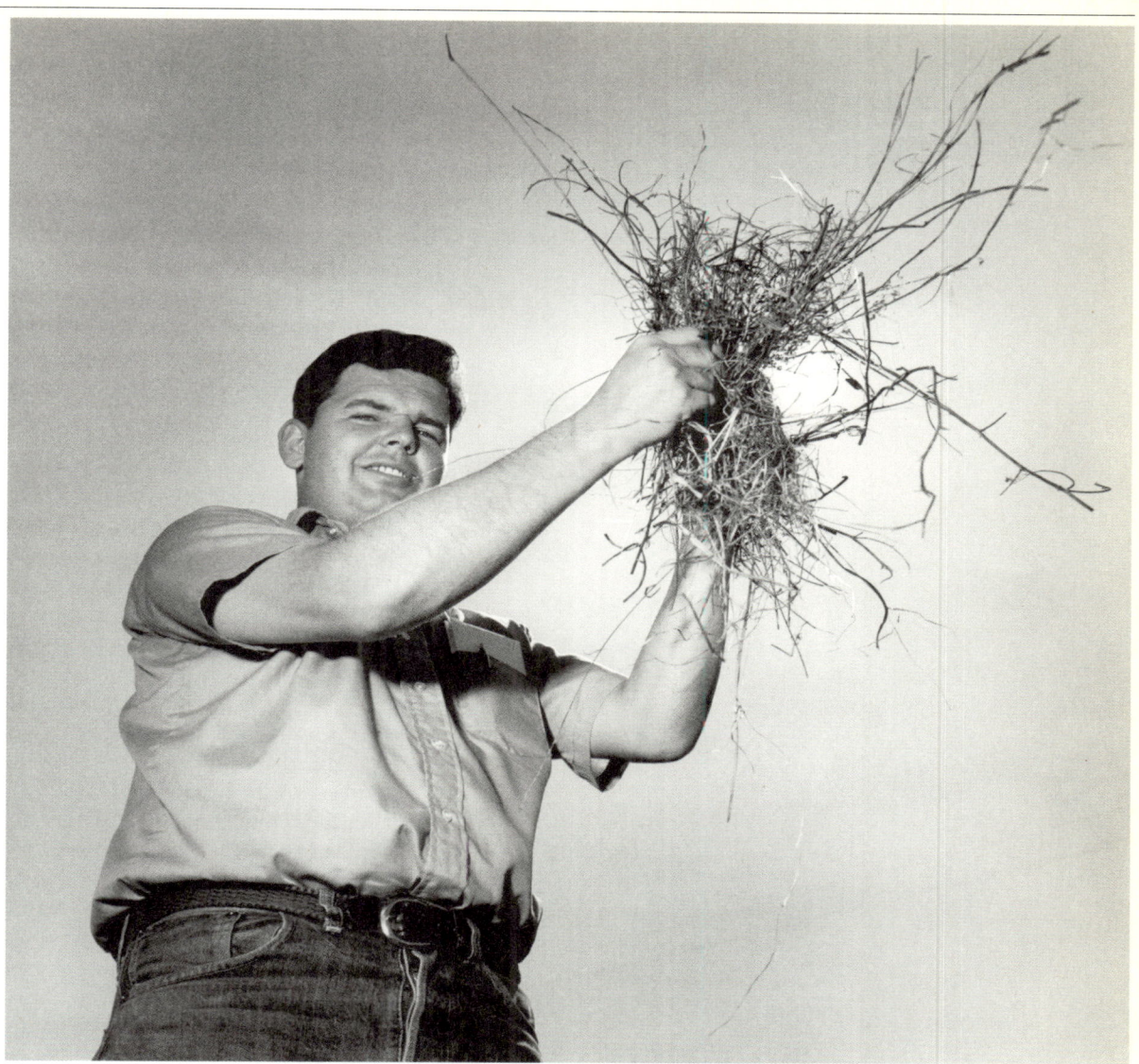

The pictures felt less risky to me, and I guessed that Gaskell had
discreetly dropped the humor from her work when it entered the
public conversation. Gaskell did eventually exhibit the sneezing
pictures in a 2006 group show called *Voice and Void* at the Aldrich
Museum in Ridgefield, Connecticut, and published an interview
about them: "I was thinking about how as a kid I had interpreted
a Bible story where the prophet Elisha brings a boy back to life
and the boy sneezes seven times. I had overlooked the miracle
and thought that sneezing had saved his life!" And I had overlooked the spiritual pantomime these pictures were performing.
The slapstick rictus in the photographer's expressions was the
revelatory shock of resurrection.

If you tell a joke in the forest, but nobody laughs, was it a joke?

—Steven Wright

William Wegman's *Crooked Finger, Crooked Stick* video from
1972–73 is a work of art that you can't help laughing at, despite
every effort. It hurts to try, and brings back childhood memories
of being unable to hold back laughter. The psychoanalyst Adam
Philips describes the feeling: "Through tickling, the child will
be initiated in a distinctive way into the helplessness and disarray
of a certain primitive kind of pleasure." In the late 1960s, a ticklish
levity overtook a set of thoughtful Californian artists that still
serves as an inoculation against congenital photogeliophobia.
If this essayist were forced to explain California to a bloom of
alien geographers, I'd show them *Crooked Finger, Crooked Stick*.
"Wow, what a neat stick. Boy is it crooked. Oh, that's nothin',

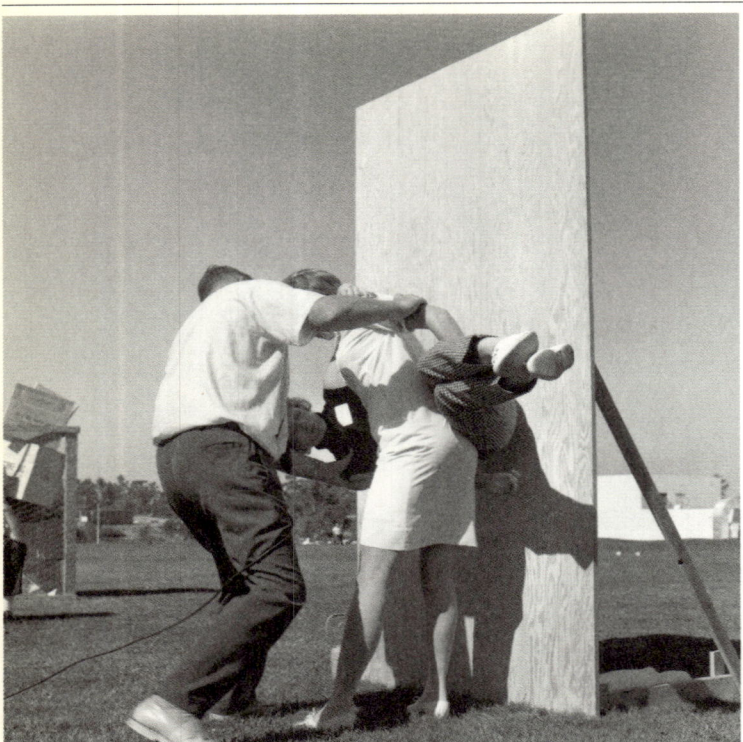

Mike Mandel and Larry Sultan, *Untitled*, from *Evidence*, 1977
© Mike Mandel and the Estate of Larry Sultan

you oughta see my finger." In slurry black and white a credulous voice—the voice of a totally nice, totally dumb guy—compares the crookedness of a finger to the crookedness of a stick. This is a work of art made in a world with no anxiety, no pain or fear. It is so unwary that thousands of years of philosophy melt away in its presence. It is not even absurd, since *absurdus*, in Latin, means "out of tune," and *Crooked Finger* hovers in a universe without dissonance. No Old Testament, no Thomas Hobbes, no Antonioni. It radiates instead with the straightforward hopefulness of the science lab. Where Rejlander hid under the mantle of seriousness in his experiment, Wegman trundles into the science lab with white lab coat flapping. The pressure is off. If it doesn't work, heck, we'll just try it again. No progress. No decisive moment.

Forget that the video was actually made in Wisconsin, and that Wegman hails from New England; he is a California artist, and this is California art: sunny, unsentimental, and utterly hilarious. These also turn out to be the perfect growing conditions for humorous photography. It was in this climate that Mike Mandel and Larry Sultan started rifling through corporate and government archives for their 1977 book *Evidence*, discovering 8-by-10 glossies of unparalleled, unintentional silliness. The pictures they collected—of science experiments and corporate folderol—evince one of photography's purest conundrums. We can know what these photographs are of, while having no idea what they are about. In this conundrum we can detect the tiniest tremor of California artists' photogeliophobia. They hide their humor in plain sight, letting it bleach bone black and white in the obvious, deadpan midday sun.

I was working this engineering job and … It wasn't a gulag but it wasn't a fun job…. So one day I was in this conference call, kind of bored, didn't really have to be there and I just started writing these Dr. Seuss poems after seven or eight years of doing just Hemingway. And that night I just brought it home and threw it on the table … and after the kids were in bed I heard my wife laughing in the other room. Like Christmas morning I peeked around the corner and she's laughing at my stuff, actually having pleasure in it…. I had just written a seven-hundred-page novel … in a Joycean voice … so to see someone taking pleasure in it was just unreal…. After that I said OK, so, you are heretofore permitted to be funny.

—George Saunders, *The Sound of Young America* podcast

Daniel Bozhkov, *Eau d'Ernest*, 2005, eau de toilette, edition of one thousand original 100-ml bottles plus 200 pirated copies; a collaboration with Ulrich Lang, New York, and Pinkar Cosmetics, Istanbul
Courtesy the artist and Andrew Kreps Gallery, New York

George Saunders is the most humane of writers. The permission he found to be funny never left him insensitive to the raging spectrum of human pain. In fact, it sensitized him to pain the way iodine vapor prepared daguerreotype plates. The history of photography's overall overseriousness starts to feel like a first date that can't laugh at the ketchup he's spilled in his lap. How to reach the fearful and distribute the Saunders vaccine to photographers? Well, the metrics tell us to look for those who don't admit to being photographers. I'm not talking A.W.U.P.s here—Artists Who Use Photography. Those folks, running from the casual veracity of the lensed image, are the most anxious to be taken seriously. The nakedest and least ashamed photographers who feel Saundersian permission to be openly funny are usually sculptors. Take Daniel Bozhkov. The photographs he makes, say, of the Hemingway-scented perfume he created in 2005 called *Eau d'Ernest*, or his crop-circle portrait of Larry King taken from the air, called *Learning to Fly over a Very Large Larry* (2002), are all bit parts in enormous, elaborate performative systems. For *Eau d'Ernest*, he didn't just make a photograph. He attended a gathering of Hemingway lookalikes in Key West and collected their input. He produced an actual scent, made a commercial for the stuff featuring robust, white-bearded Papa-types and sexy models slinking around Hemingway's actual favorite Istanbul

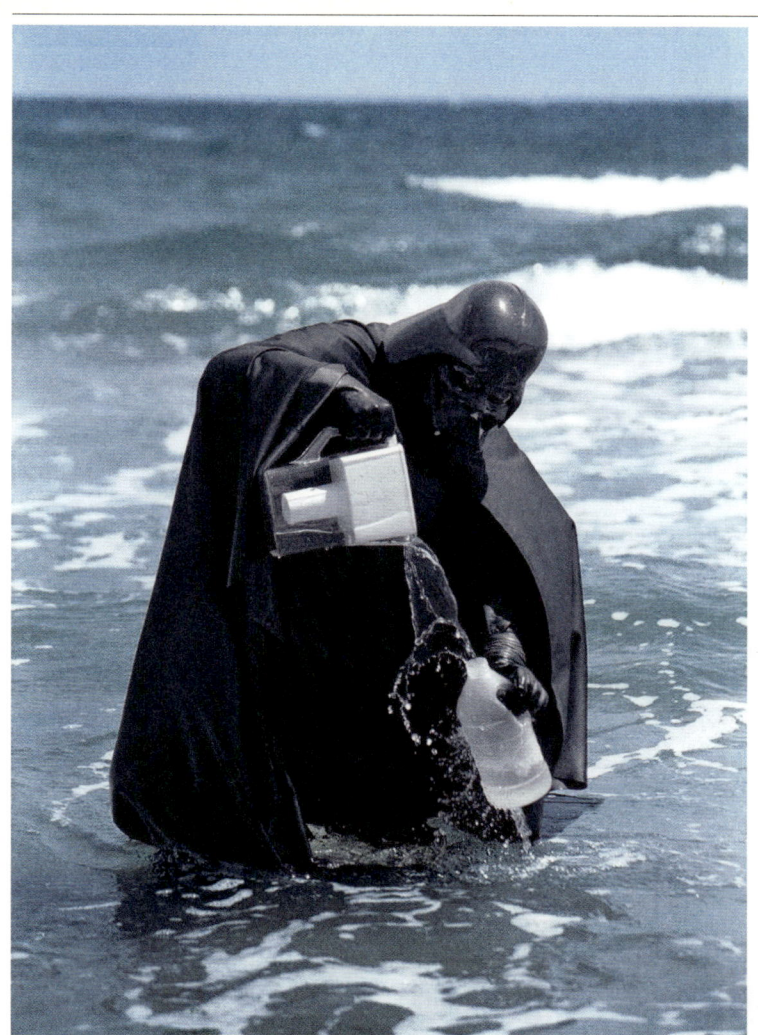

hotel. He sold Eau d'Ernest in fancy Turkish perfumeries, but also made knock-offs that were sold on the street. Bozhkov's photographs, unembarrassedly funny, are mere illustrations in cockeyed, delirious, imaginative essays about how meaning leeches into the world. The photographs themselves are far from phobic, but they're shy about standing out in public, like the joke opening a lecture at a Medieval Philology conference.

So, even the bold are fearful. I, too, am afraid. But enough about me, let me tell you a little about myself. A photographer walks into an amusement park, where his wife and little sister persuade him to go on the roller coaster. This photographer gets nauseous on escalators. As the sun sets beneath the rain, he stares at the horizon, desperate to hold onto any sort of equilibrium. He makes it through the experience feeling like Byron's Don Juan on the ship leaving Spain ("Here he grew inarticulate with retching"). On the way out, the high school kids working the ride try to sell passengers a picture that's been snapped of them on a precipitous descent. They've seen thousands of these images pop up on the screen over the long summer, and are as inured to them as to corndogs. But when the image of the photographer pops up on the screen, looking soulless and devoid while surrounding riders scream with glee, the kids break up and fall on the floor laughing. The photographer's wife shells out the nine bucks for the image in its marbled cardboard frame. It sits in the studio for years, waiting to be legitimized into a proper work of art, but ends up merely preserving for all eternity the terrible suffering of one more photogeliophobe.

Bozhkov's photographs, unembarrassedly funny, are mere illustrations in cockeyed, delirious, imaginative essays about how meaning leeches into the world.

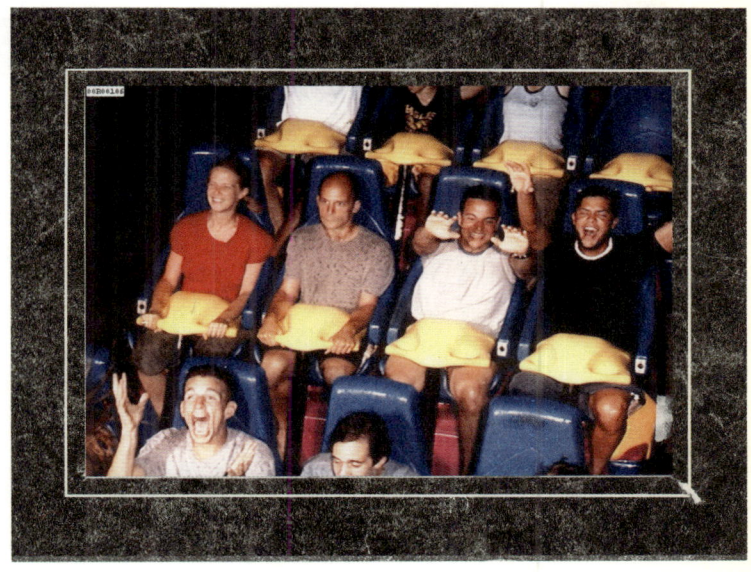

The photographer riding the "Nitro" at Six Flags Great Adventure, ca. 2002
Courtesy Tim Davis

Top:
Daniel Bozhkov, *Darth Vader Tries to Clean the Black Sea with Brita Filter*, 2000, performance on the coast of the Black Sea, Burgas, Bulgaria
Courtesy the artist and Andrew Kreps Gallery, New York

Tim Davis is an artist and writer who teaches photography at Bard College. He is currently at work on a recording of songs he's written and a set of accompanying music videos titled *It's OK to Hate Yourself.*

✂● Davis's *My Life in Politics* was published by Aperture in 2006.

Photography Knocks at the Door

Erwin Wurm in conversation
with Max Hollein

Austrian artist Erwin Wurm's principal medium is sculpture, but his ephemeral works are often realized through his use of photography. His *One-Minute Sculptures*, an ongoing series begun in the late 1980s, are documented performances carried out according to Wurm's instructions and characterized by playfulness, slapstick, absurdity, and an engagement with the ordinary. Citing a range of conceptual influences, from Yves Klein to Joseph Beuys to Bruce Nauman, Wurm's spontaneous sculptures are an intriguing form of portraiture, an awkward physical comedy of contortion and gesture. His 2012 project *De Profundis* continues this interest in the body by drawing on poses found in Gothic and early Renaissance art. Wurm once remarked that his greatest fear was of "sickness of the body and the spirit." "Maybe," he continued, "my whole work is about this fear," an observation that points to the pathos that often resides within the comedic. Here he speaks with Max Hollein, director of Frankurt's Städel Museum, Liebieghaus Sculpture Collection, and Schirn Kunsthalle, about the unique role photography plays in his work, the ways in which his projects have seeped into the commercial world—sometimes co-opted without his permission, other times purposefully, as with his work for the Austrian lingerie brand Palmers or with Hermès—and the possibilities and risks that accompany humor in art. The following conversation took place in Munich last April. —**The Editors**

Max Hollein: **In our everyday culture, and particularly in digital media, we are seeing an increasing tendency to spontaneously exchange and publish private photographs. Interestingly, these are often pictures that show people in precarious and even physically ambivalent situations. For example, there is the phenomenon known as "planking," where people stage themselves as stiff boards in public spaces and let themselves be photographed. This could be interpreted as a continuation of an Erwin Wurm sculpture. Is this something that you follow or see as part of a new development?**

Erwin Wurm: I don't directly follow it but I am aware of it. For example, there were forums on the Internet displaying posed *One-Minute Sculptures*. From the beginning, it was a strong desire of mine that these *One-Minute Sculptures*, initially made as snapshots, should appear like private photographs with a touch of clumsiness, like a private game of ineptitude. What chiefly interested me was the fact that public space is no longer only squares, streets, and house fronts. The contemporary public space for art is now the media space: newspapers, magazines, television, the Internet.

MH: **Do you consider it an interesting form of continuation that your works, thoughts, and aesthetic formulations are being picked up, copied, and actually reproduced in various contexts in the advertising and entertainment industries? Do you want to regulate this or do you see it as an interesting expansion of an idea?**

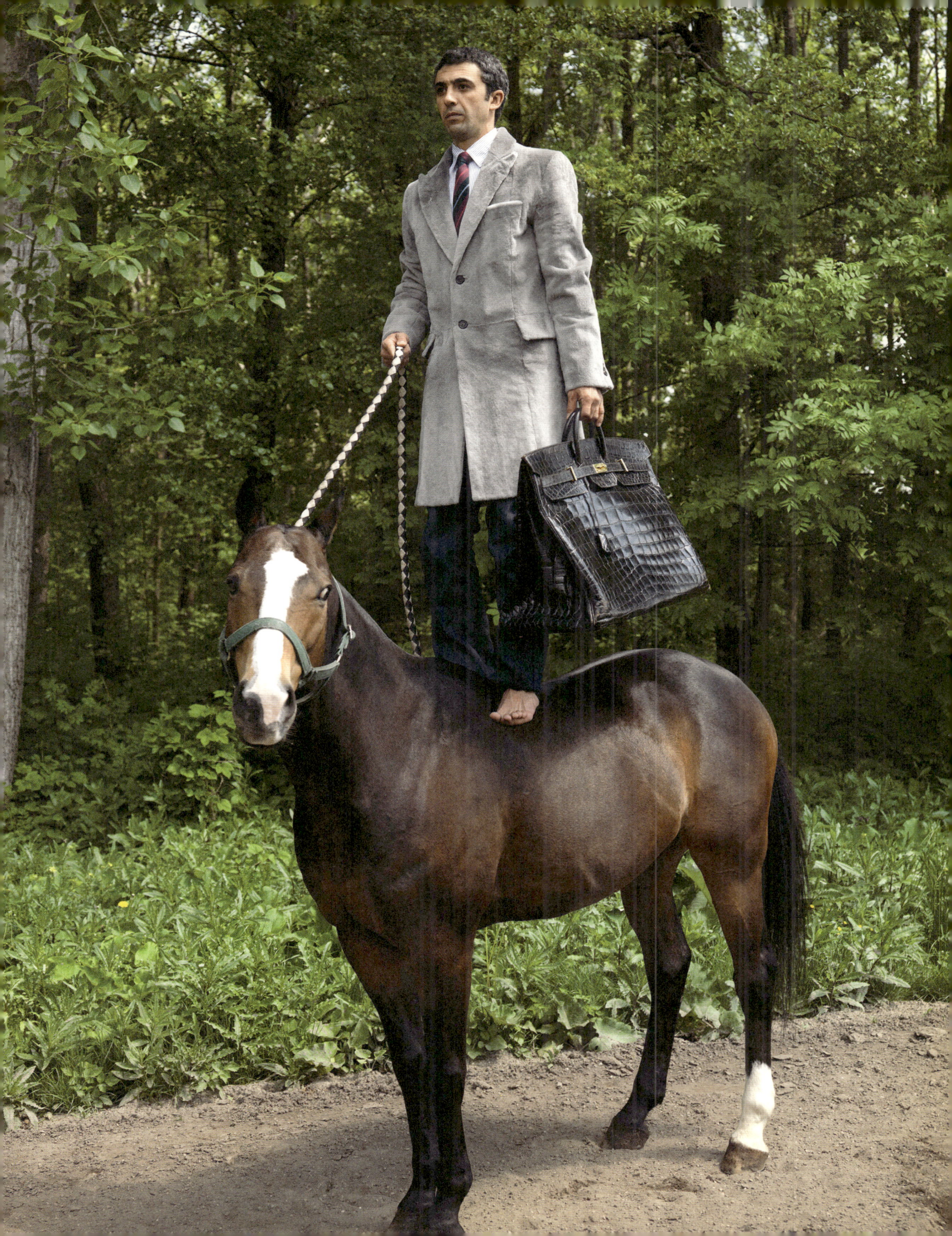

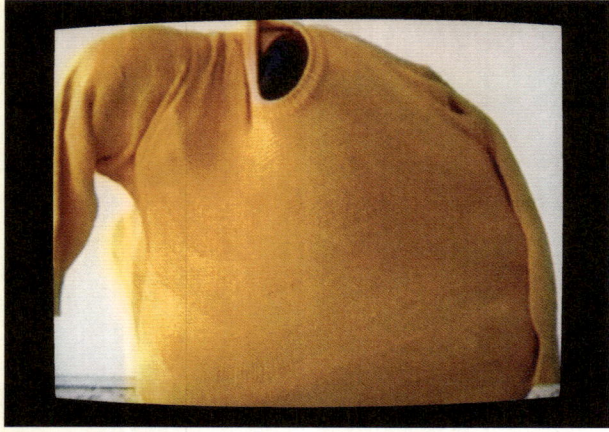
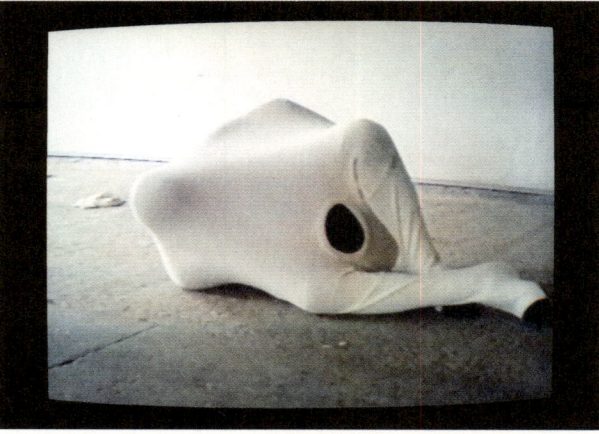
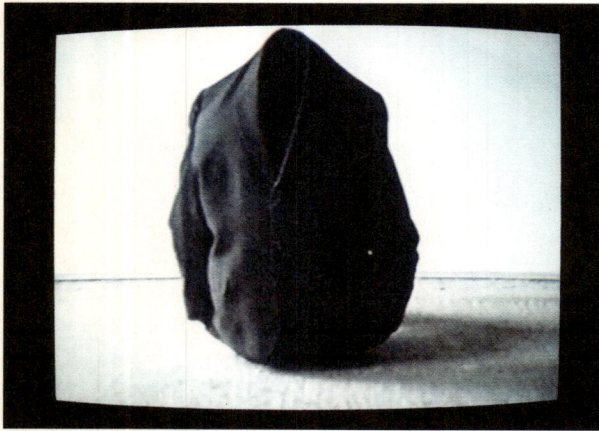
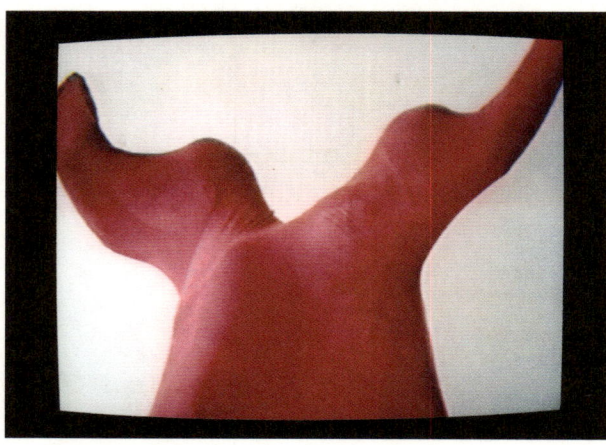

Video stills from
59 Positions, **1992**
Courtesy Lehmann Maupin,
New York

I found that the lightness that cynicism and humor produce raises us up, in contrast to pathos, which makes us seem small and presses us down.

EW: On the one hand, there is the positive element of development in the direction of the public. On the other, it comes with a danger. Take the example of Constantin Brancusi's famous *Bird in Space* [1923]. By being reproduced thousands of times, it can no longer be *seen*. I found it fascinating that the first *One-Minute Sculptures*, which were exhibited in the Bremen Kunstverein a while back, were adopted or interpreted by many viewers—for example, by fashion photographers, by musicians like the Red Hot Chili Peppers, and by fashion designers like Walter Van Beirendonck. I realized that my work had broken free, in a certain sense, and that my ideas had found their way into an aesthetic of the everyday, of the mainstream. On the other hand, it irritated me how much had been co-opted in a cheap and superficial way by advertising. My aesthetic was diverted onto completely false paths.

MH: Your work deals with fundamental questions of sculpture, sculptural practice, and the integration of other media that are normally regarded as separate. Here we are talking about elements such as text, video, architecture, photography, and lately, painting. You have defined and established them all as "sculptural" forms of expression. When did you actually begin to work with photography?

EW: It happened gradually. I was interested in the question of whether a physical action can become a sculpture, and if so, when this transition occurs. With the help of looped sequences showing someone standing still, I wanted to discover when and if this transformation takes place. Our eye … our brain is not designed to process *lack* of motion, but rather movement. The observer is inclined to project suggestions of movement onto what is seen. Afterwards I began to film this performance, this aspect of movement, this action. The result was my work *59 Positions* (1992). In that project, someone had to put on a pullover sweater, and remain for a short time in an abstruse, bizarre position

Right:
Untitled (Palmers), 1997
Courtesy Xavier Hufkens
Gallery, Brussels, Belgium

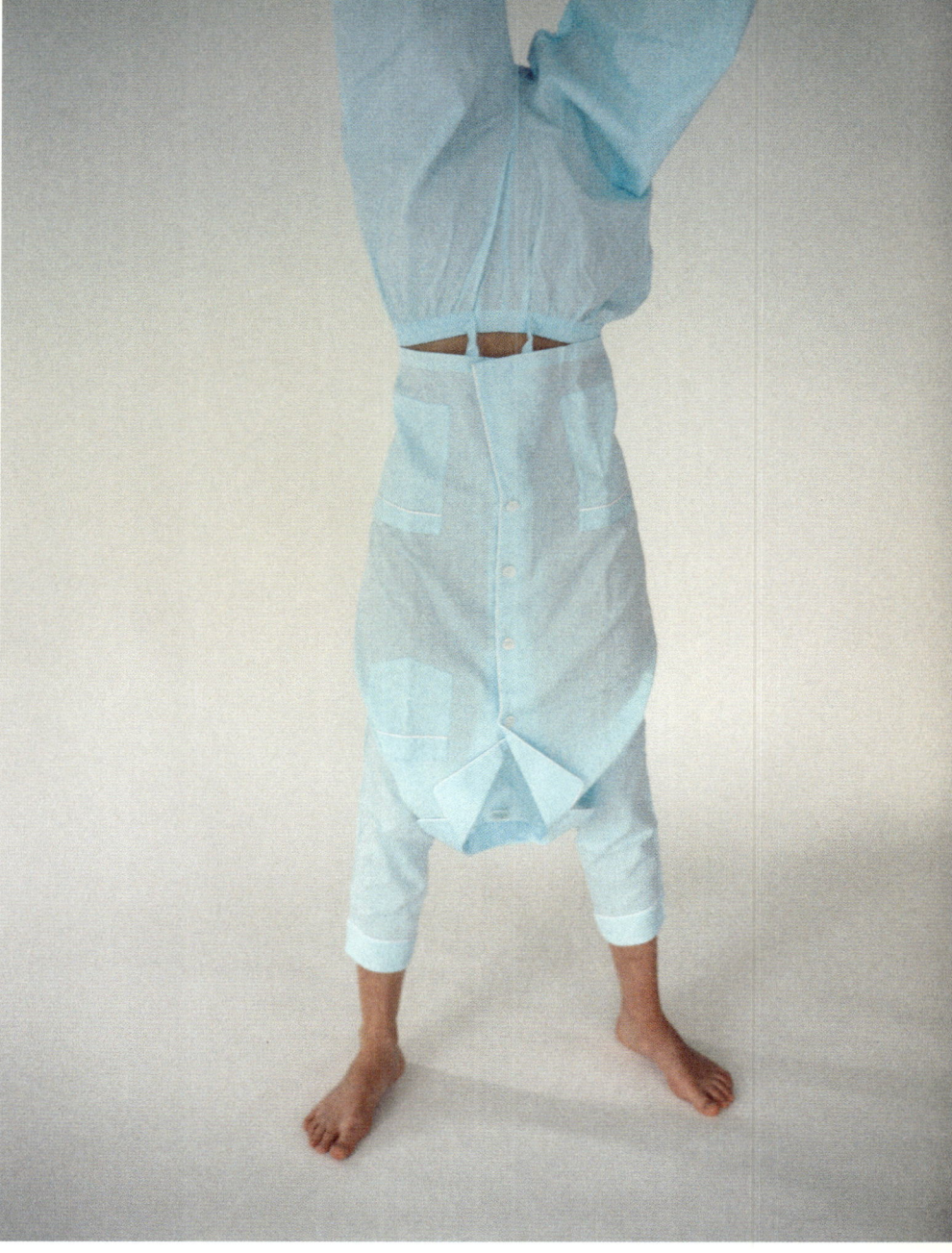

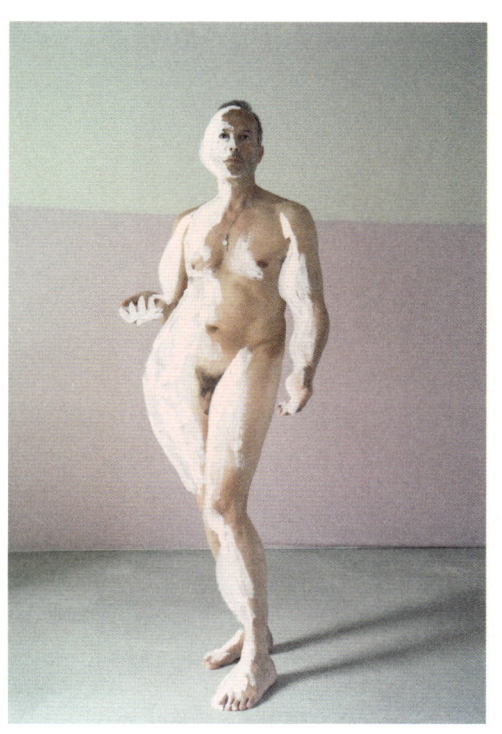

Above:
Erwin Wurm, *Untitled (Erwin) 2* from *De Profundis*, **2012**
Courtesy Thaddaeus
Ropac Gallery, Salzburg
and Paris

Right:
Untitled (Palmers), 1997
Courtesy Xavier Hufkens
Gallery, Brussels, Belgium

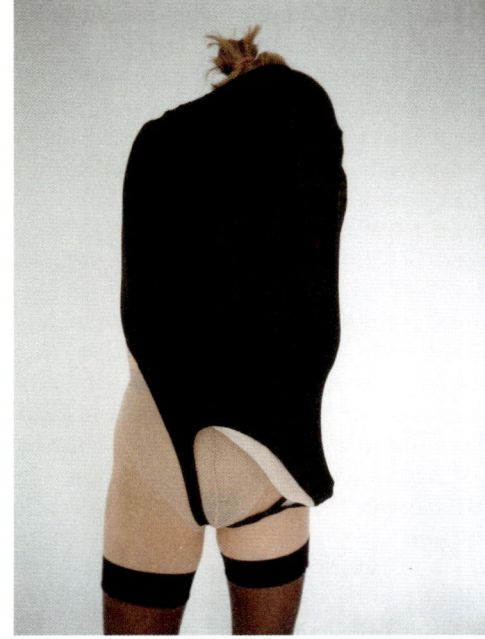

while being filmed. For the first time in my work, I left things in that I would normally have excluded, such as embarrassment or ridiculousness. Naturally you could see that someone was inside the pullover because he trembled a little bit. When the work was finished I saw that it actually looked incredibly good, even as a still picture. As a result I began to photograph.

MH: **Photography as a medium—in contrast to sculpture or painting—creates the strongest suggestion of a sort of snapshot of time, a temporary condition or momentary situation. Many of your works deal with delicate or precarious situations. There is no assurance of any sort of permanence. Photography is a medium that supports this type of sculptural form. The task here is to capture a sculptural moment whose permanence really cannot be assumed.**

EW: This is also the reason I came to photography. Naturally, the history of photography knocks at the door and wants to be let in. One walks out onto strange, scary terrain. The first photographs really were just snapshots, dramatically miserable from an aesthetic standpoint. Of course you want to improve upon that,

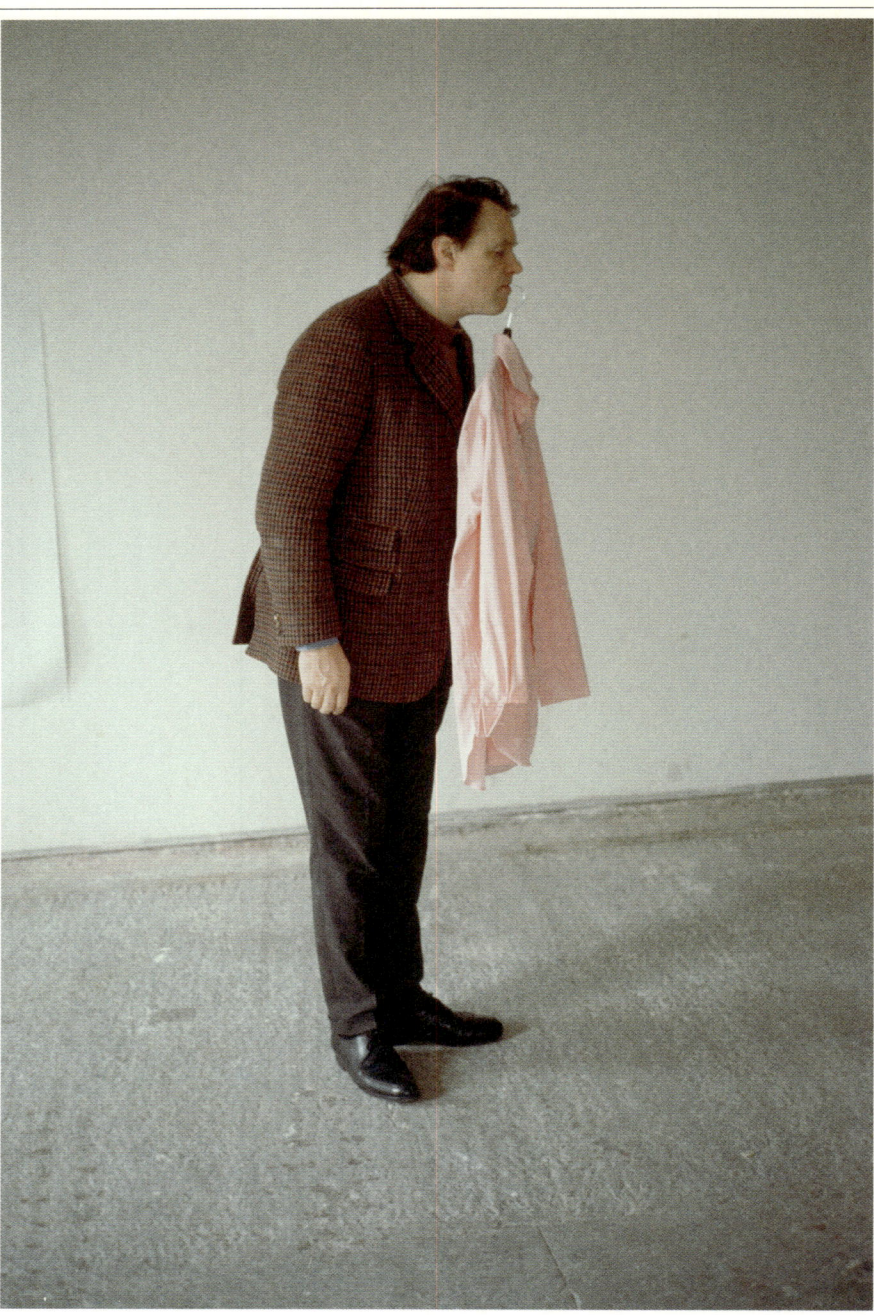

and that is where the problem begins. Those early works were defective because I was more interested in sculptural matters than in photography.

MH: **Humor, irony, and paradox play an important role in your work. However, when I think about your artistic development, I would say that your early work is based on Viennese Actionism, as well as on Minimalism, post-Minimalism, and Conceptual art. Humor plays a more subordinate role in these artistic movements. In your early *Dust Sculptures* (1990), which essentially represent spatial configuration by showing only the remainder—dust—along the perimeter where there was initially a rectangular object, I see no sign of humor. Instead I perceive the very stringent framing of an absent space and a physical *becoming*, in the tradition of Yves Klein, for example. Can you pinpoint the moment that marks the beginning of this development, where you started to employ humor and irony as conscious stylistic devices, or was this also a slow, gradual process?**

EW: During my studies Minimalist art, Conceptual art, and Pop art were the trendy directions, the valid artistic doctrine,

so to speak. But I read somewhere that if you want to be successful you have to overcome your fathers. So I began to take old discarded wooden boards and nail them together into classical figures. I consciously wanted to create something completely different by way of separating myself clearly from Minimalism, Conceptualism, etc. After a while I realized that these works were based on a counterreaction. Suddenly, I found myself included in the classification of "New Sculpture" (parallel to the "Neue Wilden," a neo-Expressionist art movement in Germany during the 1980s) because I still longed for color and went ahead and *painted* boards. But then I saw that I had been pushed into being an integral component of a movement that made me very uncomfortable after a while. This was not something I wanted, so I tried to produce something that was oppositional, rebellious, defiant.

Theodor Adorno absolutely dominated art discourse at that time. According to him, art and humor were incompatible, because art was noble, serious, and profound. I, too, came to think that the art of the twentieth century was very heavy and solemn, and that the great truths were represented with the help of pathos. I found that the lightness that cynicism and humor produce raises us up, in contrast to pathos, which makes us seem small and presses us down.

MH: This is an almost anarchical form, a subversive way of communicating. The attempt to establish easy accessibility, hand in hand with a subversive, anarchical form of overthrowing regular expectations, has enjoyed a long tradition. On the first level, an initial relationship with the public is established through humor. Whether or not the various other levels into which we may penetrate actually develop depends on the subtlety of the work.

EW: Unfortunately, many people remain stuck at the first level.

MH: How great is the danger of remaining stuck at this first level of reception? Can someone love a work too much or can one become too enthusiastic and, as a result, remain stuck at only reflecting the humorous punch line, while the more disturbing or revelatory social, personal, or art historical implications might get lost?

EW: That really is a danger. There are various possibilities that I employ either to avoid this or to attack the problem in another way. Integrating texts, for example. Some of my video works were created for this reason, in order to convey content through text.

MH: Your approach of using all media sculpturally is fascinating, particularly when you work with the grotesque. Suddenly you yourself become part of the process while you are contemplating the work. I make a conscious decision if I carry out the instructions of a *One-Minute Sculpture* and open myself up to this situation.

EW: It's up to you whether you participate or not. The sculpture still functions as a simple Conceptual work even if it remains unperformed. If a person decides to take part, however, the rest occurs only according to my will. During a certain period of time, I made a special offer that if people sent me Polaroids of posed *One-Minute Sculptures* I would sign them and return them (for a hundred euros). But I signed only those photographs that were really the way I wanted them. I excluded the others.

MH: That means that you still retained control over the complete work.

EW: I think that this is absolutely important. Otherwise things would get completely out of hand. This strategy is essential for maintaining an unadulterated work.

MH: You can see that the desire to co-opt your work and even in various ways to co-opt *you* personally is enormous.

EW: People have tried from many directions to co-opt my work, but I have usually resisted that successfully. On the other hand, about sixteen years ago I was the first artist to receive an invitation from Palmers fashion house to be part of their advertising campaign. The Palmers advertising campaign in Austria was conducted with unbelievable hype back then. The most famous models and the best fashion photographers of the time worked for Palmers. Naturally there was a great temptation to get into this line of work, especially since I was convinced that the modern public space for art was the media space. So this correlated very well with my ideas and convictions. I had underestimated the fact, however, that product advertisement has completely different parameters from those of art. And so I failed miserably! My work was not accepted, but I was able to make wonderful use in my exhibition of the pictures that I had taken. That was the first and last time. The work that I did later for Hermès was carried out on a completely different basis because the word "advertising" never came up. On the contrary, I had it contractually stipulated that none of the subjects that I developed—not a single one—could be utilized in any form for advertising or anything similar.

In the course of my development I have dealt with various issues of our times. The icon is such an essential phenomenon of our time. It doesn't matter what sort of icon, whether an architectural icon, a pop icon, or even a fashion icon. Hermès is one of the biggest fashion icons. That's why I was interested in working with that sort of icon, to poke around in that kind of work.

MH: Your work is characterized by a great variety of media and materials and also by complex production processes. Lately, however, you have turned back and begun working with wood—as a classic, perhaps a "poor" material.

EW: I have come to realize how much contemporary art suffers, or has suffered, from the fact that artists' studios have been transformed into manufacturing workshops. I have noticed that many artists do almost nothing at all themselves, but rather let their works be produced by others. That really strikes me. It irritates me because I have lost contact with my work, so to speak. And so I am trying to get that contact back again by creating everything myself, or at least for the most part by myself.

MH: In this connection photography, as a sculptural vehicle, is an ideal medium for you, because you are back in a situation where you can determine everything about the sculpture yourself and also carry out on your own what you have decided.

EW: Exactly. To me, photography is a medium that I will gladly return to for specific projects, as I did for the exhibition *De Profundis*. At present, however, I am again concentrating more on making sculptures.

(*Translated from the German by Alan G. Paddle*)

Erwin Wurm will have solo shows at the Museum of Contemporary Art, Krakow, Poland, October 17, 2013–January 26, 2014, and at Lehmann Maupin, New York, March 3–April 26, 2014.

Max Hollein is currently preparing an exhibition of Wurm's *One-Minute Sculptures* for the Städel Museum's Old Master, Modern, and Contemporary Galleries in Frankfurt am Main, to be presented next year.

Are our information-age lives all play? Brian Droitcour considers John Gerrard's computer graphics simulations and Jon Rafman's investigations of online role-playing games and Google Street View.

The Big Game
Brian Droitcour

What is *play*?

We can think of it as work's opposite. And thanks to Marx, we know that work is the transformation of nature into socially useful resources. Work is what makes the world *ours*. Play is an exchange of meanings that makes the world of socially useful things worth using.

In his 1938 study *Homo Ludens*, Dutch historian and cultural theorist Johan Huizinga argues that play is a primary condition of culture: he identifies the "play elements" in various forms of art and entertainment as traces of a primordial human drive. Huizinga argues that play can be set aside from ordinary life, a claim that may no longer hold today, when play is so fully integrated into everyday existence through information technologies. "To call all human activity play is cheap," Huizinga wrote; he insisted on the status of play as an element of culture at large. Of course there are other fields of human activity: war and murder are not play, they're matters of life and death, as is the doctor's work on bodies. The work of the miner, the farmer, the oil refiner—virtually invisible in the information economy's field of exchange—is work through and through. But notions of "serious" and "fun" have become useless in separating play from work, just as "ordinary" and "special" are useless designations in sifting play from life. Some Chinese prisons force their inmates to play the online role-playing game World of Warcraft to collect game-world treasures and sell them to gamers abroad for the profit of their captors. These days, play can sometimes be no fun at all.

When play enters art now as a theme, it is different from the "play element" that Huizinga identified as the trace of art's origins. It has come to constitute a way of seeing the world: play as the defining condition of life in a world buffered from nature by a cloud of information.

John Gerrard is an artist known for his "simulations"— three-dimensional models of places and the things that happen in them. These aren't videos; they have no beginnings or endings. Some of them—such as his series of derricks shot on North American oilfields in 2009 and 2010—index work that is unseen and unknown by most of his audience. But recent projects take simulation itself as their theme. In *Exercise (Djibouti) 2012*, sixteen athletes, dressed in red and blue, jog in a figure eight, describing the infinite track of a Möbius strip, with pauses for rest every few minutes. Their shadows follow them, dark and even, yet slightly askew to the artificial sun, and this small displacement makes the shadows strange enough to be a reminder of the algorithm that produces them, and its divergence from nature.

Similarly, Gerrard's *Infinite Freedom Exercises* (2011) varies slightly from reality, and in the friction of rhythmic gestures against the languidly shifting viewpoint and the even more slowly changing sunlight, which follows the computer's clock. By the side of the road in an Iranian desert, a man in fatigues performs the exercises that soldiers do to practice shielding themselves from missile fire. But Gerrard's subject is not a soldier, he's a dancer. His gestures aren't exercises, they're choreography. The difference between work on the body for its preservation and the aesthetic play of motion matches the difference between the origins of the images and the simulation that Gerrard has assembled from them—a gap aligned with the one between nature and play. Significantly, Gerrard's simulations are built on game engines—the software frameworks used for rendering

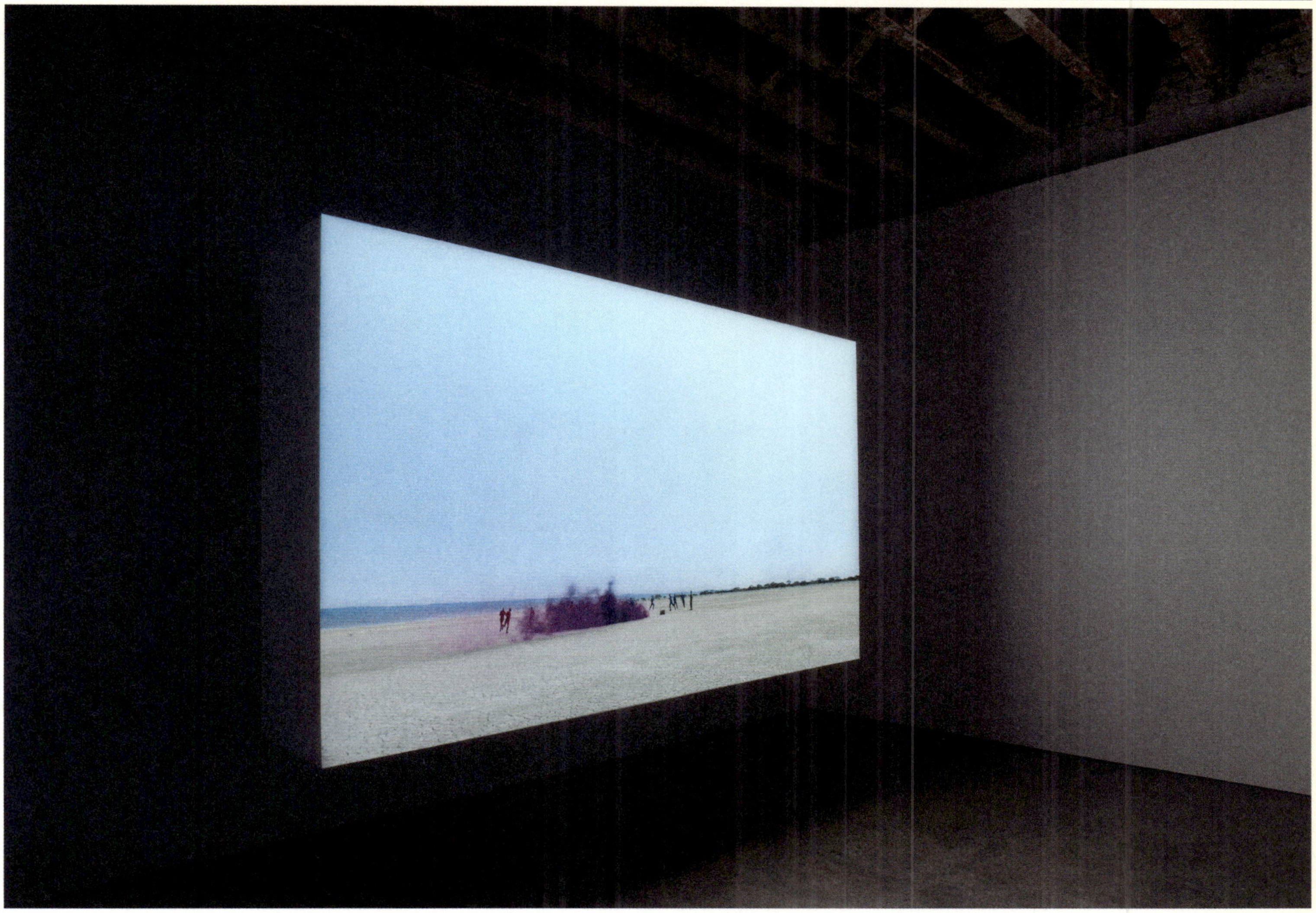

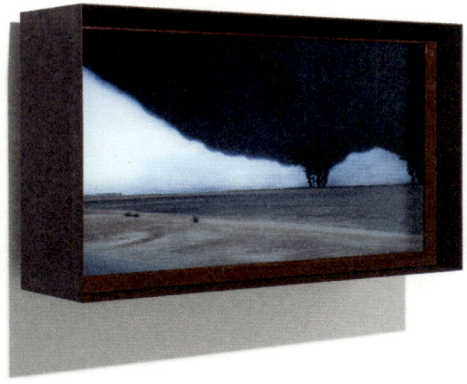

Top:
John Gerrard, *Exercise
(Djibouti) 2012*, 2012
(installation view)

Bottom:
John Gerrard, *Burning Oil
Fields (near Abadan, Iran)*,
2013 (installation view)
Courtesy the artist and
Simon Preston, New York

graphics, modeling the physics of collision and combat, and managing the artificial intelligence of characters in computer games. Game engines model the world in code and images, just as the choreography in *Infinite Freedom Exercises* models the body's movement in the world. A photograph makes an image from the world, but a simulation makes a world from a set of images, and from rules that encode the relations among objects in those images. *Exercise (Djibouti)* was commissioned for the cultural program accompanying the 2012 Olympics, and Gerrard's men in red and blue are modeled on the bodies of Olympic athletes. When exhibited alongside the muted militarism of *Infinite Freedom Exercises* (as it was this past spring at Gerrard's New York gallery), *Exercise (Djibouti)* is a reminder of the Olympiad's origin as a way of sustaining competitive conflict among cities without war. As a model of mortal combat, sport produces a field for the continuity of culture.

Whereas Gerrard starts each project by traveling to a desolate location where nature remains hostile to humanity, and where play is still separate from everyday life, the artist Jon Rafman concerns himself with the expanses of desire that are accessible from any computer. Since 2009 Rafman has collected screenshots of scenes he finds when surfing Google Street View—the map of photographs taken and stitched together by a nine-eyed mobile robot, and offering us the world as data. His project succinctly speaks to the possibility of photography as the capture and repositioning of images made by machines. Most of Rafman's work involves wandering in game worlds, and in that context his Google project, titled *9 Eyes*, aligns the condition of photography to play. Second Life, an online community where users design avatars and environments to

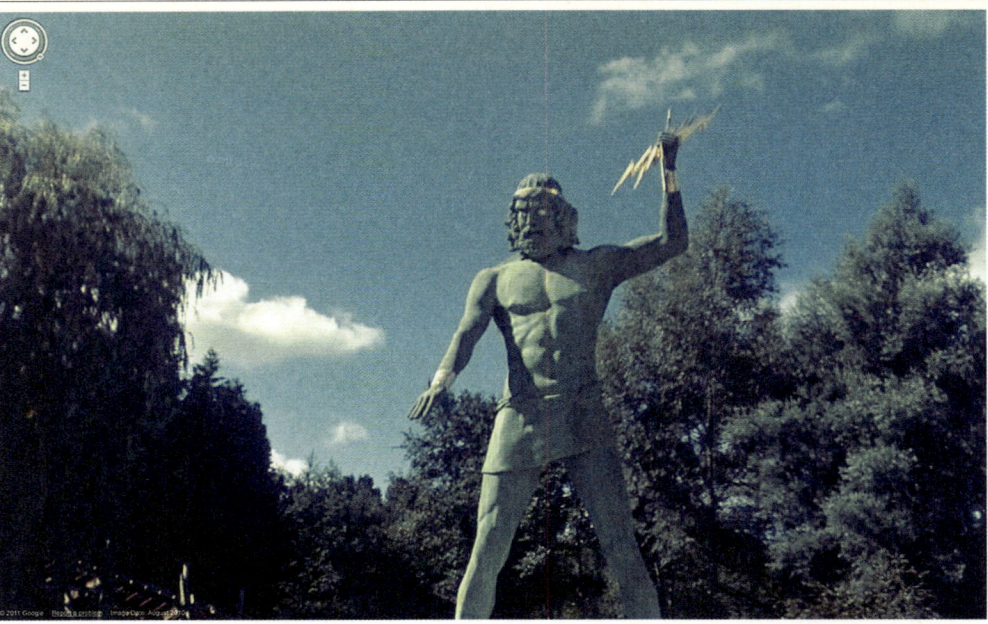

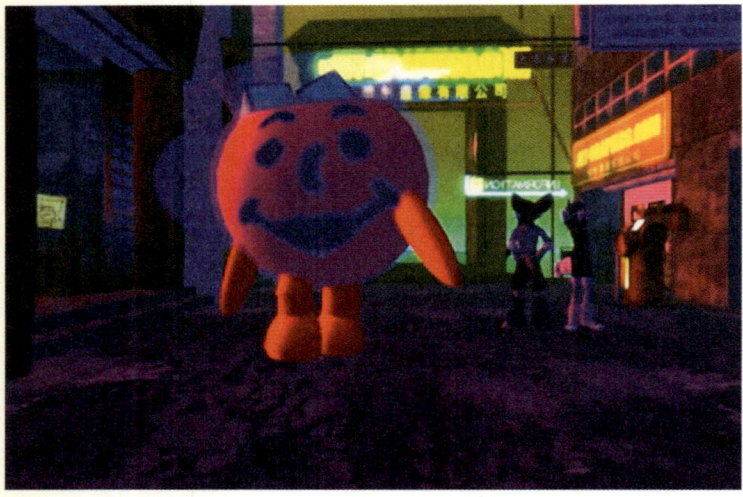

For these artists, information technology is an engine of reality and of games, a way of organizing life that erases the distinction between the two.

visualize their fantasies, is a world Rafman has explored as the avatar "Kool-Aid Man." The artist's eye—ethereally present like the Google van's nine—swells into the bulbous pitcher of Kool-Aid, with a sugary smile of dumb bemusement permanently fixed to its surface as it visits Second Life's fantastic landscapes, its strip malls and sex clubs, its alien discos and ruined temples. *Kool-Aid Man in Second Life* (2009–11) exists in several forms— as a series of videos and as still images—all captured onscreen with Second Life's built-in camera function.

Rafman's more recent videos swap the avatar for speech. They don't have a proxy body like Kool-Aid Man, but rather a first-person narrative in Rafman's own voice. He draws footage from Google Earth and Second Life, from mapping applications and games. He implicates play in the computer-aided navigation of the world; it is a theme in the plots of his videos, whose protagonists are *flâneurs*, gamblers, gamers. His *Codes of Honor* (2011), a memorial to New York's defunct Chinatown Fair Arcade, tells a story of gaming as a thrilling realm of mastery for kids that collapses in a void at the threshold of adulthood. It's heavy, the nostalgia that follows the short lifespan of the champion gamer. Rafman's *Remember Carthage* (2013) begins in Las Vegas, that playground in the desert. The narrator loves the simulations that fill the streets, the newness of the reproduced ruins of world culture, but even enveloped in play he is disturbed by the presence of other people. A longing for absolute solitude makes him restless. He travels to Tunisia in search of the Uqbar Palace Resort, "the Vegas of the Maghreb," a pleasure zone planned for the middle of the Sahara but abandoned halfway through construction. As he wanders the desert, he keeps thinking he sees the half-built copy of Carthage's ruins, but it is only the shifting dunes. Throughout his journey he fantasizes about being the last man alive, the sole survivor of a deadly pandemic. What Rafman's narrator wants is the condition of the computer game to become the total reality of the world. He wants pure play: the circulation of signs without people, with no one but him to recognize it and to know it.

Rafman's works in progress borrow mountainous landscapes from the fantasy role-playing game Skyrim and street scenes from the latest edition of SimCity, the urban-planning simulator. Like Second Life, these games have an expansive notion of play. They are bound by rules and by the limitations of their game engines, but they mask those confines by simulating as closely as possible the contingencies of life—just as Second Life depends on its users' unpredictable imaginations to expand and thrive. These games

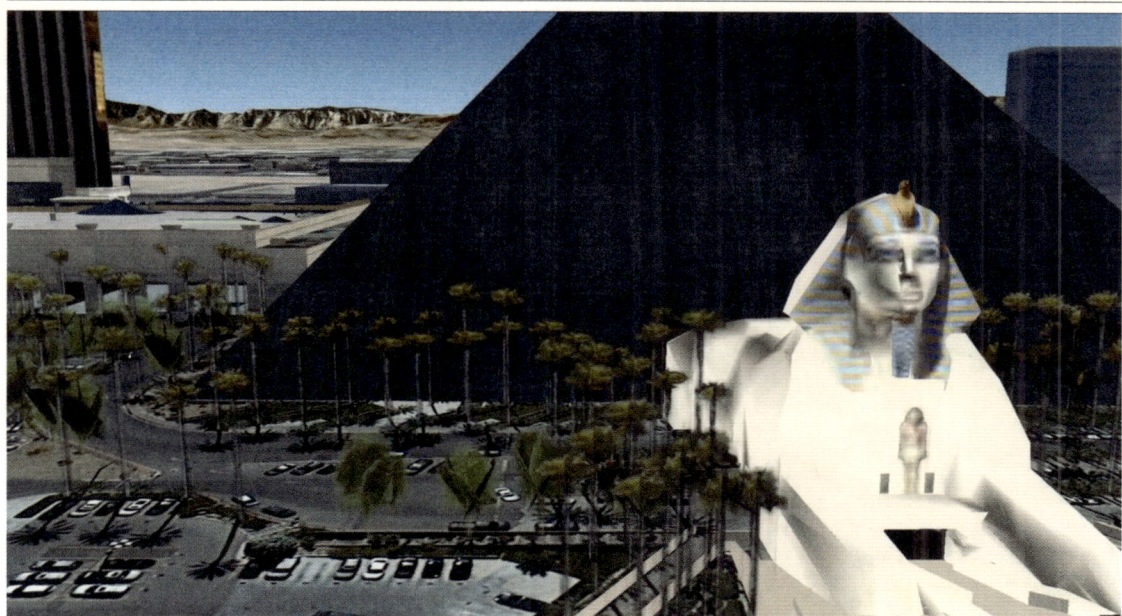

**Still from Jon Rafman,
Remember Carthage, 2013**
Courtesy the artist, Zach
Feuer Gallery, New York, and
Seventeen Gallery, London

are vast. They extend their reach into the everyday lives of the people who engage with them, who operate through the logic of avatars in their daily communication on Facebook, who win points and prizes for mundane consumption on Foursquare.

While Rafman is a scavenger of game engines, grafting pieces of readymade models to his narratives, Gerrard works with teams of programmers to build his own. The construction of playlands in the desert in *Remember Carthage*—whether in Nevada or the Sahara—are baroque instances of man demonstrating mastery over nature. Control doesn't bring satisfaction; it only opens up new possibilities, which in turn open up new kinds of desire. Rafman indexes the infinity of fantasy in his promiscuous distribution practices: his art comes in the form of websites, DVDs, PDFs, posts to his Tumblr or Vimeo accounts. Gerrard's works are self-contained and monolithic. They are software programs, but they're attached to solid substrates, like the huge white slab that holds the projection in *Exercise (Djibouti)*. For all the weight of its monumentality it flows as a double of real temporality. Gerrard's works are limited in space; Rafman's, in time. But with an open-endedness in the opposite category each alludes to the vastness of play.

Information technology is the ground for both of these artists as an engine of reality and of games, a way of organizing life that erases the distinction between the two. Filmmaker Harun Farocki has also explored these ideas, in works such as *Serious Games* (2009–10), a documentary about the use of computerized simulations for training in the U.S. military. His two-channel video installation *Parallel* (2012) traces a history of computer graphics from the quasi-logographic representation of trees, water, and clouds by keyboard characters on empty black screens to contemporary digital models that are at least as deeply detailed as the trees, clouds, and water in the world. From ciphers to simulations, all the images shown by Farocki were made for games. *Parallel*'s voiceover is a critique of mimesis; its subtext is that play is never mimetic. It belongs to a world that operates by transfers of information, by exchanges and models: models that are more beguiling and more readily available for interaction than the alien objects they simulate. This world, not a natural one, is the one we live in. Huizinga defined *play* as markedly separate from ordinary life. But those boundaries look false now—as false as "virtual reality" sounds as a description of the Internet, to which so many people carry a portal in their pocket. Play and technology have become inextricably tied to each other, and both are inexorably fused with life.

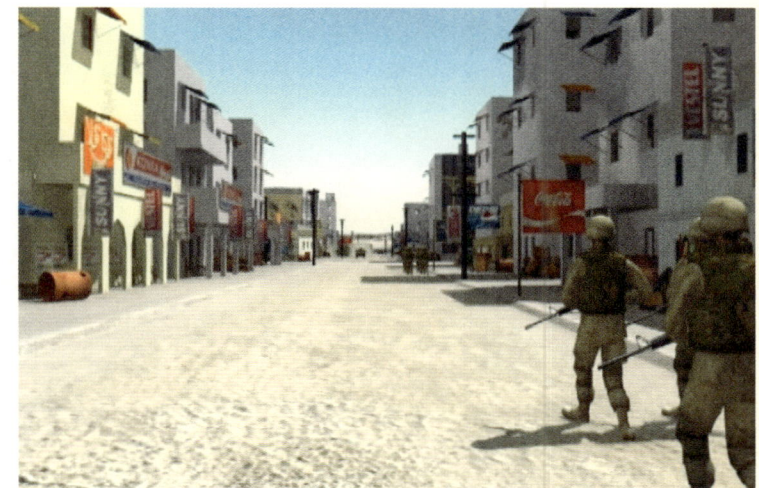

**Still from Harun Farocki,
Serious Games (I–IV), 2010**
Courtesy the artist and
Greene Naftali, New York

**Brian Droitcour is a writer, translator,
and curator. He lives in New York.**

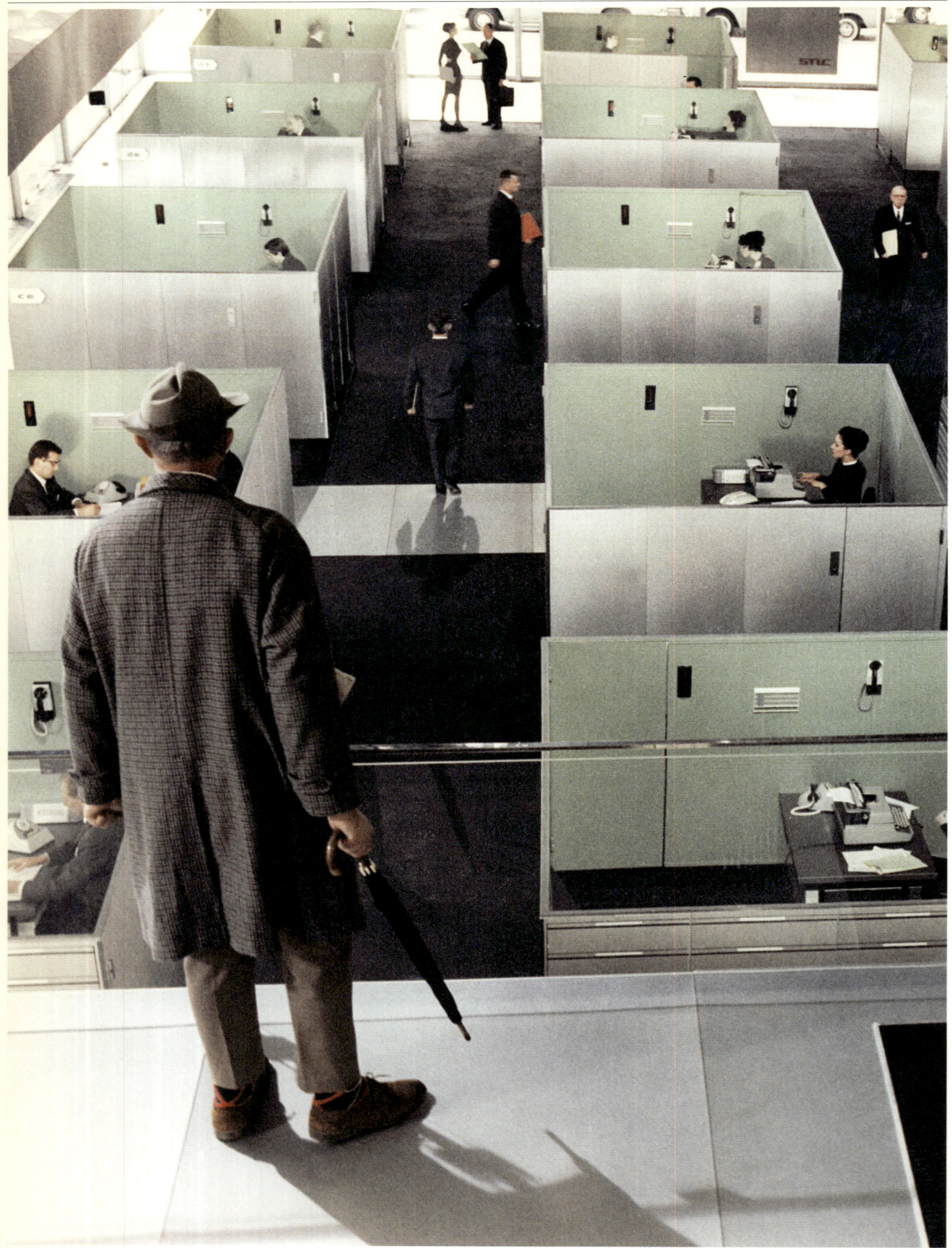

Jacques Tati's legendary 1967 film is a masterpiece of physical comedy and a send-up of modern living. Visually generous and shot in 70mm, the film continues to resonate with still photographers.

Photography and Jacques Tati's *Playtime*
David Campany

Playtime (1967) is the great labor of love crafted over three years by the maverick French filmmaker Jacques Tati. It was shot in 70mm on a set purpose-built at the edge of Paris, and its genesis is the stuff of legend.

Tati was a slow-moving perfectionist who had made the international hits *Les Vacances de Monsieur Hulot* (*Mr. Hulot's Holiday*) in 1953 and *Mon Oncle* (*My Uncle*), an Academy Award winner, in 1958. In each film Tati plays Hulot, an affable middle-aged bungler at odds with the rhythms and values of contemporary society. *Playtime* was intended as his magnum opus, an enormous canvas on which to lay out his affection for and misgivings about high-tech modern life.

The star of the film was to be a deliriously detailed steel-and-glass cityscape. Constructed at enormous expense, it was dubbed "Tativille" by the press. High winds blew it down and Tati rebuilt it. Shooting was frequently suspended when financial backers got worried. Tati mortgaged the rights to his previous films and sunk all his wealth into the project. The budget spiraled, eventually topping seventeen million francs: it was the most expensive French film ever made up to that time.

Playtime has hardly any plot. Hulot the scatterbrain comes to the sterile city for a meeting. Where is he from? The suburbs? The countryside? The past? All we know is he's out of step with this place. He interacts with various minor characters—secretaries, elevator attendants, shopkeepers, bureaucrats. He crosses paths now and again with a young American woman on holiday but there's no romance. He goes to a newly opened restaurant-nightclub and leaves as dawn breaks on another day. That's it. The skeletal narrative is the barest excuse to string together a series of moods, observations, and set pieces, of which there are plenty. The first cut was 155 minutes long.

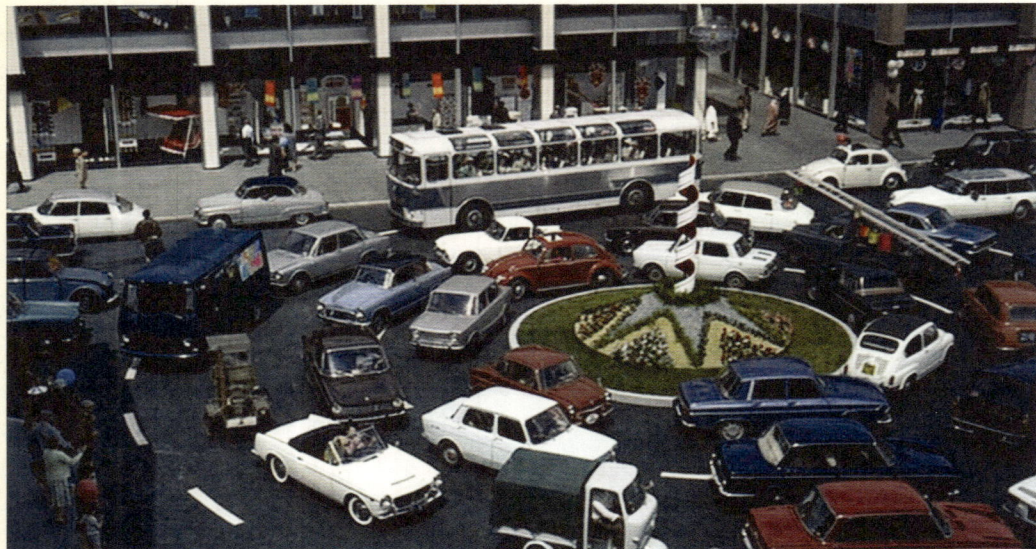

Left:
Film still from
Jacques Tati's *Playtime*,
1967

Playtime features no well-known actors. Tati reduced even himself to a character in the ensemble cast. The film has no close-ups either: it's mostly shot in medium and wide views. Upon the film's initial release, *Playtime*'s distribution in Europe was limited to movie theaters with 70mm projection and stereo sound. In America it was released in 35mm and monaural, but not until 1973, and in a version cut by almost an hour. Even so, it lost a fortune. While reviewers recognized its brave mastery, technical innovation, and unique take on life, it came to be seen as a great folly. *Playtime* was the work of a charismatic hero of popular culture undone by vaulting hubris. Today, however, it is understood as an idiosyncratic and unrepeatable work. In a recent poll of international directors and critics it was rated the thirty-seventh best film ever made.

Paris loves (and hates) its *grands projets*, those big statements of civic and cultural pride: new museums, reinvented districts, and show-stopping architectural statements. The largest of these has been La Défense, the business and shopping area built in the west of the city in the 1980s and '90s. As its grassless and treeless concrete piazzas sprawled and its crystal towers sprouted, many commentators were reminded of Tativille. The similarity was uncanny. Life had imitated art but had missed the point. *Playtime* was a movie, a series of images, a city to be inhabited imaginatively and allegorically, not actually. Today so much of our urban fabric looks great in photographs but is unpleasant to live with. Through the harsh anomie of our city experience, the befuddled bonhomie of Tati feels like a last affectionate moment.

More recently *Playtime* has struck a chord with many photographers, but not always in the same way. For some it's the epic vistas of ultramodern urbanism, their sharp geometry muted by a palette of blues and grays. Tati wanted the film to look almost as if it were shot in black and white. For some, the incongruously pastoral views of traffic jams and faceless buildings foreshadow the aloof panoramas of Andreas Gursky. For others it's the way the people of this "everycity" move as one, like a live-action version of a street photograph that can be paused at any time as a frame of formal harmony. Or perhaps it is Tati's comic body language, performed at a deliberately slow pace so the camera can relish his every bend and twist, like an underwater ballet. This is chaos choreographed, like a complex tableau photograph by Jeff Wall.

Playtime is also a commentary on photography as a social phenomenon. We see an excitable pack of snapping tourists, advancing into this alien world with cameras outstretched before

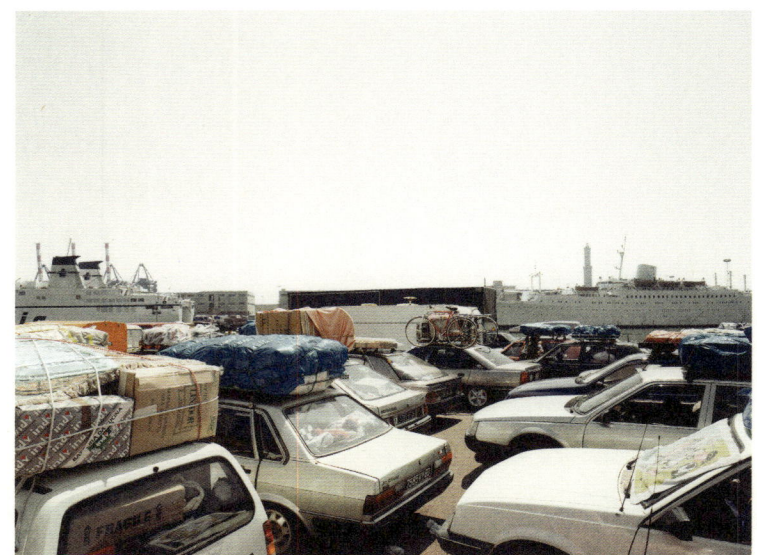

Andreas Gursky,
Genua (Genoa), 1991
© 2013 Andreas Gursky/
Artists Rights Society (ARS),
New York/VG Bild-Kunst,
Bonn; courtesy Gagosian
Gallery, New York, and
Sprüth Magers, Berlin
and London

More than anything, I suspect photographers enjoy the film's overwhelming generosity to the viewer. Each shot offers so much and is held for so long that the eye can wander about the frame.

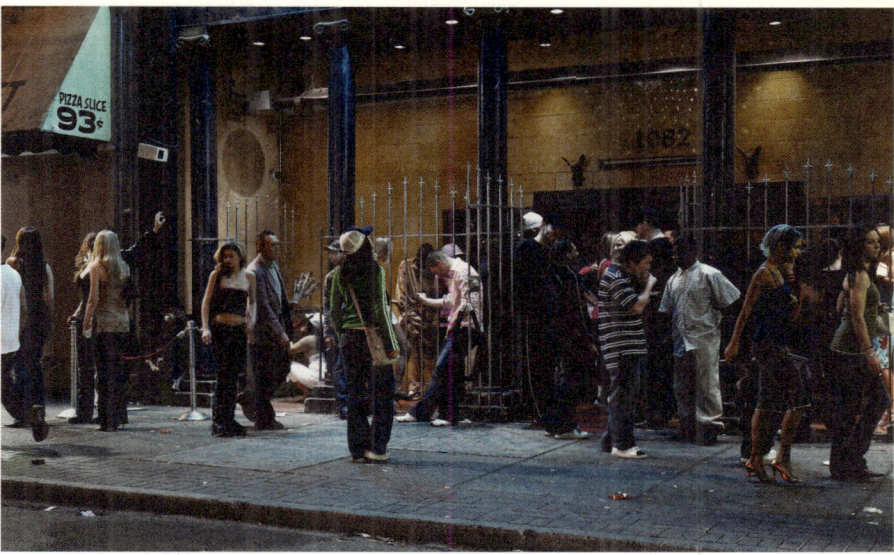

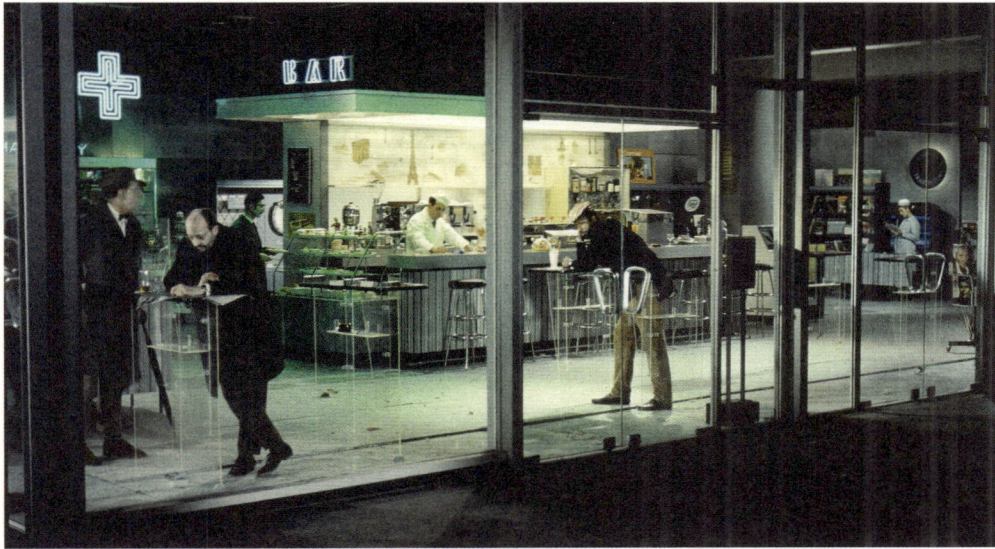

them. Hulot waits in a corporate lobby where the only decoration is a suite of austere portraits of company heads that seem to glare down upon him. There is a comic gaggle of paparazzi at the airport, swirling about their prey. Wistful scenes of Parisian clichés swing into picture-perfect view when reflected in shining glass doors. The Eiffel Tower and the Sacré-Cœur haunt this new place like spectral images from ancient times.

Perhaps photographers enjoy the fact that although this is a film of epic scale, it is clear the humanity and charm come from the smallest and most ephemeral things. A luggage label flapping on a suitcase, like a tethered bird. A pastor pausing unwittingly beneath the halo of a circular neon light. Two nuns walking down a godless corridor, their wimples bobbing in unison. And *Playtime* has more gags about the invisibility of glass than the whole history of silent film. But more than anything, I suspect photographers enjoy the film's overwhelming generosity to the viewer. Each shot offers so much and is held for so long that the eye can wander about the frame. How rare for a movie-goer to be free to take in the variety of surfaces and the array of color-coordinated extras going about their lives in the middle and far distance. It really is a series of pictures in motion.

We can enjoy the knowledge that whatever cinematic illusion *Playtime* conjures for us, this is predigital cinema. Somehow or other what we see on screen really was there. Or was it? The office blocks of Tativille were built in forced perspective (some were just a couple of meters tall) and could be moved about on wheels to improve the compositions.

The steel columns were not steel but wood covered in matte photographs of steel that reduced light reflection. And when Tati's money ran dry, the army of extras was partly supplemented by full-size photo-cutouts, placed strategically among the living.

I confess I have a soft spot for films that fail financially, especially those of great artistic ambition. Nobody wishes such failure, but when it happens it is a sign that culture is not entirely predictable and cannot be reduced to its economic determinants. So the pleasure of such films is always a little guilty, a little cultish, a little parasitic even. No matter. We have *Playtime* now. It is our film.

David Campany is a writer and curator.
His books *Gasoline* (MACK) and
Walker Evans: The Magazine Work (Steidl)
will be published this year.

What Do You See?
Sophie Calle in conversation
with Melissa Harris

Melissa Harris: What was the genesis of the original project *Last Seen*?

Sophie Calle: I had an exhibition in Boston that opened in January 1990 at the Institute of Contemporary Art. I visited the Gardner Museum, and I became obsessed by Vermeer's *The Concert*. Every time a journalist wanted to interview me about my ICA show, I arranged for the appointment to take place in front of the Vermeer. It was an occasion for me to go back there more often. About a week after my show closed, the painting was stolen. I learned about the robbery because Sheena Wagstaff —she had interviewed me in front of the Vermeer—seemed to suggest at the end of her article that maybe *I* took the painting … something like that, in an ironic way, obviously. So when I went back to Boston, at the Gardner I saw this absence: no other art had been placed in the space where the stolen work had been.

MH: Isabella Stewart Gardner's will stipulates that the arrangement of the works in the galleries can never be altered.

SC: Yes. And it's because of her will that I had this idea. It's because of the will that the absence was so *displayed*. In any other museum, they would have put something else where the work was missing. So the will was the departure point for the idea, and I proposed a project to the museum—and they immediately accepted, even in a very complex period for them.

MH: How did the concept evolve?

SC: I had already done a similar project called *Ghosts*, not about works of art that had been stolen, but ones that were missing from collections because they were on temporary loan—first in June 1989 at the Musée d'Art Moderne in Paris and then in October 1991 at the Museum of Modern Art in New York. So the idea was already more or less floating.

MH: Does it make any difference that *Last Seen* and *What Do You See?* address something that has been stolen, as opposed to out on loan?

SC: Yes, there is more feeling—like when somebody dies as compared to just leaving for the month. I did not compare the texts, but I think there is more nostalgia when the work is stolen. It is more intense.

MH: Do you have certain rules or constructs that you apply to each project?

SC: It depends on the project. In this case, when I learned of the stolen paintings, I could see how I could go on with that same system I had started with the works on loan in *Ghosts*. In 1991 for *Last Seen*, I asked curators, guards, and other staff members at the Gardner to describe for me their recollections of the missing objects.

(*continued on page 64*)

On March 18, 1990, one of the most brazen art thefts of all time took place at Boston's Isabella Stewart Gardner Museum. Two men dressed in police uniforms made off with thirteen of the museum's treasures, including Jan Vermeer's *The Concert* (1658–60), Govaert Flinck's *Landscape with an Obelisk* (1638), and three works by Rembrandt. The violation was devastating to both the Gardner's staff and the museum-going public. As Pieranna Cavalchini, the museum's curator of contemporary art, notes, it was as if the institution "had been raped and ravaged."

A year after the crime, in 1991, French artist Sophie Calle created the project *Last Seen*, a response to the theft that was both poetic and provocative: alongside photographs of the museum's newly empty walls she hung panels of text—people's recollections and observations about the absent works.

Absence serves as a primal trigger for this artist. Over the years, many projects by Calle have dealt with missing protagonists —strangers, lovers, at times even herself—and with the conundrums of identity and relationships. There is often a cat-and-mouse quality to her investigations and experimental games. (Is it any wonder the artist named her cat Souris—or "Mouse"?) Someone is following, someone is eluding, someone is being tricky, someone is being watched, someone has disappeared. Calle is often her own most malleable medium: playacting and protean identities are her methods; truth and fiction are her playthings. She has been called an "artist sleuth"—the perfect respondent to the Gardner robbery.

Twenty-three years later, the stolen works have still not been recovered. In 2013 Calle was invited back to the museum, where she created a new project about the missing works, titled *What Do You See?* As Cavalchini observes: "I have always imagined [Calle] as a sort of therapist for the museum— although I do not mean to imply that she was a do-gooder." The robbery was, of course, sensationalized by the media. "It made sense, then as now, to allow the public to see the theft through a cultural lens, through an artist's eyes." The new body of work, as well as that of 1991, will be presented at the Gardner beginning October 23, 2013. I spoke with Calle last April about both projects.
        —**Melissa Harris**

Sophie Calle,
The Clairvoyant, from
What Do You See?
2013

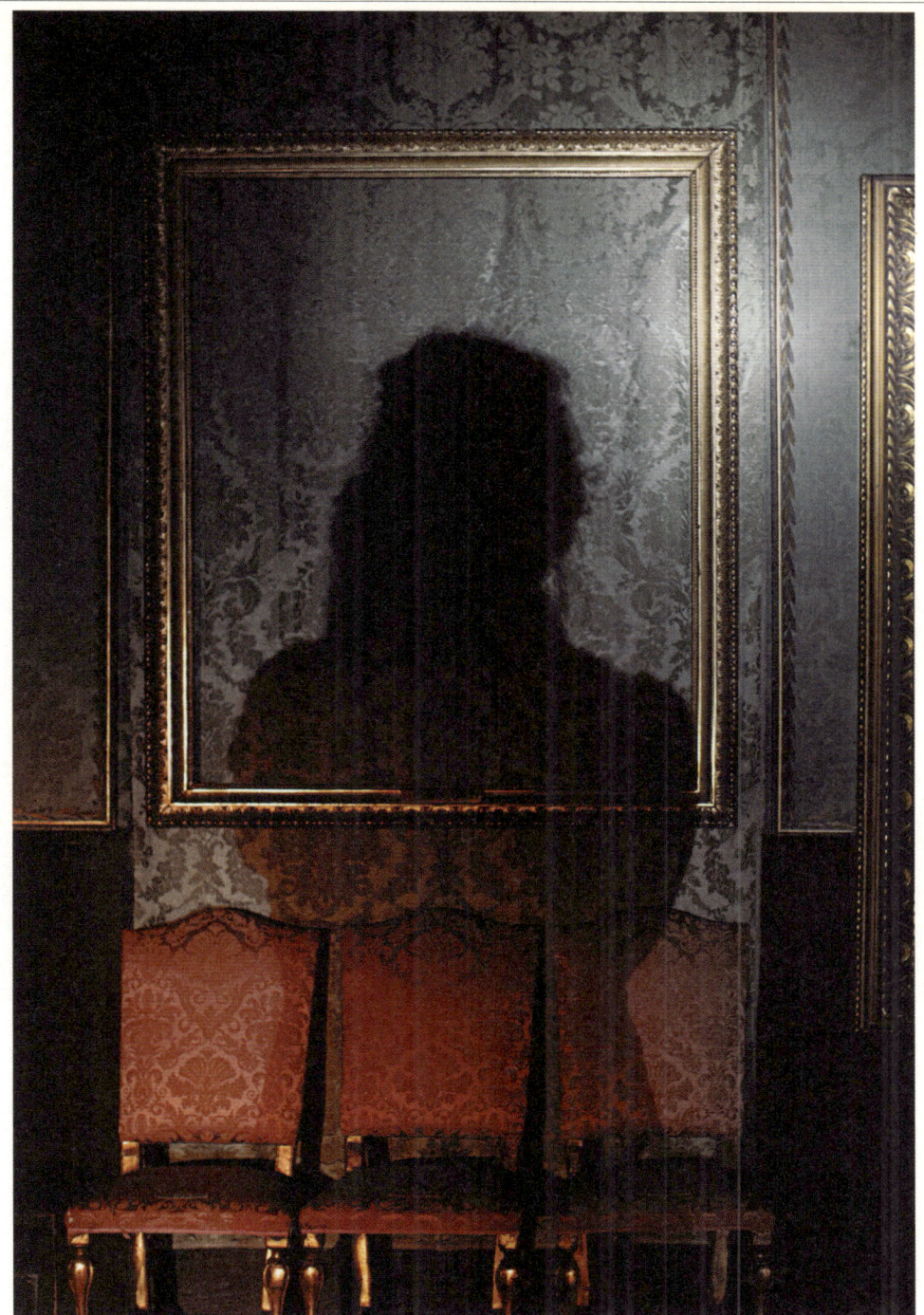

I asked the clairvoyant Maud Kristen what she saw in those empty frames.

Ghosts fill the frame, as if the theft had freed the characters, had allowed them to leave that frozen representation while staying on-site. I feel that they are more present in their absence. The visitors' gazes held them back, but now they can wander around the museum. They have that physical freedom one has in the dark, the pleasure of living one's life without being seen…. What I mean is that even if the canvas was burned, the woman who posed for it is not disfigured. It's as if, having been divested of her body, she was then divested of her image. What I see in this opening is alive and joyful.

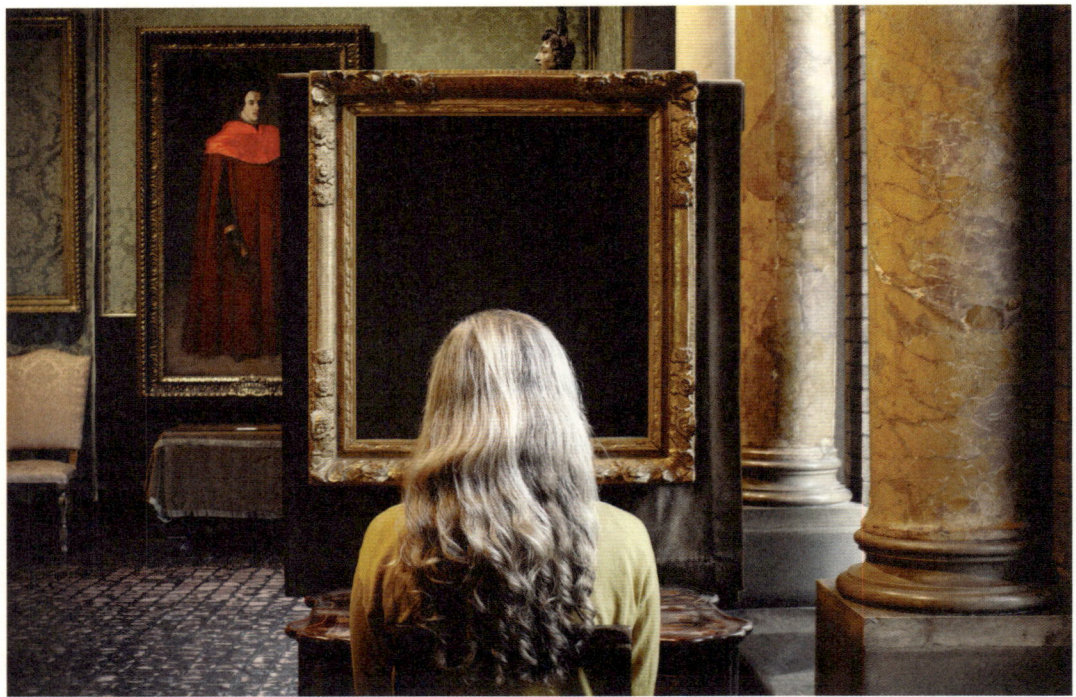

When I stand in front of this empty space, I see a woman deep in concentration playing the harpsichord, and the woman on the other side just about to emit a note from her body. And I hear music playing ♦ I see a very old wooden frame with no picture in it, and behind it a brown background, a velvet cloth. That's all there is. There's no reason for this frame to be here. What am I supposed to see? This empty space represents space, just space ♦ The picture arises. I contemplate a painting stronger than its absence. If you know this work you see it better in the velvet than on a reproduction. I see people making music. You are looking at this silent picture but you're aware of music being made in the painting. A lute player with his back to you, a woman at a harpsichord and a woman singing, palpable. In my dreams I mostly see her. I am so attached to her that I should be able to know where she is ♦ I don't see much of anything. I see an empty frame, and behind the frame is this very dark fabric. I certainly see a solemn space. A little bit reproachful ♦ I see colors. On the left, the yellow sleeve of the woman, the trapezoidal red shape of the back of the chair and then that blue… I see the luxurious jacket the singer is wearing and the shadowy foreground with that rich, oriental carpet over the table. I see three colors, that sort of dance across the surface. It's red, yellow, blue—it's Mondrian ♦ I see flashes of what is supposed to be there. I see *The Concert*. When I give people a tour, I point over and I say: this is *The Concert*. But there is nothing there. Except a framed space that represents frustration ♦ I see a black fabric, a little bit spooky. It says I could put anything I wanted inside the frame, but the blackness seems to be fighting against my desire to imagine something in there ♦ I've never seen this picture in person, so I see crime scene pictures. The frame lying on the floor, in the middle of the room, with broken glass contained within. The chalk they put around the body—that's what this frame is to me. But it never goes away; you see the body every day ♦ It's a sad and nostalgic image. I see textures and nuances. I see this soft light washing over the velvet. I see this dark shadow to the right, and this very pale horizontal line across the center. I see this tiny layer of dust, especially on the lower left-hand edge. And of course, because the velvet is so spare and simple, I focus on the frame, the gold-etched outlines of flowers and the larger floral shapes, almost like sunflowers, around the edges. The outside is very charged and the inside very quiet. And, for whatever reason, I have this slight feeling that the frame is looking at me ♦ I see a frame that shows an absence. I see something everyone is denied the pleasure of seeing. I see a loss just indescribable. I see my impossibility to ever see the real thing ♦ Today I just see velvet, but of course there's much more ♦ My job is to bring it back, so I see my failure. I see this void even in my nightmares. There is a car, and, in it, a painting with a plastic bag over it. I take the bag off and it's not the painting that I want. But I know that one day, in the middle of the night, I'll receive a telephone call: *Vermeer is back*.

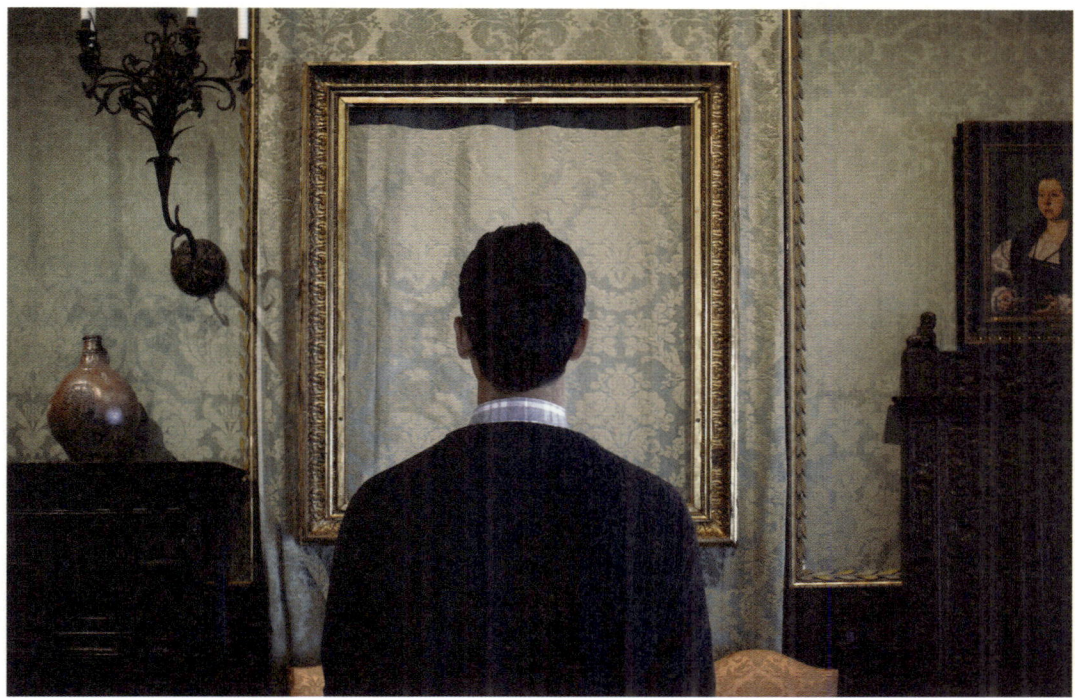

I don't see something very communicative. I see a frame and nothing in the frame. You know it's an absence, but you don't know an absence of what ♦ I see a vacant space that's not vacant. I see a space of meditation on what's missing. I see a frame that doesn't really stand in as a substitute or an understudy for the painting, a frame that makes the absence of the painting striking. It's just a holding place. A space that shows a painting is gone and reminds you it will come back ♦ All I can see is that ghost, that missing child, between the man and the woman. I'm focused on this wonderful sort of secret, remembering the absence more than the painting. It was more fascinating for what you couldn't see than for what you did. I'm connecting the loss with that child who may have been painted out because he died. And now, everyone's gone ♦ I can picture their faces perfectly—a man and a woman—but this painting never meant much to me, and why anyone would take it—that's just a mystery ♦ I see the tremendous amount of varnish we've built up around Rembrandt, so we can't really see Rembrandt anymore. Maybe that's why the frame is empty ♦ I see sacrilege. I see a frame that makes the absence of the painting striking. I see an amazing void that reminds you of the power of something so simple as canvas with paint on it. I see a space that can't be filled by anything else. Replacement would be dishonest; it would give us the sensation that we are acting as if there weren't a huge loss ♦ I don't feel the public needs to be reminded; I just like the way the frame looks. I like its dimensions, the way it crowns these chairs. I love the framing of the damask pattern behind. I see a lot of roses. That's what I see. I see bouquets. I don't think that you would pay the same kind of attention to them if they weren't framed ♦ I just see a narrative. I see that once there was a painting, and it is gone. But I thought I would see more of the absence, I thought it would be more "missing." This empty frame is a great idea conceptually, but at first, I didn't even notice that this was *the* room. Then when it's pointed out, you see the absence ♦ Maybe I'm just tired, for me there's nothing there. But if you didn't have the frame, people would think there's a gap ♦ Knowing that this frame once held a masterpiece, I can look at it in two ways: I can see it as this sad emblem of a terrible loss, the fabric representing a Rembrandt that doesn't exist. Or I can look at it as a celebration of this exquisite silk ♦ It almost looks like a curtain. Like before a play. Except it's not hiding anything and there isn't much to look at. I imagine they took out the painting? Maybe they meant to leave it that way to exercise people's imagination ♦ I see an attempt to draw attention to the frame. It might be because the frame isn't always looked at, it's always what's in the frame ♦ It's hard to imagine a painting, because it's gone. And that's the point of leaving the frame there. They want to make us believe it's not ♦ I see something very vague. It's been so long. This painting was already quiet and sad and absent ♦ I see the portrait of a couple, in a storage facility somewhere...

MH: What made you decide to revisit this site and the idea now?

SC: Pieranna Cavalchini invited me last year to show *Last Seen* at the Gardner, and while discussing this with her, she told me there was a change since my last visit: the empty frames were back on the walls. When I saw the new installation, I proposed a new version of the project. When I did *Last Seen* in 1991, the sense of absence was kind of unclear—just something missing—but now the absence was totally *framed*. So it made me desire to do it in a different way.

MH: How did you decide whom to interview for *Last Seen* in 1991, and then for *What Do You See*?

SC: The first time I asked people to describe the missing paintings, I didn't ask museum visitors—I asked only people who had very regular knowledge of a missing painting to describe their memory of the work. Obviously, the people who clean it didn't describe it the same way as the curator, who did not describe it the same way as the restorer. Each one described the missing painting from his own angle.

For *What Do You See?*, I included random visitors to the museum. And I didn't ask people to describe the missing paintings—I didn't even mention there *was* a missing painting. I just asked people: "What do you see?" Which is not the same question at all.

MH: Did you include some of the same people that you had asked the first time?

SC: I don't think so. Except for the museum's director, Anne Hawley. But it was not the same question, so I didn't care if it was the same people. In *What Do You See?*, I asked a lot of visitors, people coming by, just anybody entering the room. And, for the people working in the museum it was whoever wanted to do it. Pieranna asked around and found five, six, seven people who were interested in participating. I just asked them: "What do you see?" After, if they asked me why, I told them why. Every person spoke about four of the missing works: Flinck's *Landscape with an Obelisk*; Rembrandt's *Storm on the Sea of Galilee* and *A Lady and a Gentleman in Black*, and Vermeer's *Concert*.

MH: Did you interview a diversity of people—in order to have a diversity of responses?

SC: Yes. I did that for the sake of the portrayal. When you do a portrayal, you ask people to describe the *whole* body, not only the eyes. So to have a portrait through these different angles, it's the way to have a more complete portrait. When I did the project in 1991, you could kind of see there was an empty spot on the wall, but in the new project, it's a *frame* that you see. So now it's a "work." What I was interested in is: Do people see the absent work, or do they see a piece of material? What do they see inside the frame? In a museum, a frame is rarely empty. So it's something very unique.

MH: In 1991, were you interested in how much people actually remembered of the original painting?

SC: I was interested in the poetic picture that appears through, you know, the collective memories of everybody.

MH: Do you have a personal feeling about any of the works that were stolen? Do you care whether they are returned?

SC: That's my own problem; it's not part of this project. Yes, I would prefer if the work comes back—just to be able to look at it again. But if I wanted to give my personal feelings, I would be inside the text. Who knows? Maybe I am. If I was in it, and I wanted people to *know* that, I would say it. So if I don't say it, it means … that I don't say it.

Maybe everything is invented. Maybe I interviewed no one. Who knows? Since none of the texts has a name attached to it, you don't know who said what.

MH: Well, one of the texts has a name attached to it: *What Do You See?* includes the comments of a clairvoyant. How did that come about?

SC: I had made a project called *Where and When* [2008] with a clairvoyant. I was talking about that project to Anne Hawley at the museum as I was working on *What Do You See?*, and she said something like: "Oh, you should ask your clairvoyant where the paintings are." Since I was asking people what they see, it *was* about vision, in a way. So I thought it would be interesting to know the vision of a clairvoyant.

MH: Did she come to the museum?

SC: No. I brought her photos of the actual paintings that were stolen, and I brought her the photos that I took of what is there now, with the frames.

MH: You pair this text by the clairvoyant with an image of your own presence—your shadow against one of the frames. So we get the ruminations of someone who was *not* there and the shadow of the artist who *is*. Why did you make that photograph?

SC: The people at the museum offered me something lovely—a night visit, simply for the pleasure of it. They showed me around the museum with a flashlight. It was beautiful. I just had to make that picture.

MH: When you first walked into the galleries this time, what resonated most?

SC: What surprised me was the *mise en scène*—how the absence was so staged. It was very striking for me, since my own work—from the first project to the latest one—is often in some way about absence: a man who goes away, somebody who dies, something that's not there. Then I arrive in a place where the absence is totally organized. It was miraculous in a way.

Sophie Calle will have an exhibition at the Stavanger Art Museum in Norway this September; in October her work will be on view at the Isabella Stewart Gardner Museum, Boston, and at Paula Cooper Gallery, New York. Next year, she will take part in the Sydney Biennial.

Melissa Harris is the Editor-at-Large of *Aperture* magazine.

Pictures

Jo Ann Callis, from the series ca. 1976, 1976
Courtesy the artist and
ROSEGALLERY, Santa Monica

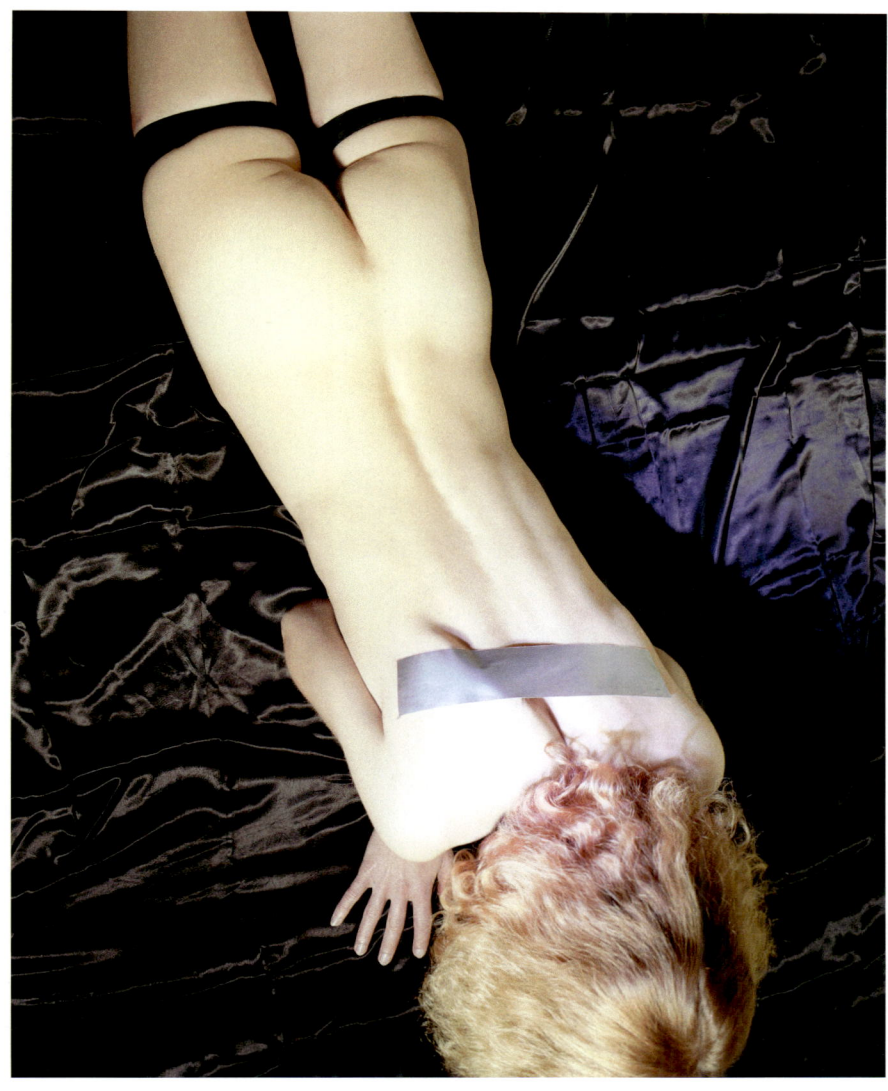

J'aime—je n'aime pas. —Roland Barthes

Human beings are shaped by desire. We hope and yearn for what we do not have, driven by thoughts of the people, things, and experiences we covet. Our longings may appear as cravings; conversely, they may crop up as but innocent ripples, pleasantly skimming the surface of consciousness. When sexually invested, our longings accelerate, unleashing powerful urges, fantasies, and erotic fixations. "My body is not the same as yours," Roland Barthes once famously said, elucidating both the origins of our erotic attractions and the pulsating rush of human desire.

Jo Ann Callis's color photographs from the mid-1970s take a fetishistic delight in human bodies. Naked, vulnerable, and tied in myriad places, the androgynous men and women in her pictures seem both enchanted and faintly repelled by the circumstances in which they find themselves. Callis was inspired by Pierre Molinier's doll-like self-portraits and the twisted mannequins of Hans Bellmer, and her subjects attempt to enhance their pleasure in ways that are simultaneously playful and therapeutic, sticking their hands into pools of honey, tying nylon threads around their breasts, and rubbing their alabaster skin against luxurious fabrics. Faces are conspicuously and tellingly absent, buried in pillows or covered under waves of hair and a soft satin glove. A line along a woman's back suggests a surgical incision mark, or the tingly sensation of fingers running down one's spine. A heap of black sand sprinkled on skin conjures feelings of bliss or something more sinister. Callis is playing a game of *what-does-this-feel-like*, rendering physical sensations—sand, satin, hair, nylon, viscous honey on skin—in ways one might find erotically pleasing and titillating, or not. Rendered in photographic form, these double-edged fantasies achieve a degree of realism that is not for the squeamish, teetering as it does between the sumptuous evocation of physical delight and the sobering acknowledgement of emotional pain.

Callis has long exploited the photographic process to narrative ends. A teacher at the California Institute of the Arts and widely regarded for her conceptual work with three-dimensional objects and images of people in mysterious settings, she has worked both in black-and-white and color photography, sculpture, painting, set design, and digital imagery. While she uses the camera often, she never pursues the medium as an end in and of itself, employing it instead as a studio tool to capture the pleasures and terrors of female life. The resulting pictures are both seductive and unsettling, tantalizing visions of interior states that attest to Callis's singular vision of the delicate tension between what feels good and what doesn't, between what is desired and what is allowed. The photographs selected here are but a preview of Callis's œuvre: beautifully composed, with an unfailing eye toward color and texture, yet laced with the raw shivers of anxiety that run through her work like a chilling undercurrent.

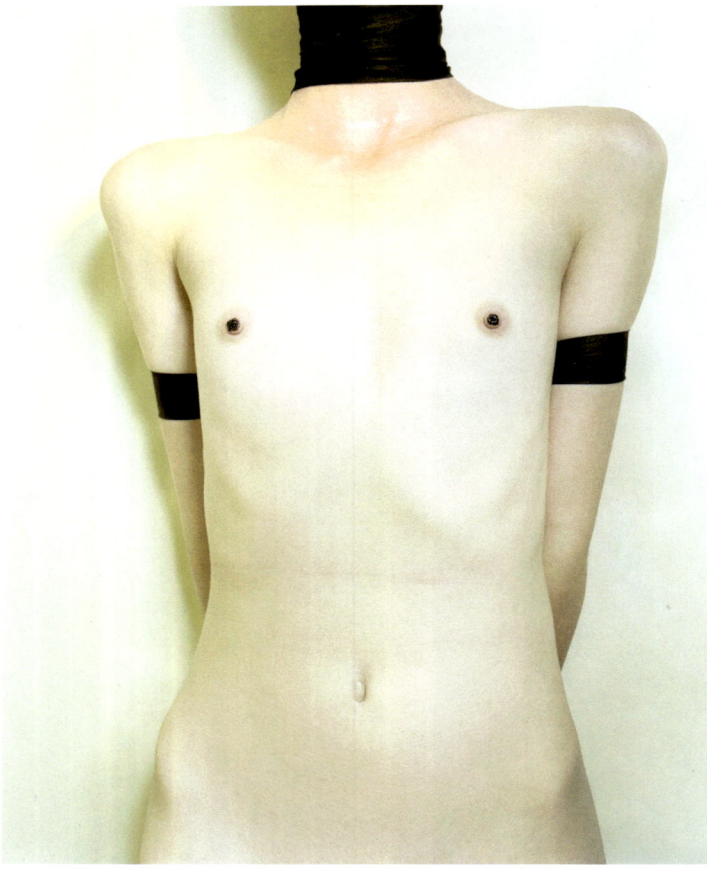

Jo Ann Callis
ca. 1976

Claudia Bohn-Spector

Claudia Bohn-Spector is an independent writer and curator living in South Pasadena, California.

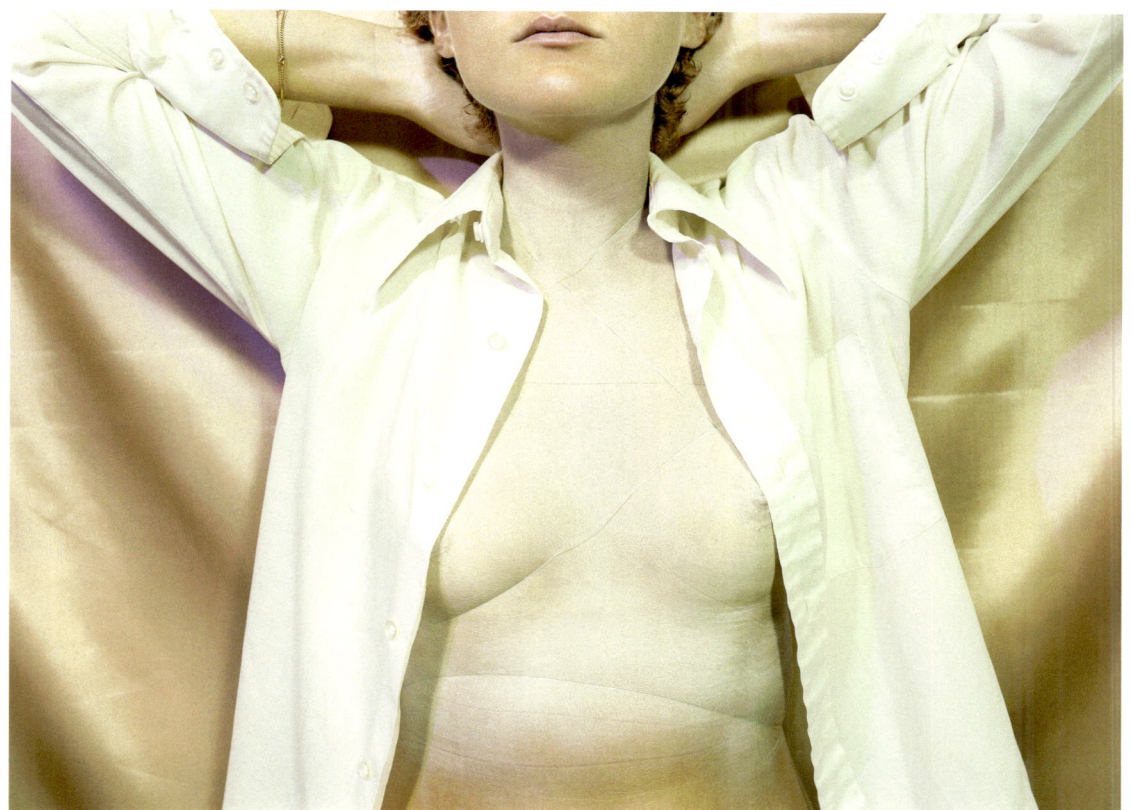

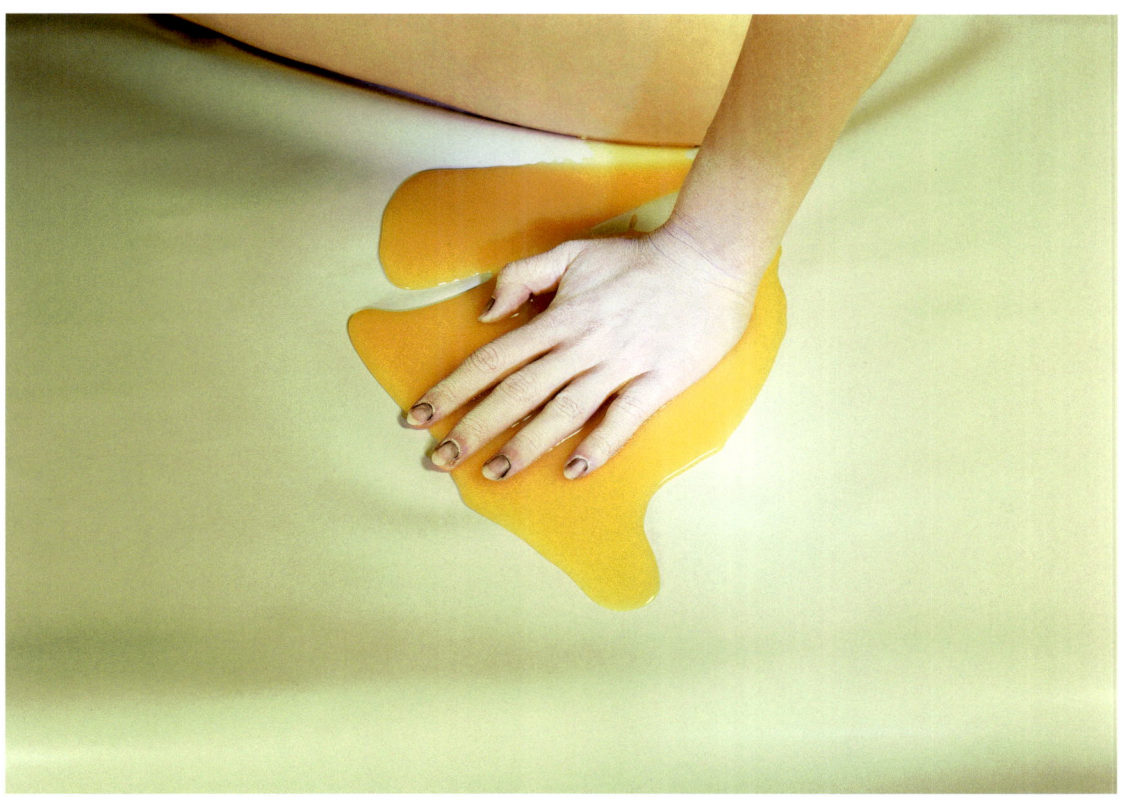

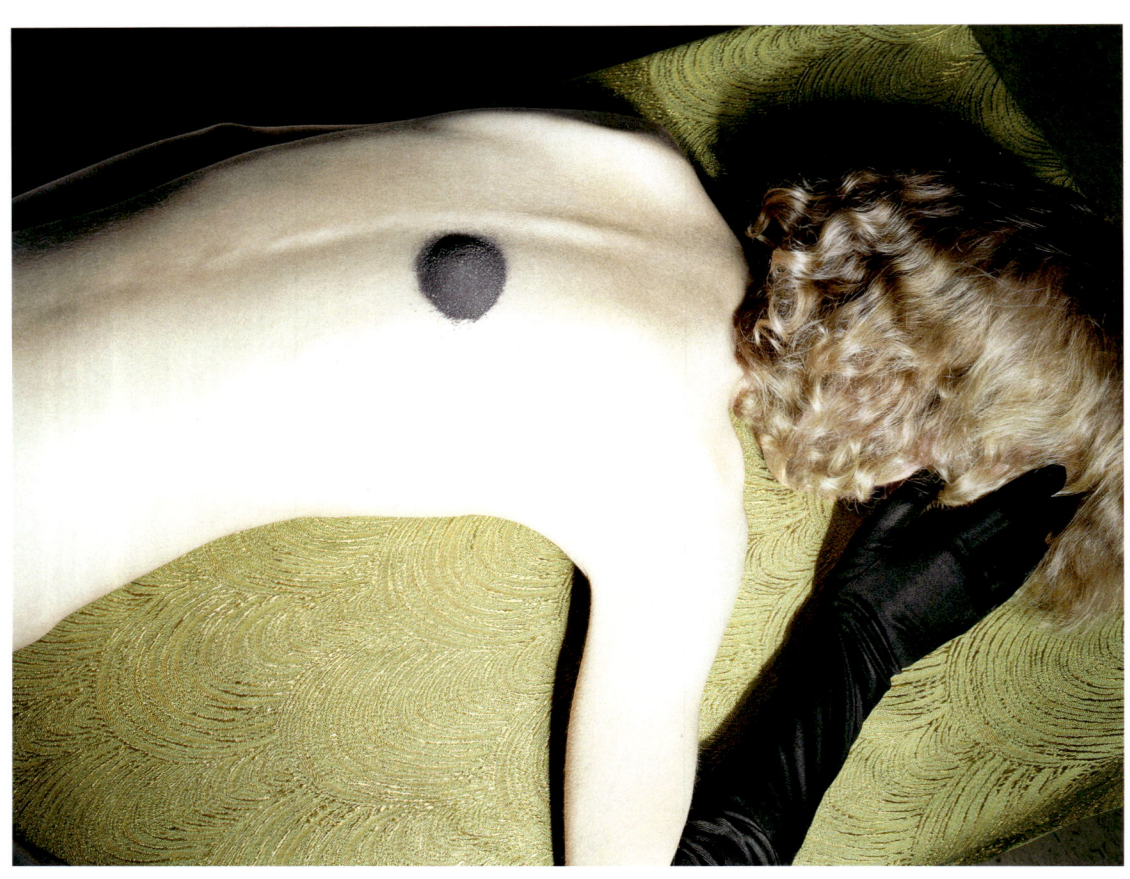

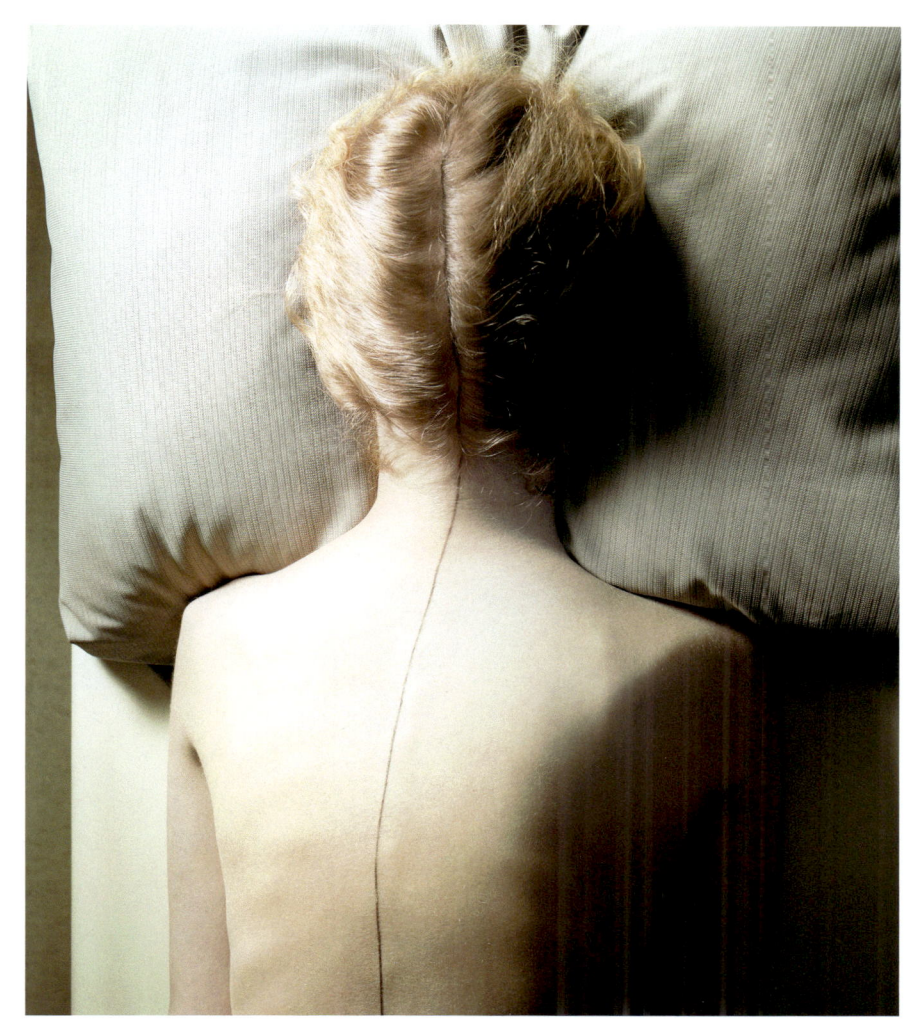

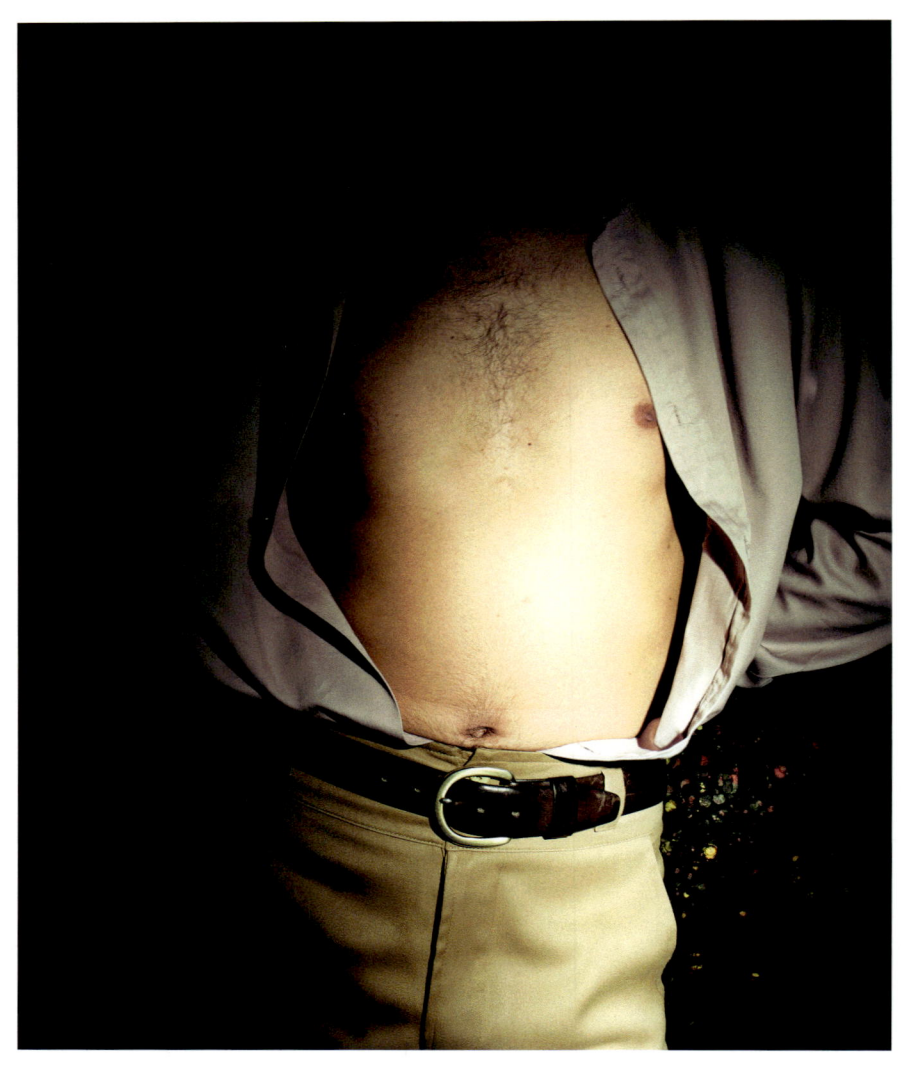

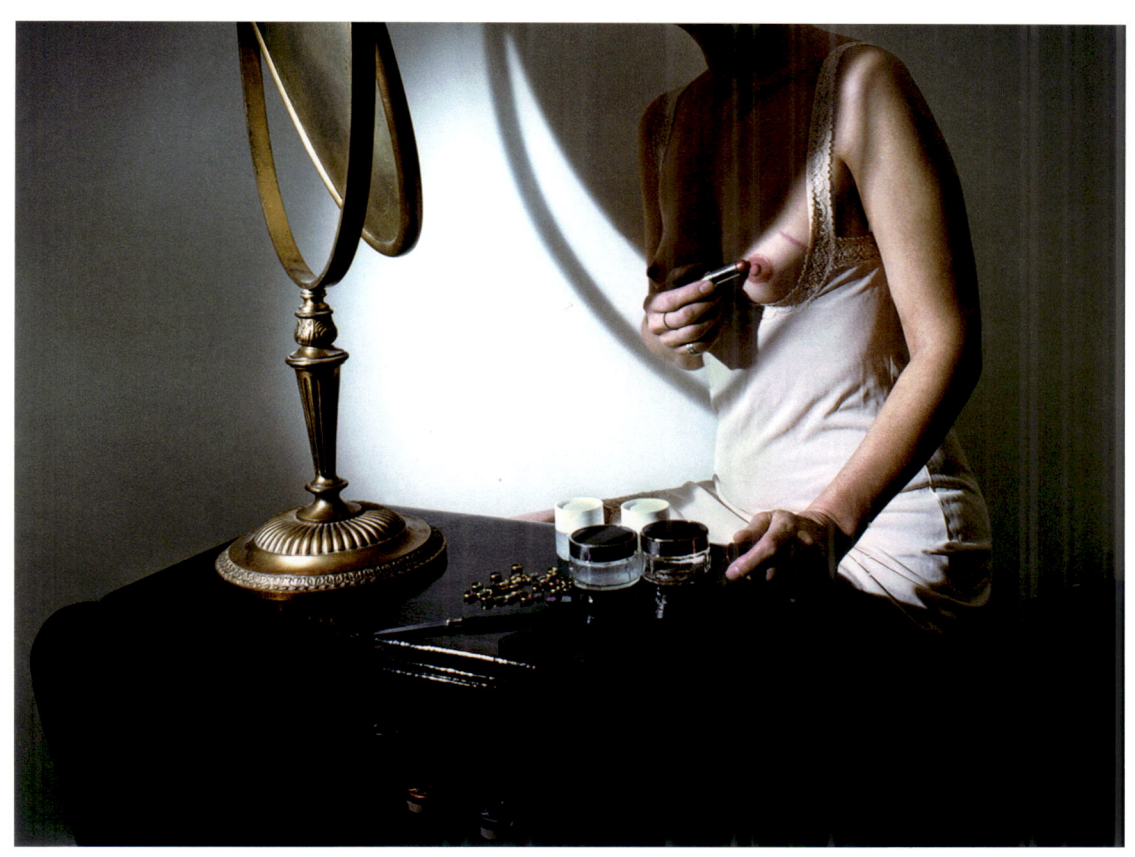

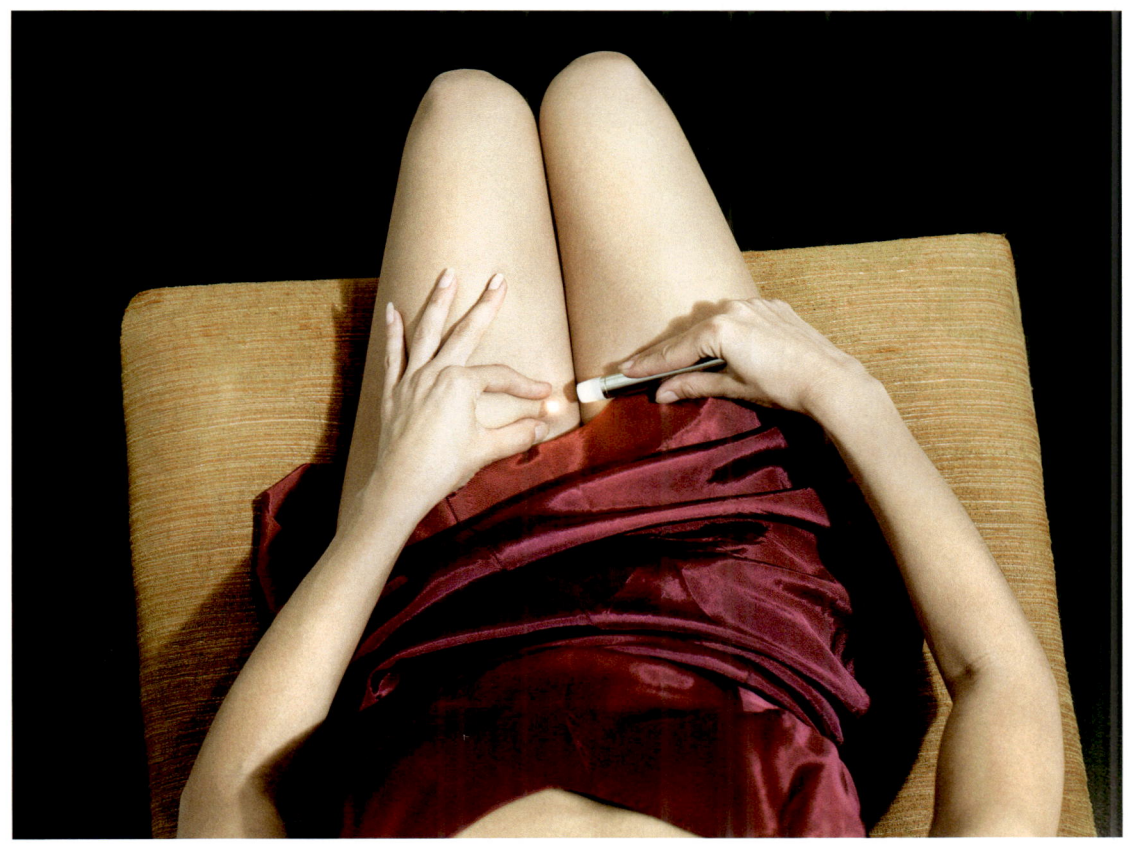

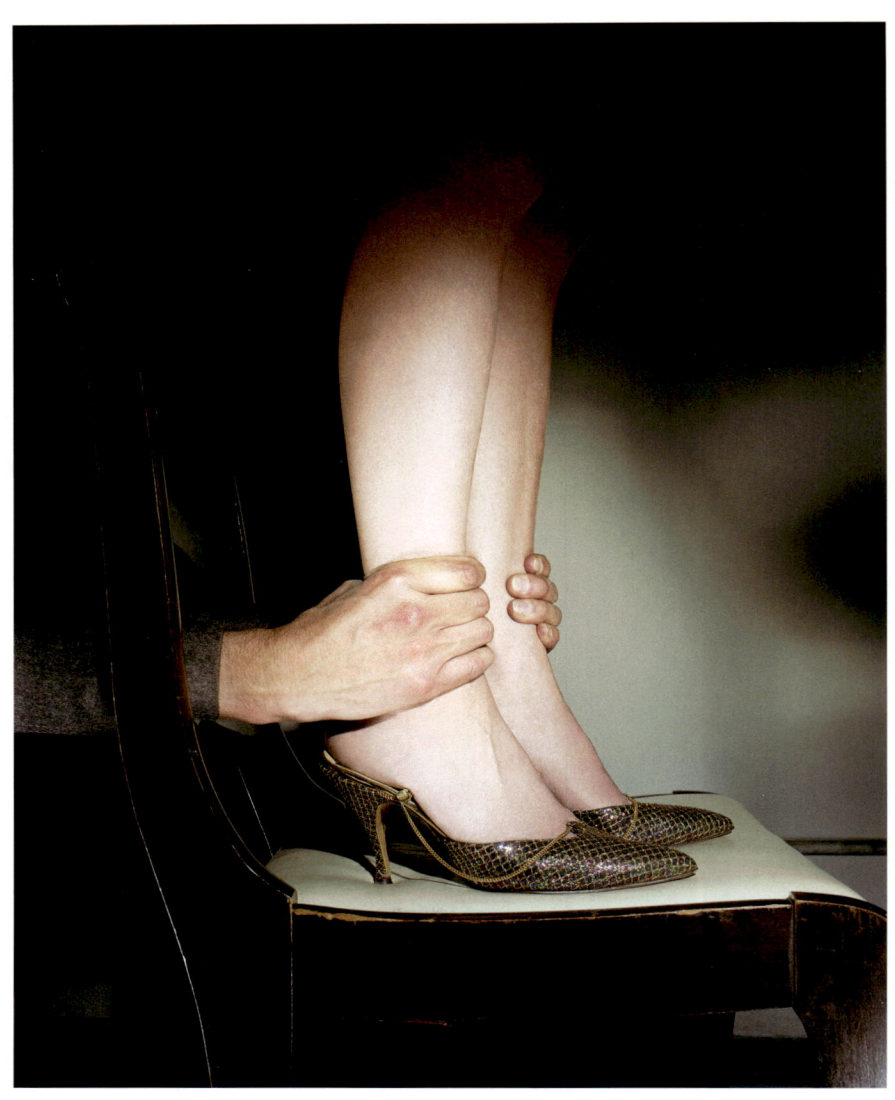

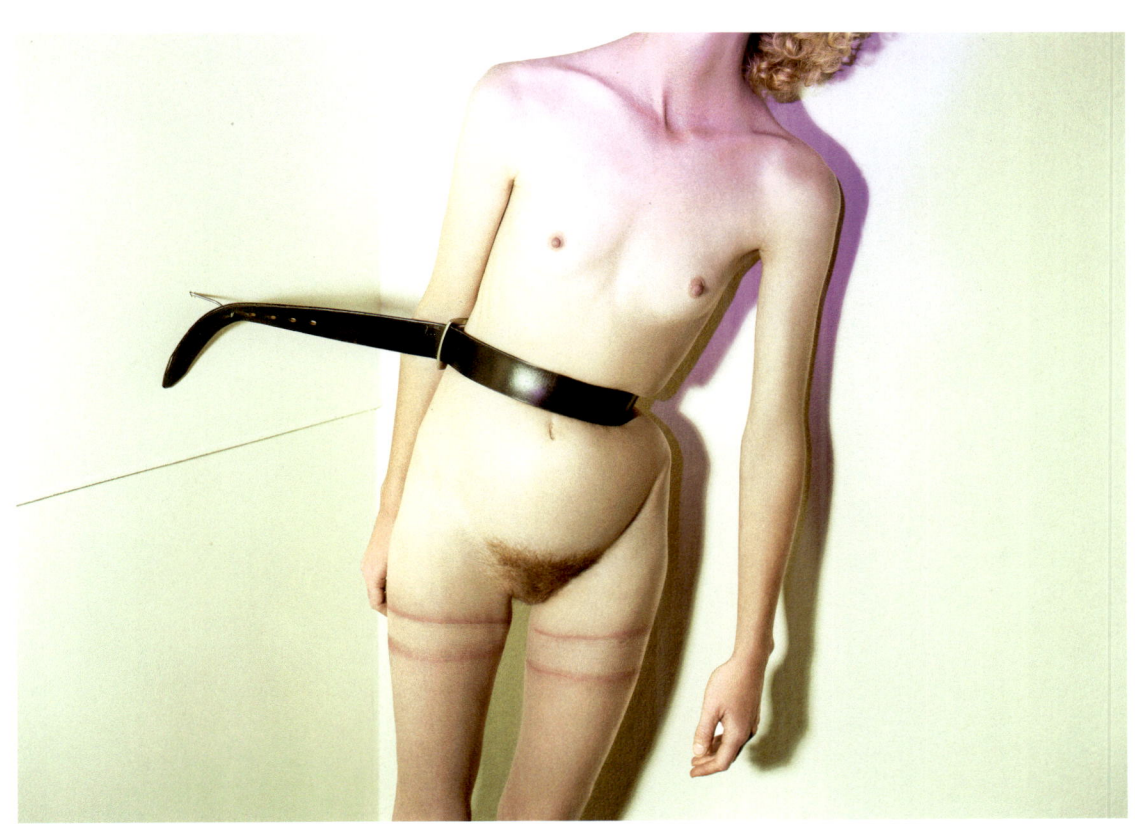

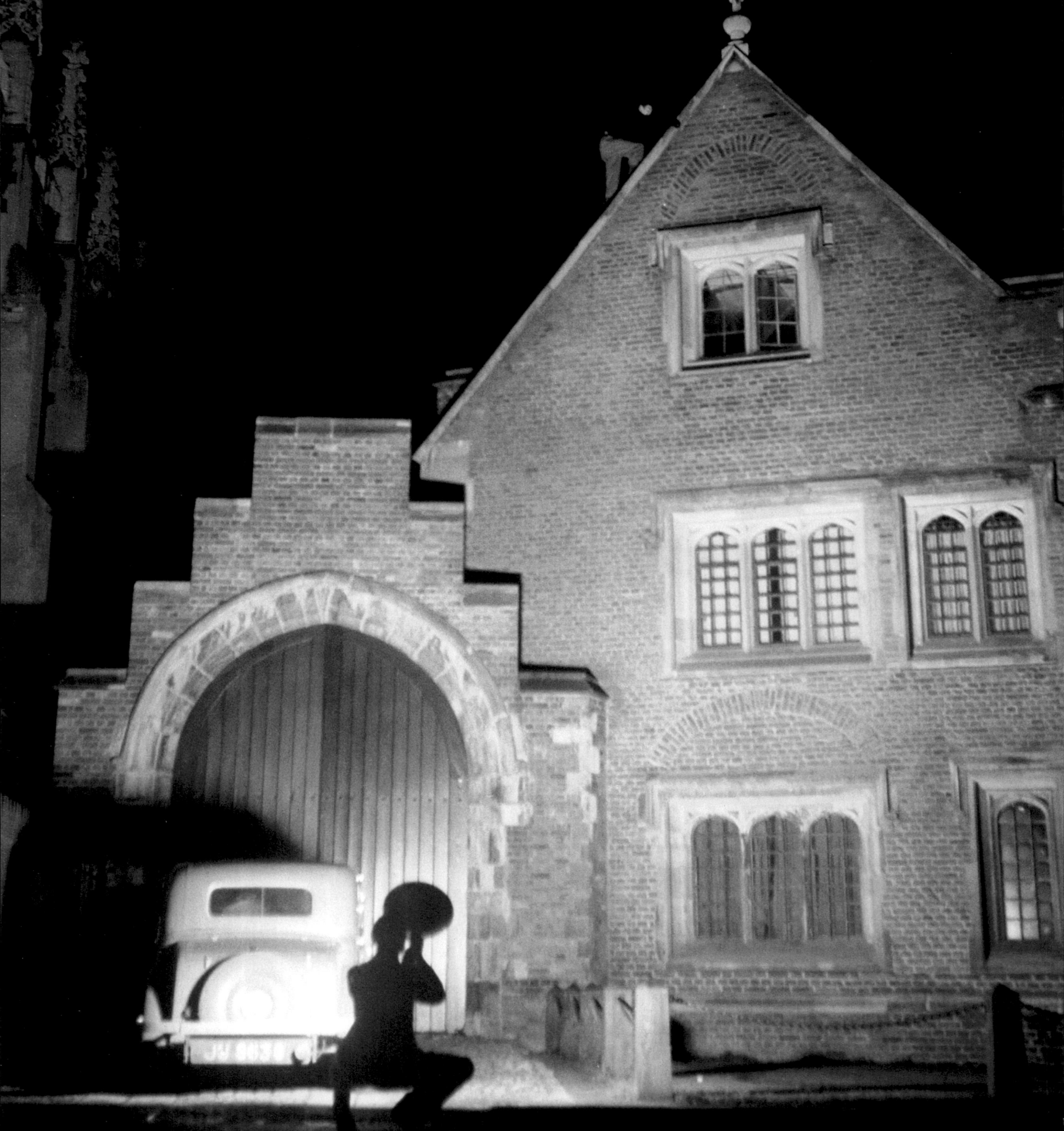

Opposite: The Ivy Arch,
St. John's College,
St. John's Street

"A much more genteel climb is getting on to the Ivy Arch, fifty yards to the south of the Main Gate. The name dates back to the days when it was covered in ivy; since then it has had a shave, and is now quite spruce-looking. Architecturally, it is rather unimaginative. Built to conceal the fact that behind the gate it adorns is a vulgar backyard, it goes up in broad steps to a veritable plateau on the top."
—Climber's note

Night Climbing

Ian Jeffrey

Ian Jeffrey is an art historian. Among many other projects, he was a major contributor to *Thirties*, a comprehensive survey of British art and design before the war, presented in 1979 at the Hayward Gallery, London.

Thomas Mailaender will exhibit *The Night Climbers of Cambridge* this September at Roman Road Project Space, London.

Why should Thomas Mailaender, a contemporary artist known for his impudent provocations, want to present us with photographs of students climbing on the roofs and walls of colleges at the University of Cambridge in the mid-1930s?

The Night Climbers of Cambridge was first published in 1937, by Chatto & Windus, a respectable publishing house in London. (The book, illustrated with photographs, was recently reissued by Oleander Press.) Mailaender, attracted by this peculiar venture, bought the original pictures and assembled them as a traveling exhibition. An odd choice, at first sight, but Mailaender has always been attracted by makeshift spoofs and charades. Nothing attracts him more than a tacky stunt where all the seams show. He is at home in the soft underbelly of the Internet, where self-satisfied egotists hog the limelight as they compete for delusional awards. In one noteworthy presentation he features as a beaming prize-winner holding on to outsize checks. He has a fondness for shaky facsimiles and rackety cover versions. His pictures of Algerian vehicles, piled high with possessions and discards, taken at the port of Marseille, look like nothing so much as a Joseph Beuys exhibition chanced upon in transit.

Mailaender is a saboteur. Bathos is his mode. His targets are credulity and complacency. He finds contemporary life, which includes contemporary art, ridiculous, pathetic, and entertaining. Long ago, before the night climbers plied their saucy trade on the walls of Cambridge, he would have been at one with Austrian writer Karl Kraus, who also appropriated pictures. Kraus's *leitmotif*, you will remember, was the hanged body of the separatist Cesare Battisti displayed on a board in the moat of the Castello del Buonconsiglio in 1916 as part of a group portrait of executioners and accomplices all happy to be involved. Kraus saw it as a conclusive indictment of the Austrian Empire.

The Cambridge adventurers fit Mailaender's bill precisely. Maybe they meant no real harm. All the same they were climbing, which was a man's business carried out regularly and hazardously on rock faces in the Lake District and in Wales—and sometimes in the Alps and on Everest where George Mallory and Andrew Irvine came stylishly to grief in 1924. In this context fooling around on the buttresses of King's College or St. John's couldn't be taken seriously. The night climbers, headed by Noël Edward Symington, were, one might think, *asking* to be held in contempt.

They weren't even doing anything very unusual, for any amount of famous names had amused themselves on those famous walls—Geoffrey Winthrop Young, for example, a famous alpinist and author of *The Roof-Climber's Guide to Trinity* in 1899. What set the new generation apart was its interest in publicity. They photographed themselves in action, using flash—which drew the attention of passing policemen. They were, that is to say, interested in staged events, and at the time such events were popular in the British press: studio pictures, for instance, of films in the making and of early TV shoots at London's Alexandra Palace.

Meanwhile, in the real world the Spanish Civil War was in full swing—Guernica was bombed in 1937. In depressed Britain the government was at its wits' end and the unemployed were up in arms—the famous Jarrow marches protesting unemployment and poverty also took place in 1937. The night climbers, cheeking the authorities and policemen, played their studiedly inconsequential part in this ghastly montage, and it is on this state of affairs that Mailaender has put his finger.

This page, top:
Flashlight, bulbs, rucksack, camera, ropes, and men

This page, bottom left:
Lion chimney (narrow climbing passage), Fitzwilliam Museum

"They took a photo of me at the top of the chimney. This chimney, above one of the lions at the north-east corner, is of an ideal width, with vertical grooves to keep the feet (and body) from slipping sideways."
—Climber's note

This page, bottom right:
Note on the verso of the photograph, "The Face of [Gonville and] Caius [College]"

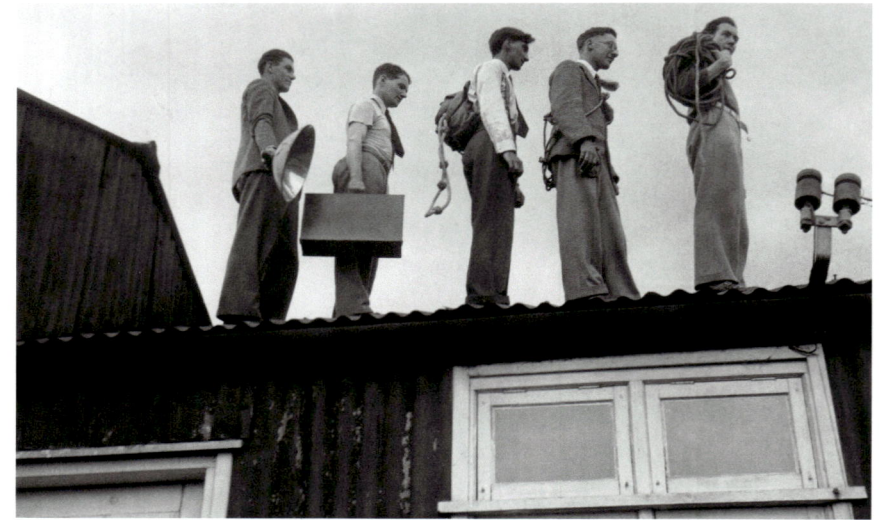

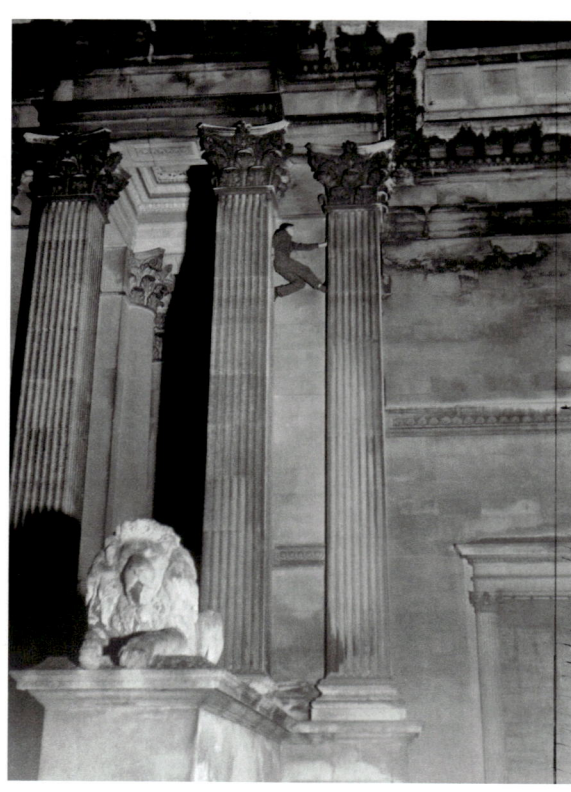

16.

The Face of Caius.
Some feet lower down the climber must do a hand-traverse on a ledge after climbing the bars of a window to the right. The statue helps him higher up.

This climb must be done to reach the top of the Senate House from the ground.

Not yet described in the book

THE SOUTH FACE OF CAIUS.
The stone is very sound, or the climb would be impossible.

Opposite:
Trinity College, Fourth Court climb

"Reaching the second ledge. The pipe is too close to the wall at this point to help, unless the windows by the climber's feet are open."
—Climber's note

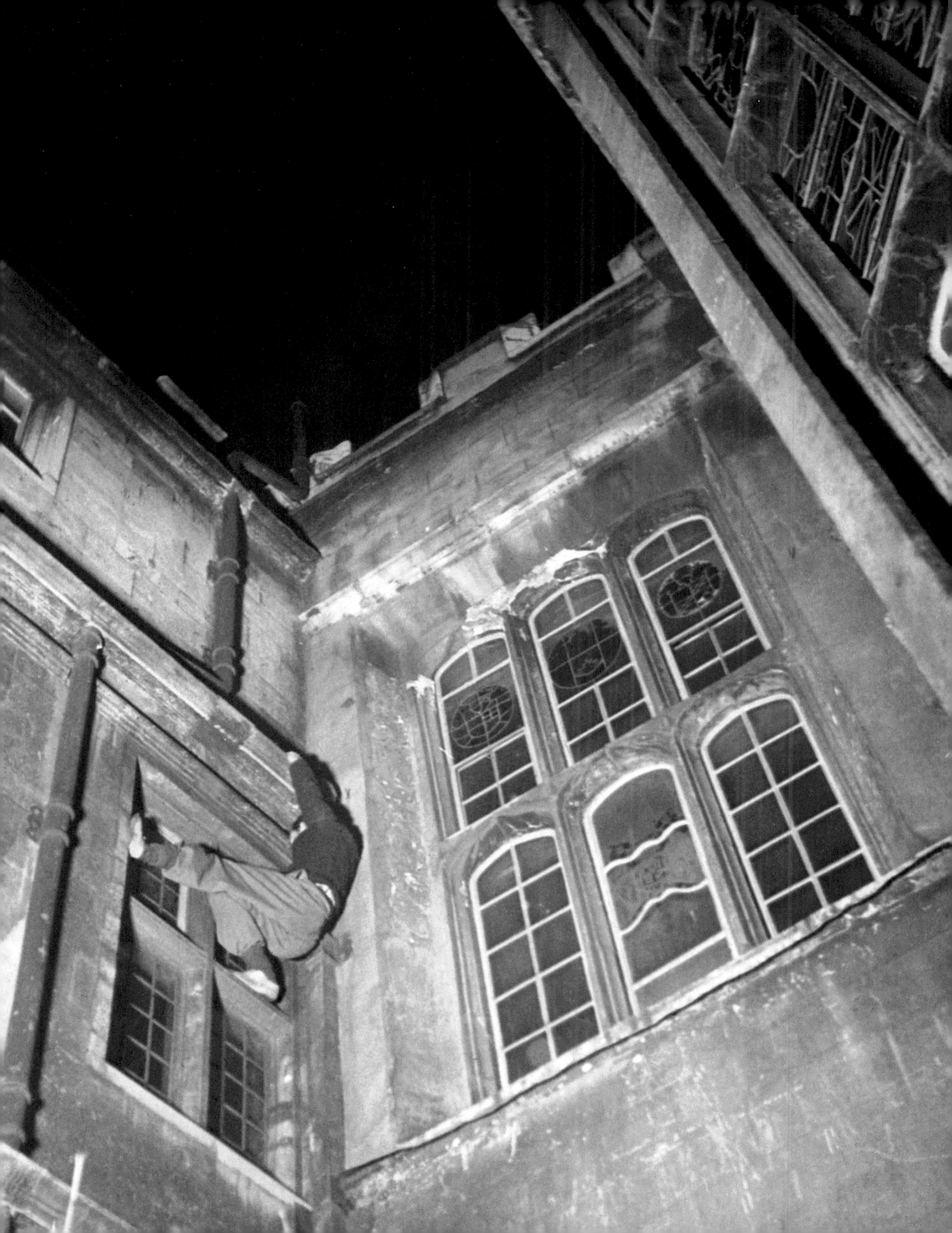

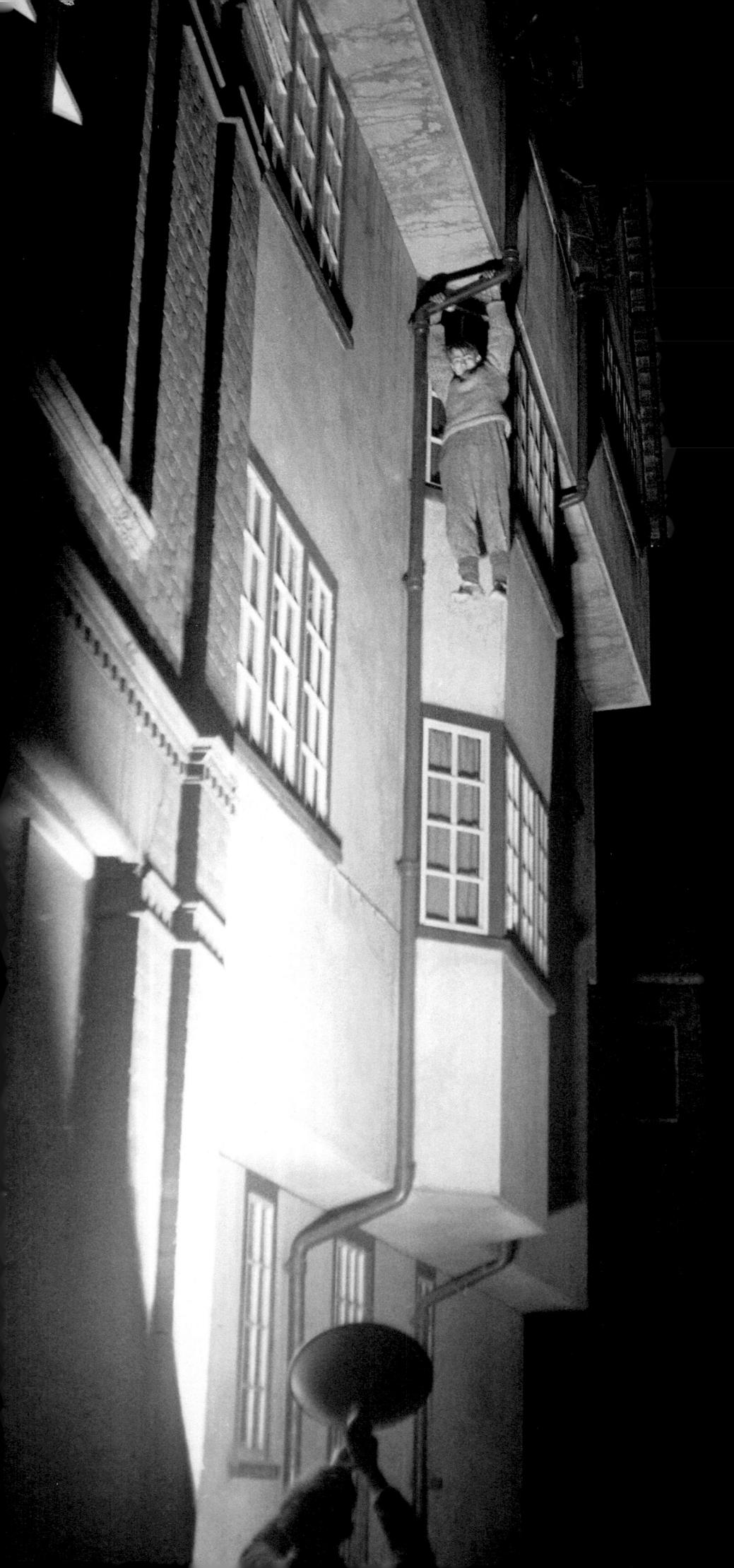

This page, top right:
"Tottering Tower," Old Schools, Trinity Lane

"Standing on the parapet of the roof, one holds on to a gargoyle with the left hand and to a ridge above it with the right hand…. At the top there is a good view of the lighted town, and little or no chance of the climber being seen by inquisitive eyes. The name 'Tottering Tower' was given because two of the party swore that the top of the pinnacle swayed just before the photograph was taken."
—Climber's note

This page, left:
Note on verso of photograph, "Tottering Tower"

This page, bottom right:
King's College Chapel (shown: Noël Howard Symington)

All photographs © Noël Howard Symington, *The Night Climbers of Cambridge*/Collection Thomas Mailaender

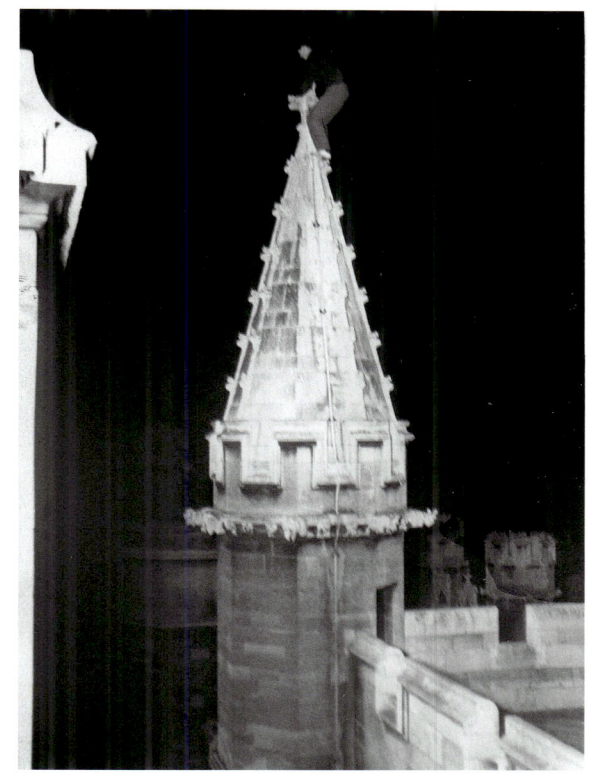

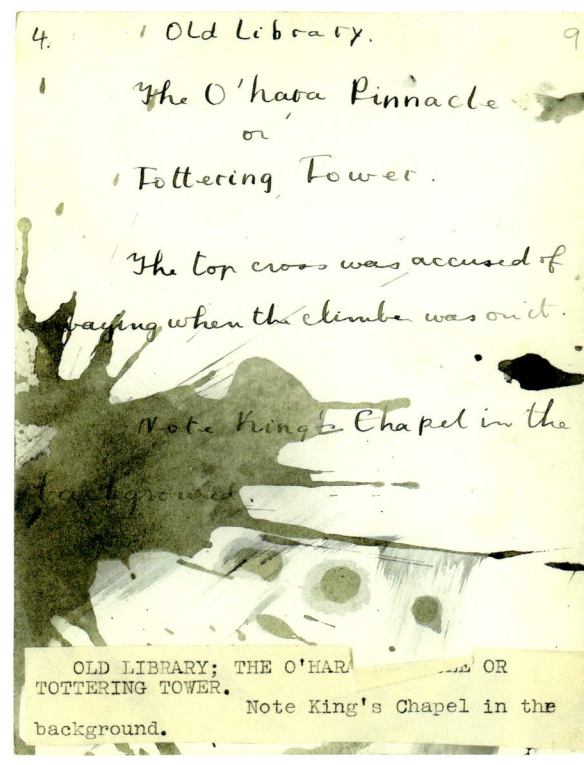

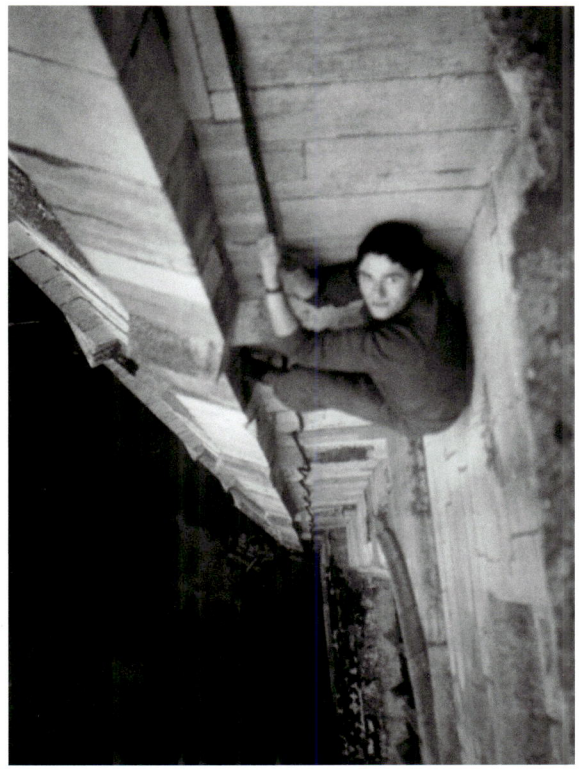

Opposite:
Back up Garrett Hostel Lane to Trinity Lane

All photographs made at the University of Cambridge, ca. 1937.

Japan's Showa period lasted sixty-four years, from 1926 to 1989. Kazuyoshi Usui's *Showa 88* is set in a world that doesn't exist, projecting twenty-four years into the future of an era that has long since ended: it is a speculation on what things would be like if the Showa period had continued to the present day. Usui looks for the remnants of it in Osaka, Kyoto, Chiba, and the *hisaichi* (the devastated area in Japan's northeast)—though not in Tokyo, which is for Usui a gray zone of prescribed organization, social codes, and sexual mores.

Showa culture is vivid and overwhelmingly pink-toned in the quasi-documents Usui has generated. This is his version of a cyberpunk world where future and past are mixed. Although many Japanese urban centers have experienced gentrification and a routing-out of the seedier areas, there remain enclaves where the "stench of flesh" (as Usui puts it) is still pungent. And it is into this world that Usui introduces his troupe of players: a traveling minstrel (a B-grade Kabuki performer), a blind shaman, Butoh dancers cast as *yakuza* (Japanese mafia), and a young geisha girl—although the extent of the *mise en scène* is never quite clear in this project, or who is truly a player, and on what level.

In this imagined alternate reality, the fictional precinct that Usui's photography revives is a typical *akasenchi,* or red-light district. As was common practice through-out Japan's history, such areas were separated from the rest of town, usually located on the other side of a bridge: crossing over it is a process of leaving reality and its restrictions to enter a fantasyland. But even this realm of carnal pleasures is not entirely godless. Spirits abound here, and they are acknowledged and respected. The area is punctuated with red *torii* gates (shaped like a capital letter A); like those found at all Shinto shrines, they represent the passageway between the mundane and the sacred. In Usui's work—and typical of the *akasenchi* in reality—even in places of debauchery the *torii* are present. We also see their shapes on the pavements of side streets, reminding passersby not to defame the gods.

Showa 88 is an homage to the "pink zone" that exists between black and white: the zone where life and death coexist, which fosters a particular type of play and exuberance that allows for darker shadows. The easy coexistence of the profane and the sacred is what makes the perfume of *Showa 88* so appealing and nostalgic—but this is nostalgia for a world that never was. It is the beauty of a plastic cherry blossom that these images bring to life: the beauty of a fabrication.

Kazuyoshi Usui: Showa 88

Ivan Vartanian

Ivan Vartanian is a publisher and producer based in Tokyo, active under the label GOLIGA.

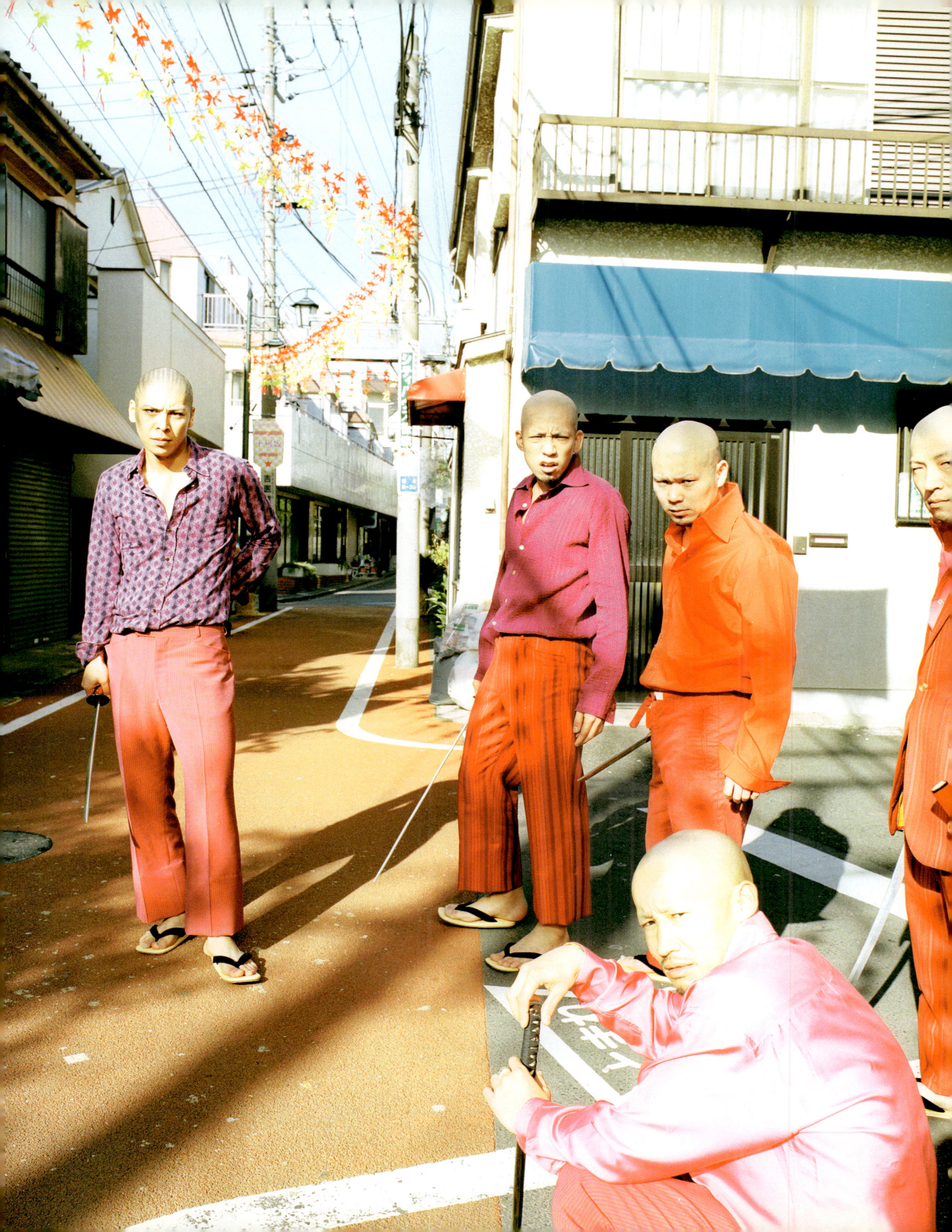

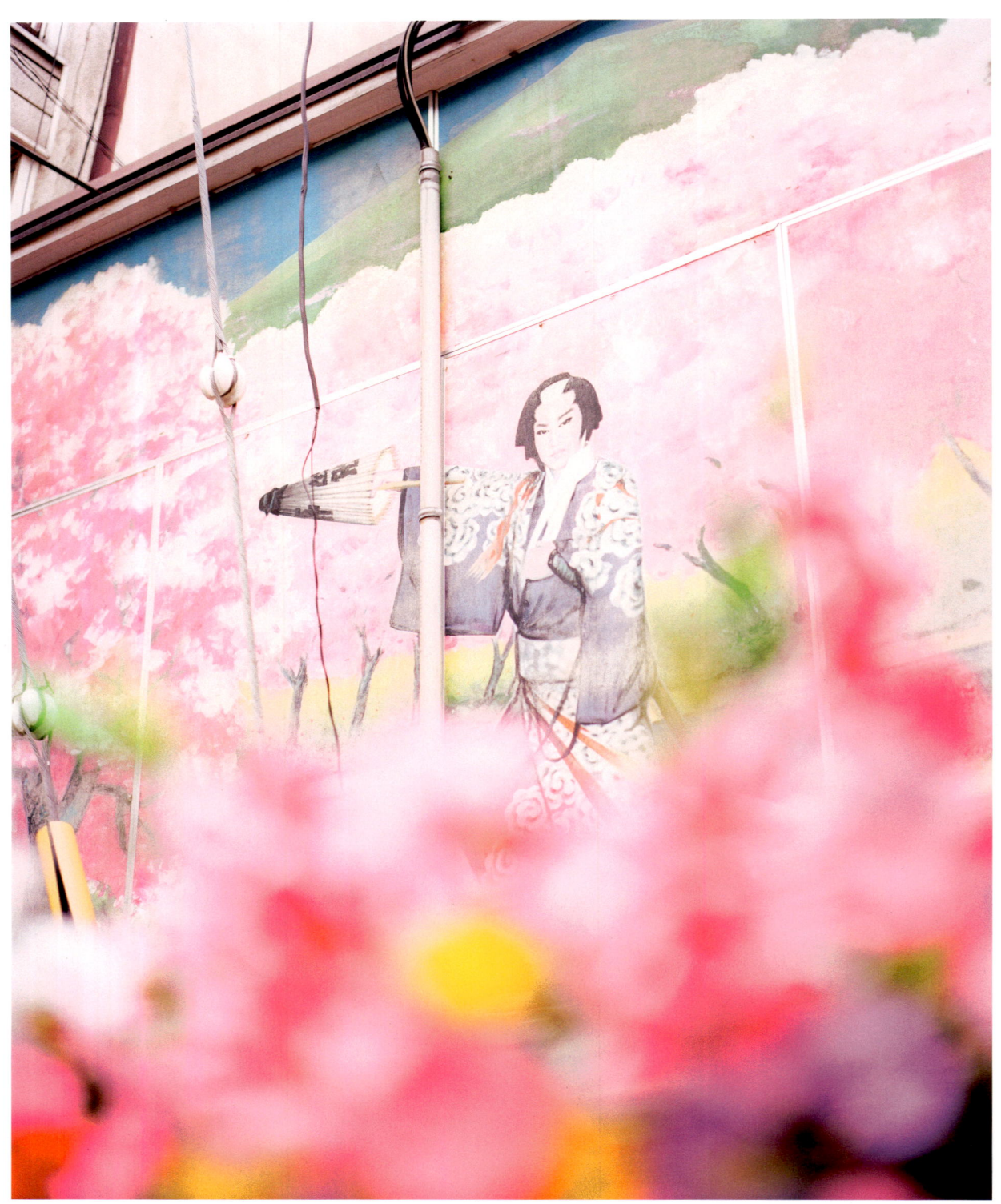

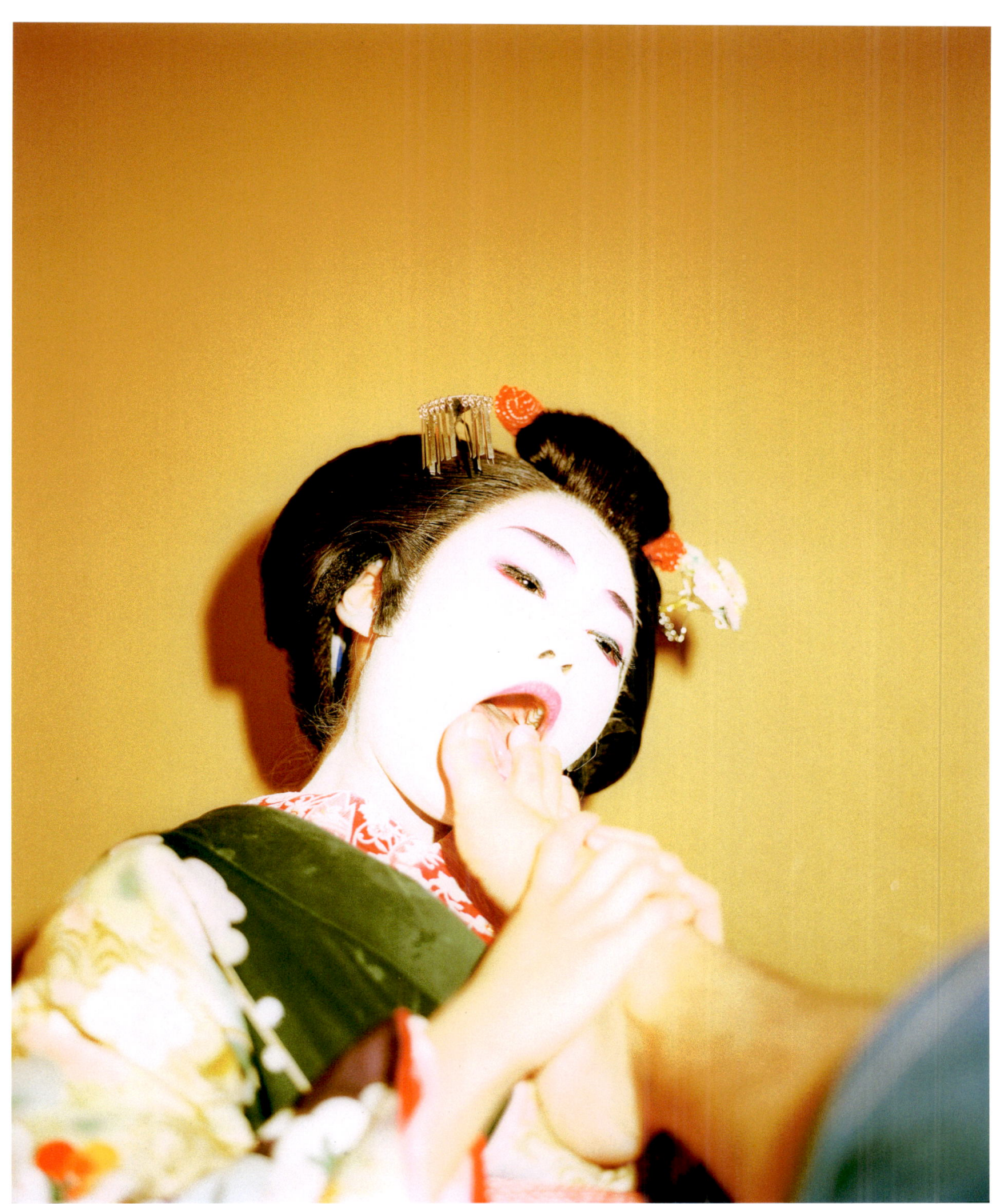

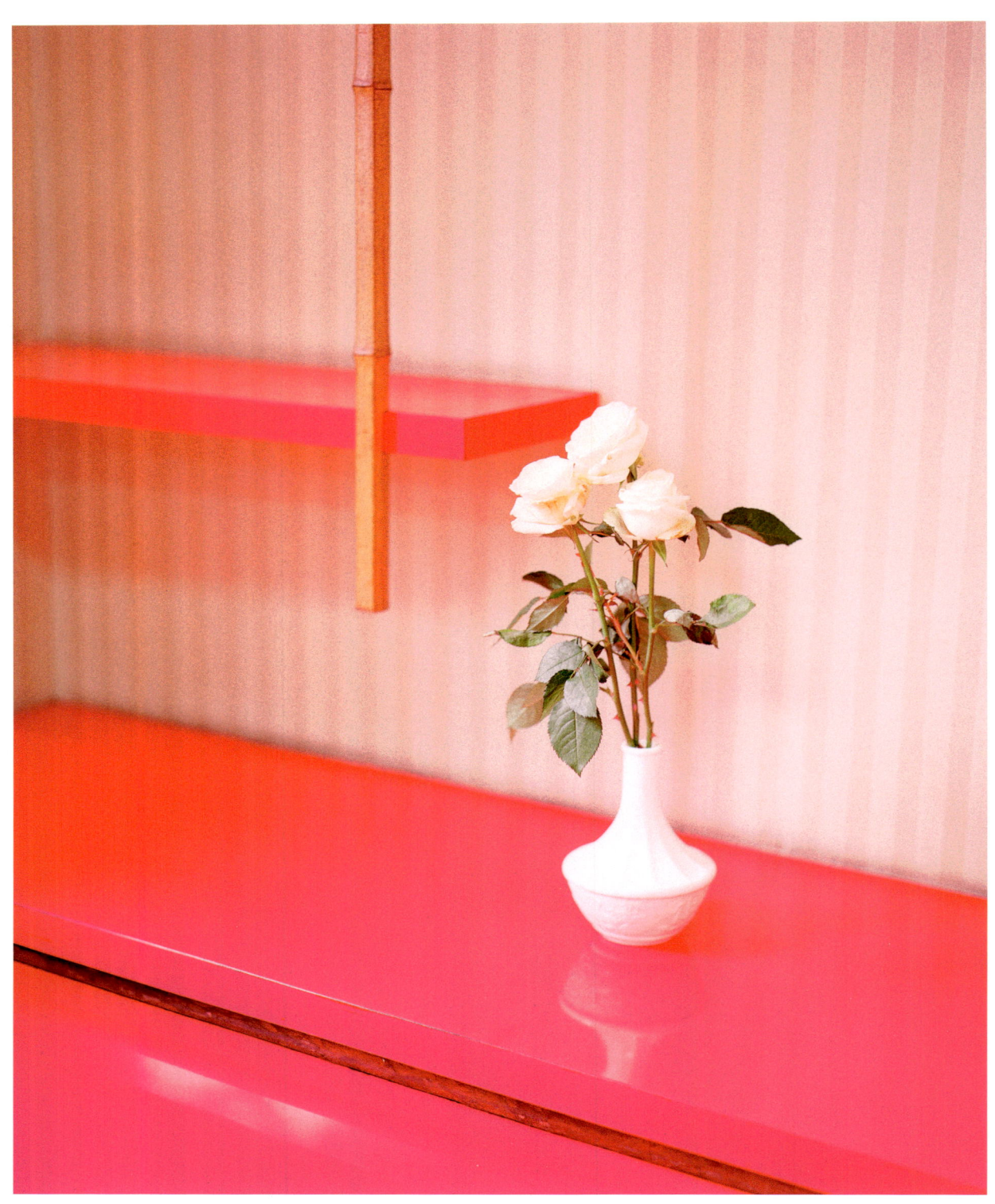

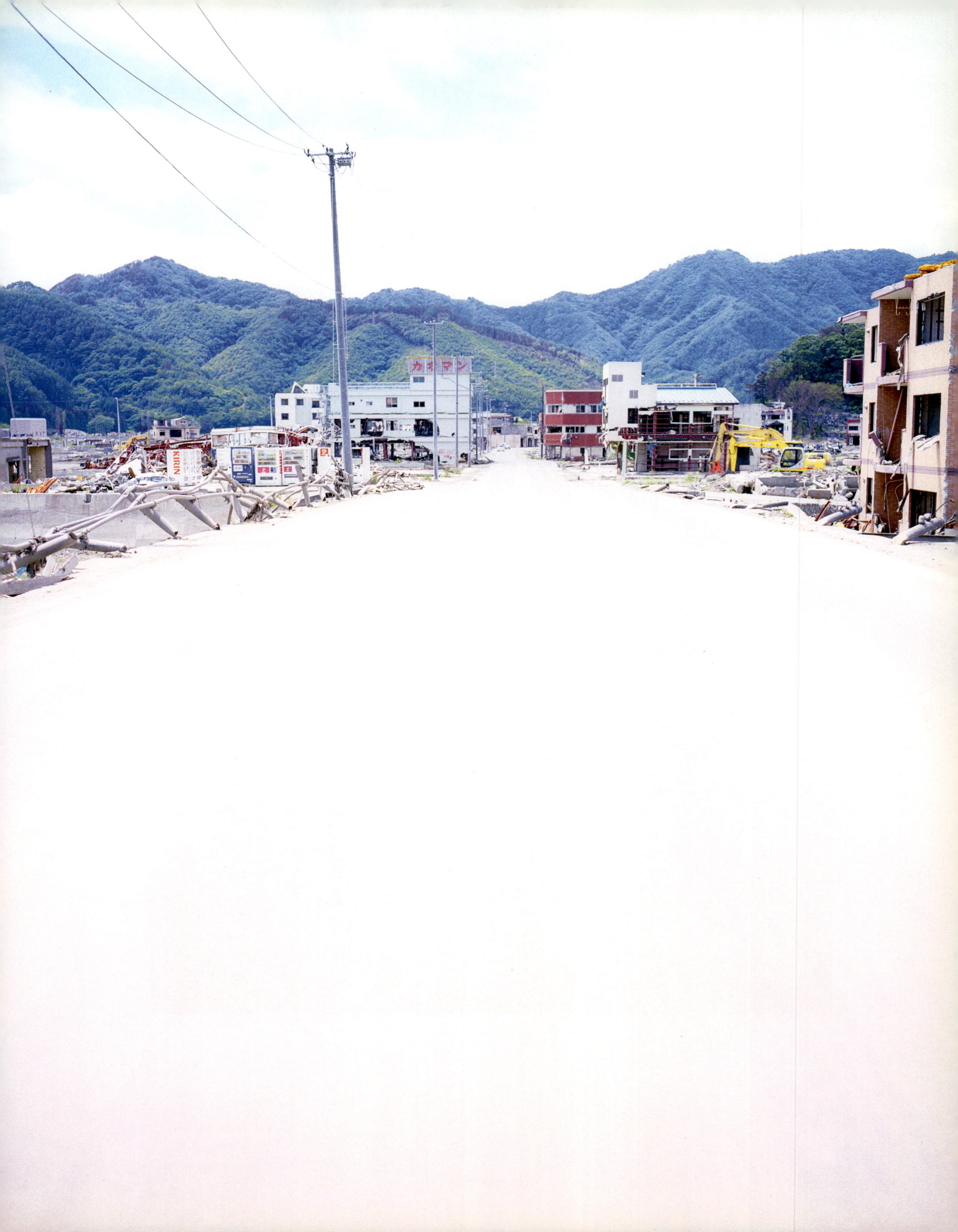

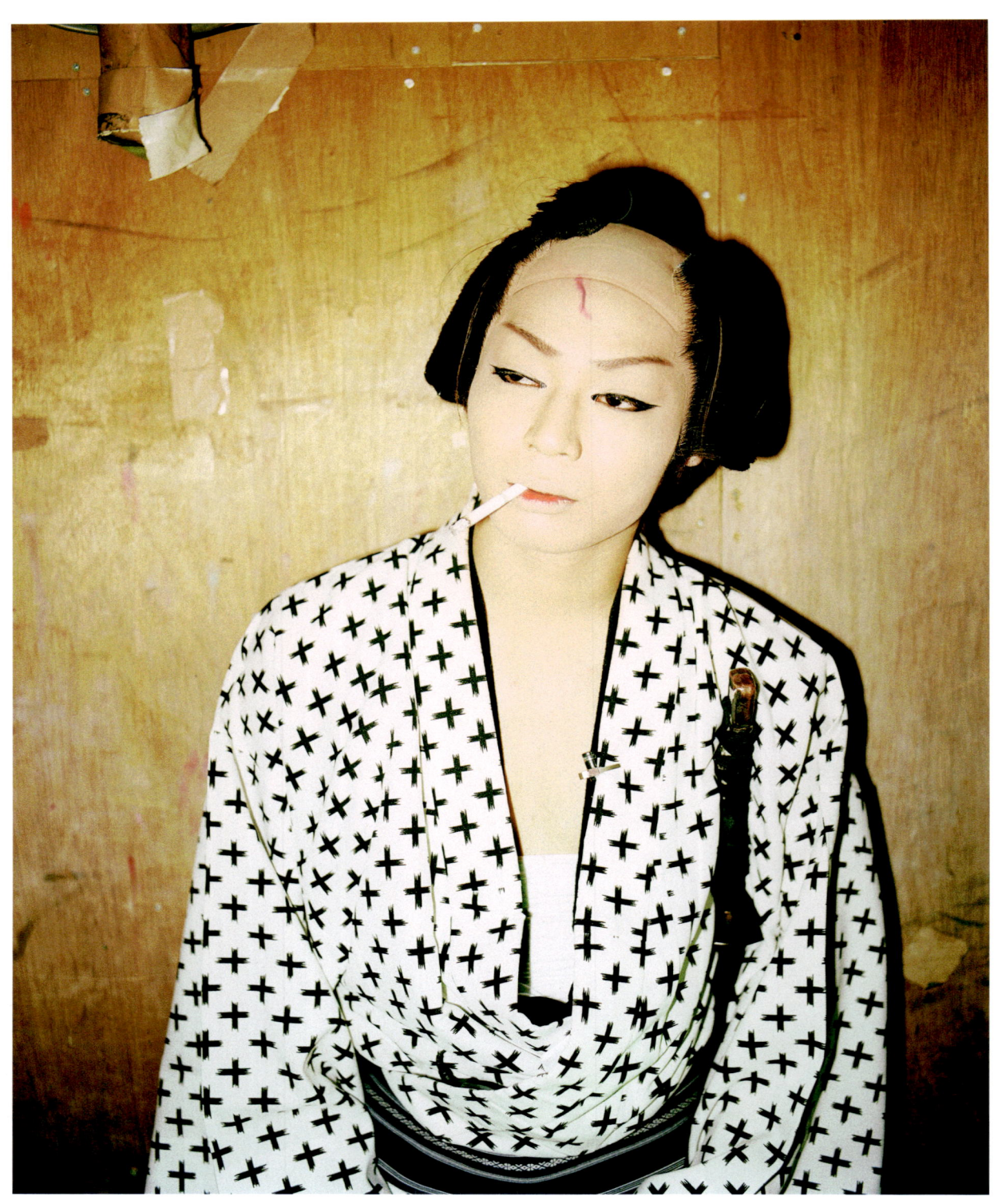

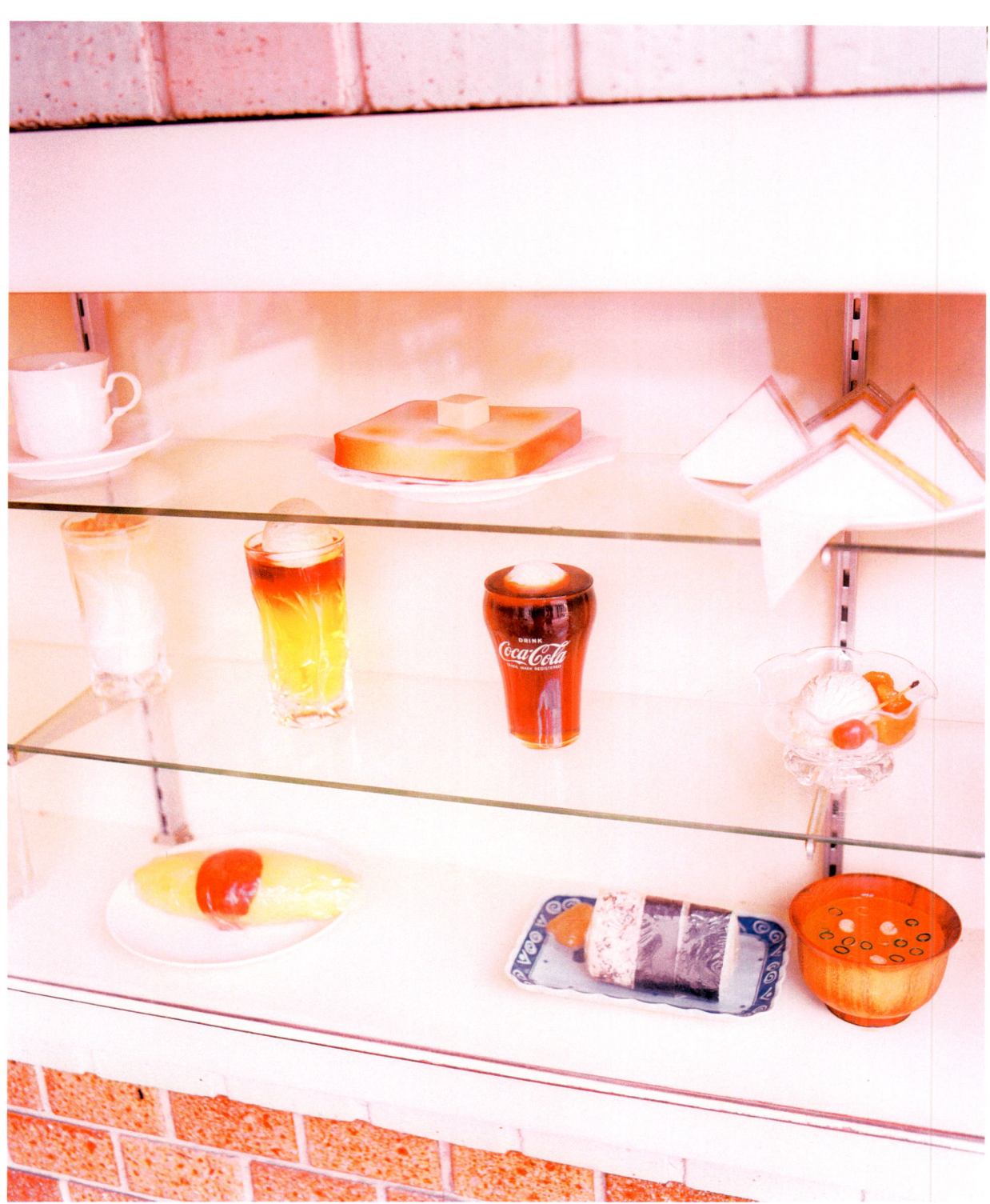

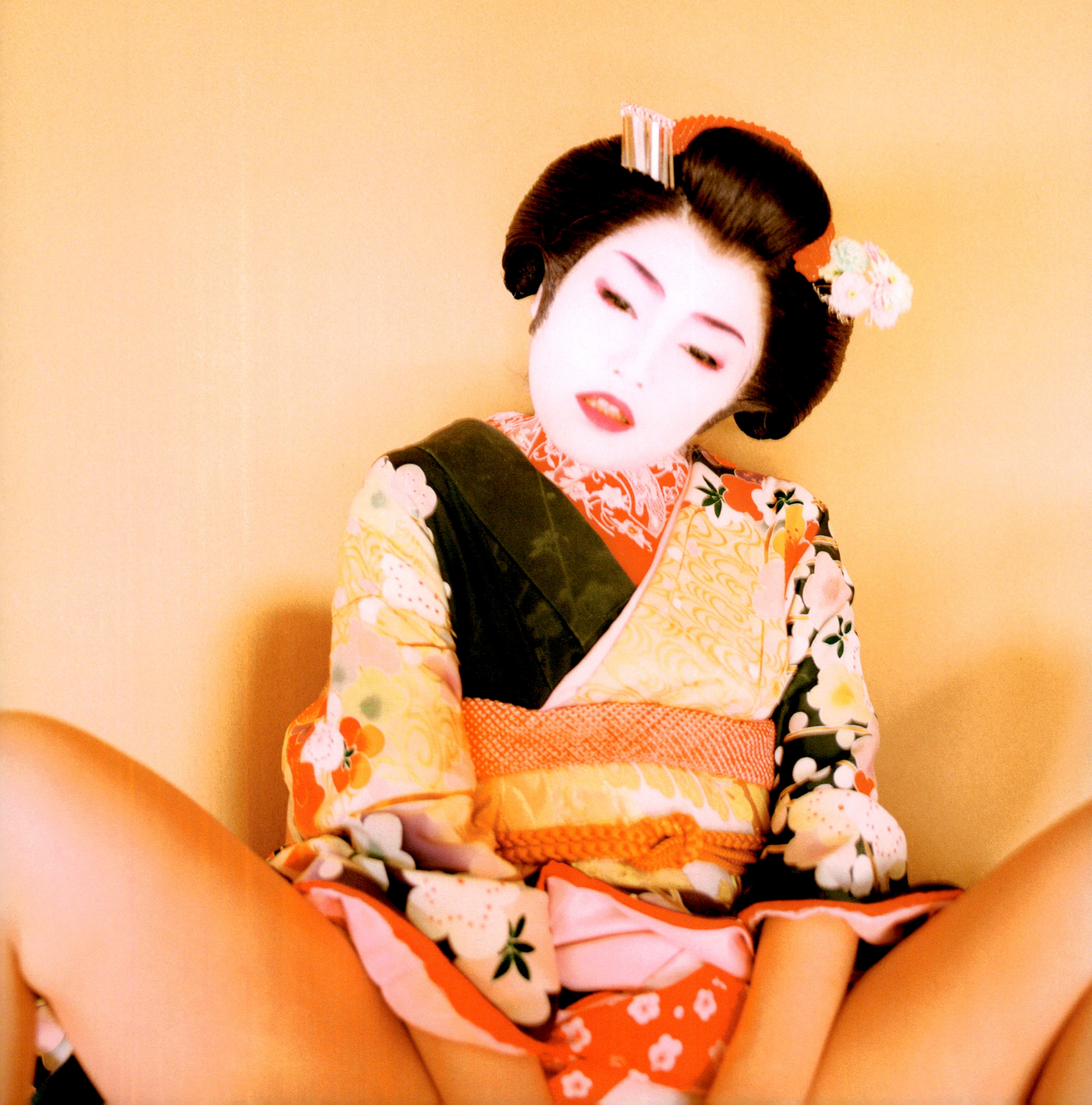

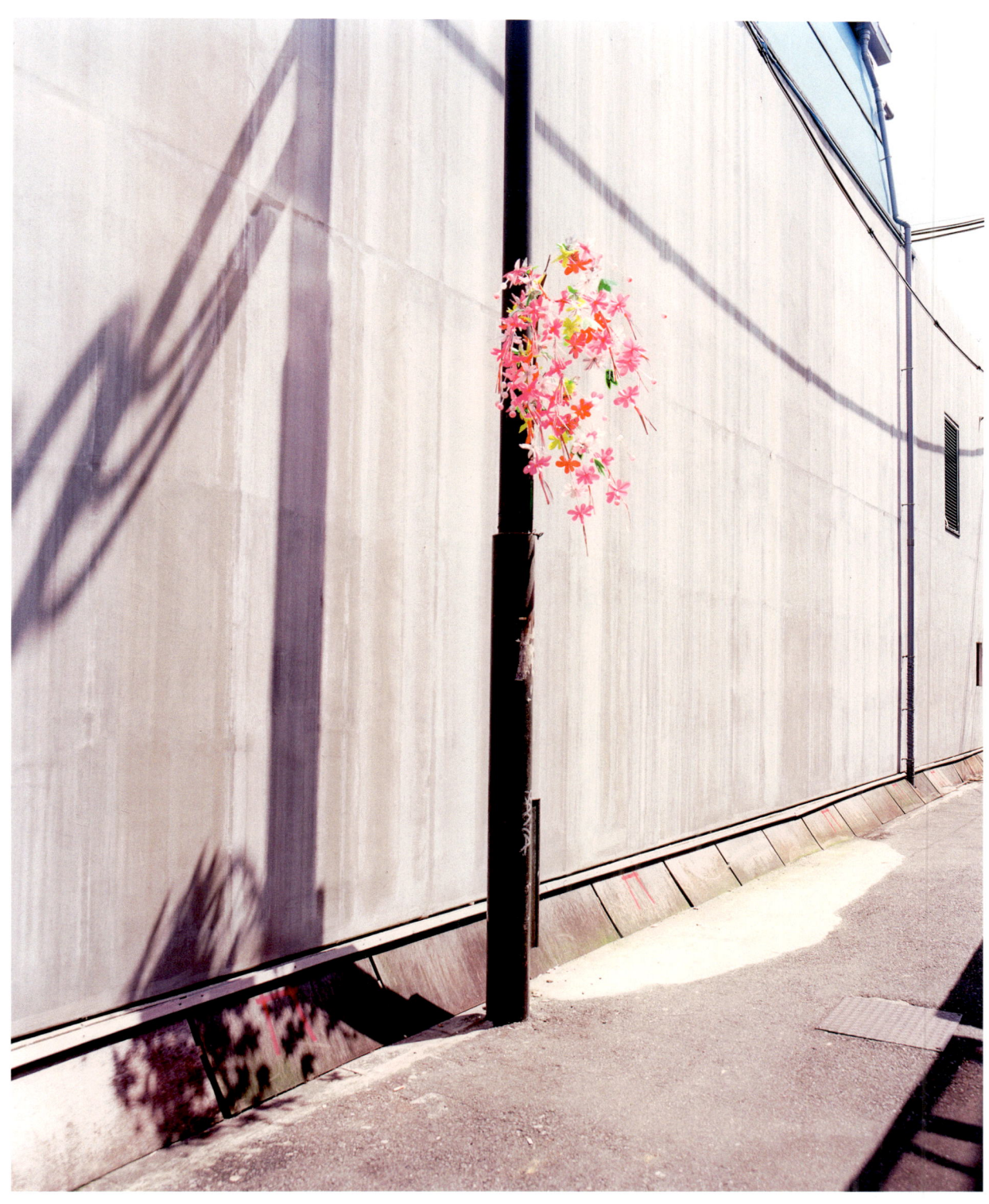

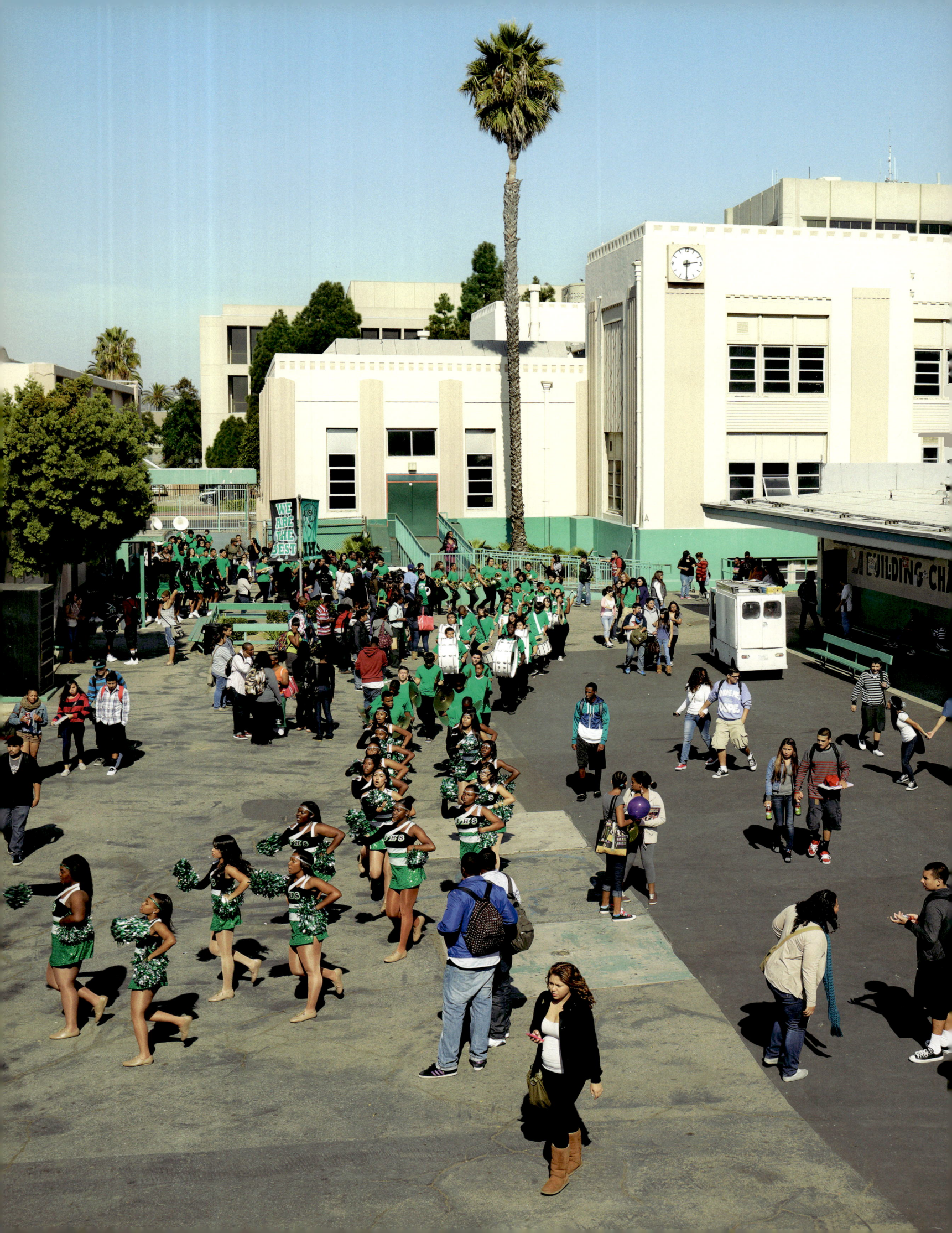

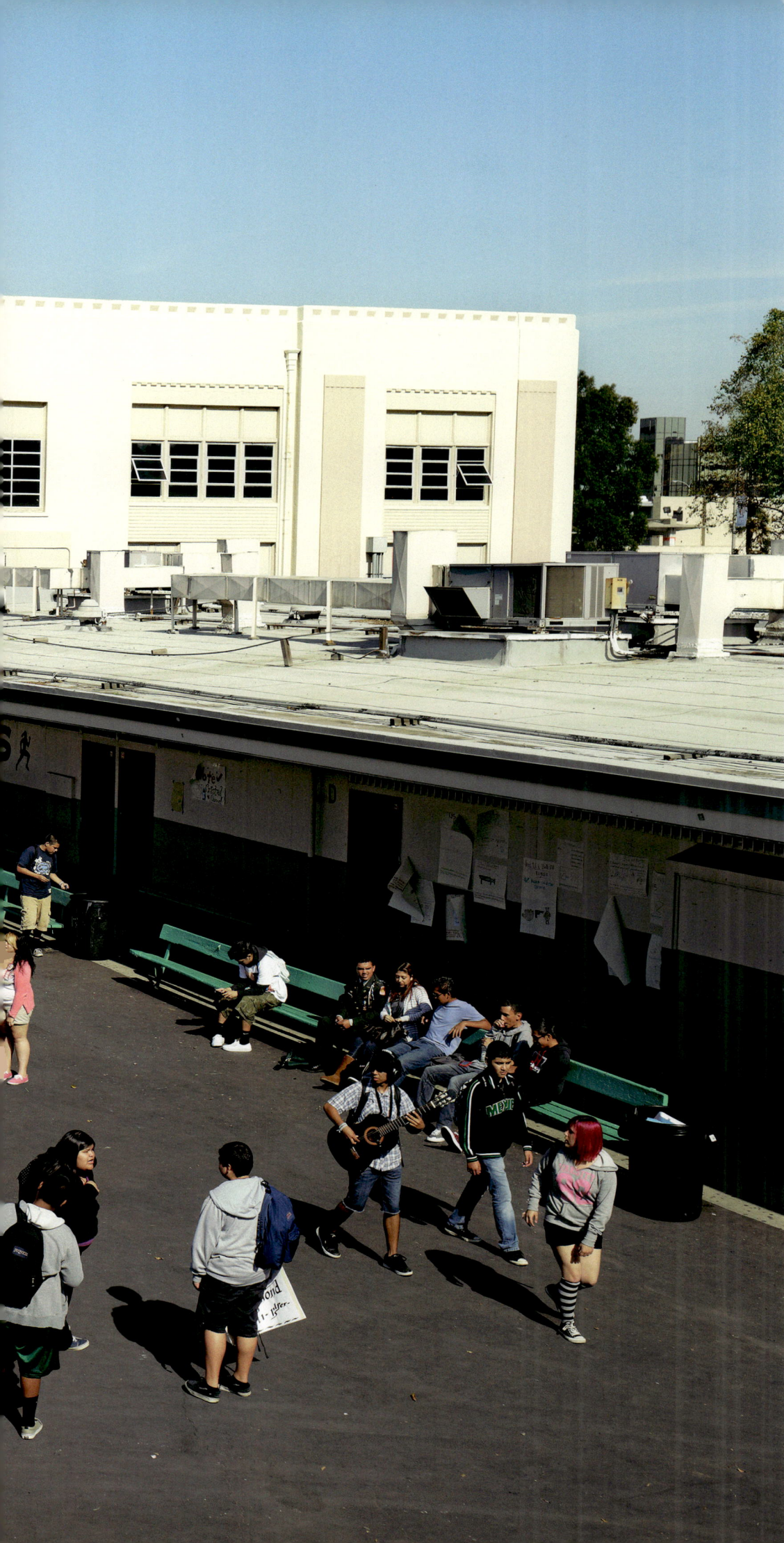

James Mollison's projects are defined by original, conceptual conceits applied to serious social or environmental issues. His 2010 book *Where Children Sleep* recorded children's sleeping spaces across the world and socio-economic strata. The series was originally commissioned by Fabrica—the Benetton-sponsored communications think tank that also publishes *Colors* magazine— with whom Mollison has worked for fifteen years. He continues to play a leading role in developing the visual language of *Colors*, provoking interest in international subjects as did his predecessors, Tibor Kalman and Oliviero Toscani.

For his latest work, seen in these pages, Mollison undertook a global consideration of children at play, a project inspired by the photographer's own memories of the character-forming school playground of his youth in Oxford, England, where he negotiated relationships and his sense of place in the world. Mollison looks for narratives within children's playtime behavior unfolding in varied landscapes that address the diversity and inequality to which they are exposed. There is clearly an attraction here to the mythic romance of childhood innocence, but this is offset—if you look closely—by alarming scenes.

James Mollison: Playgrounds

Chris Boot

Chris Boot is the Executive Director of Aperture Foundation.

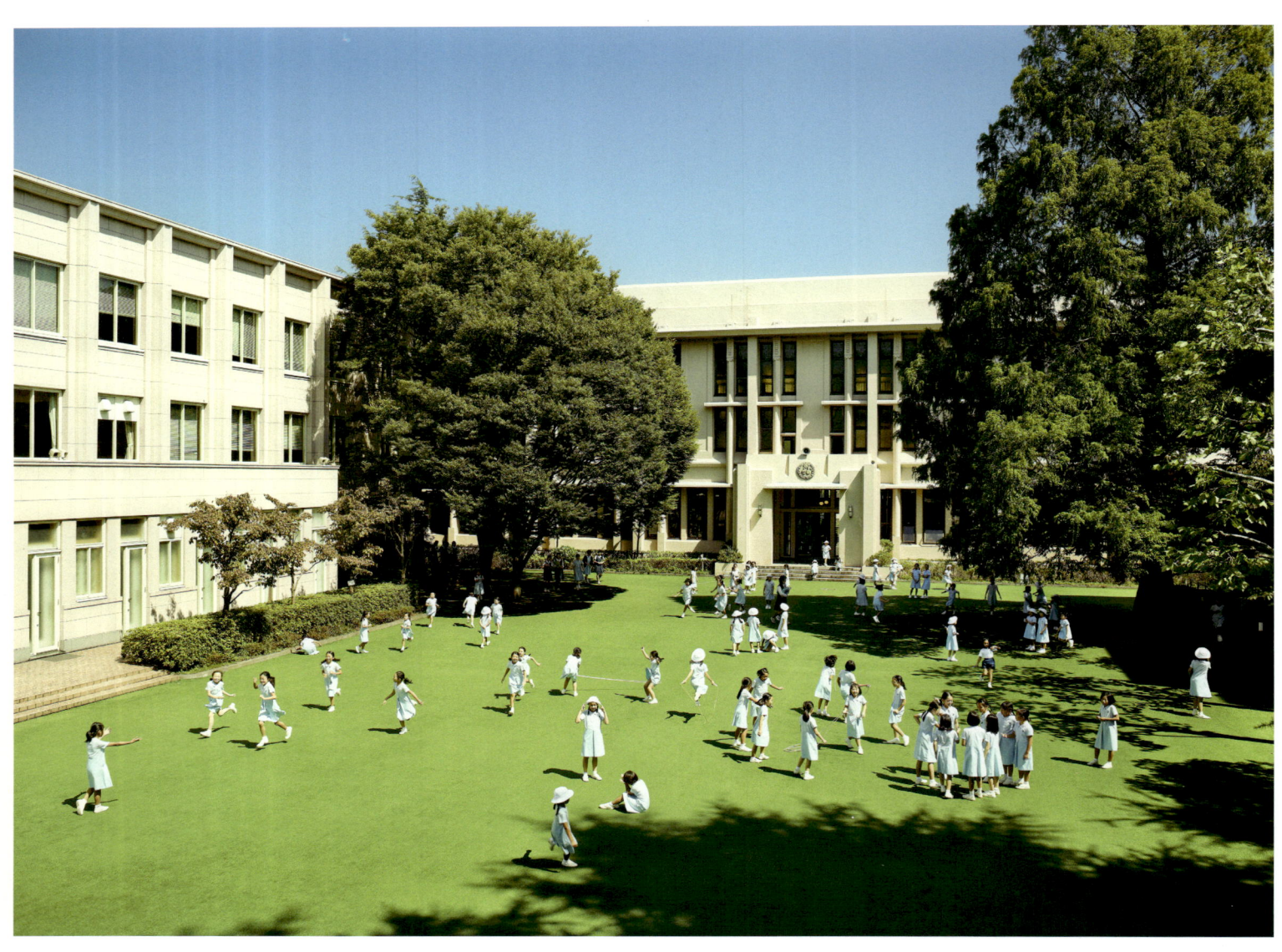

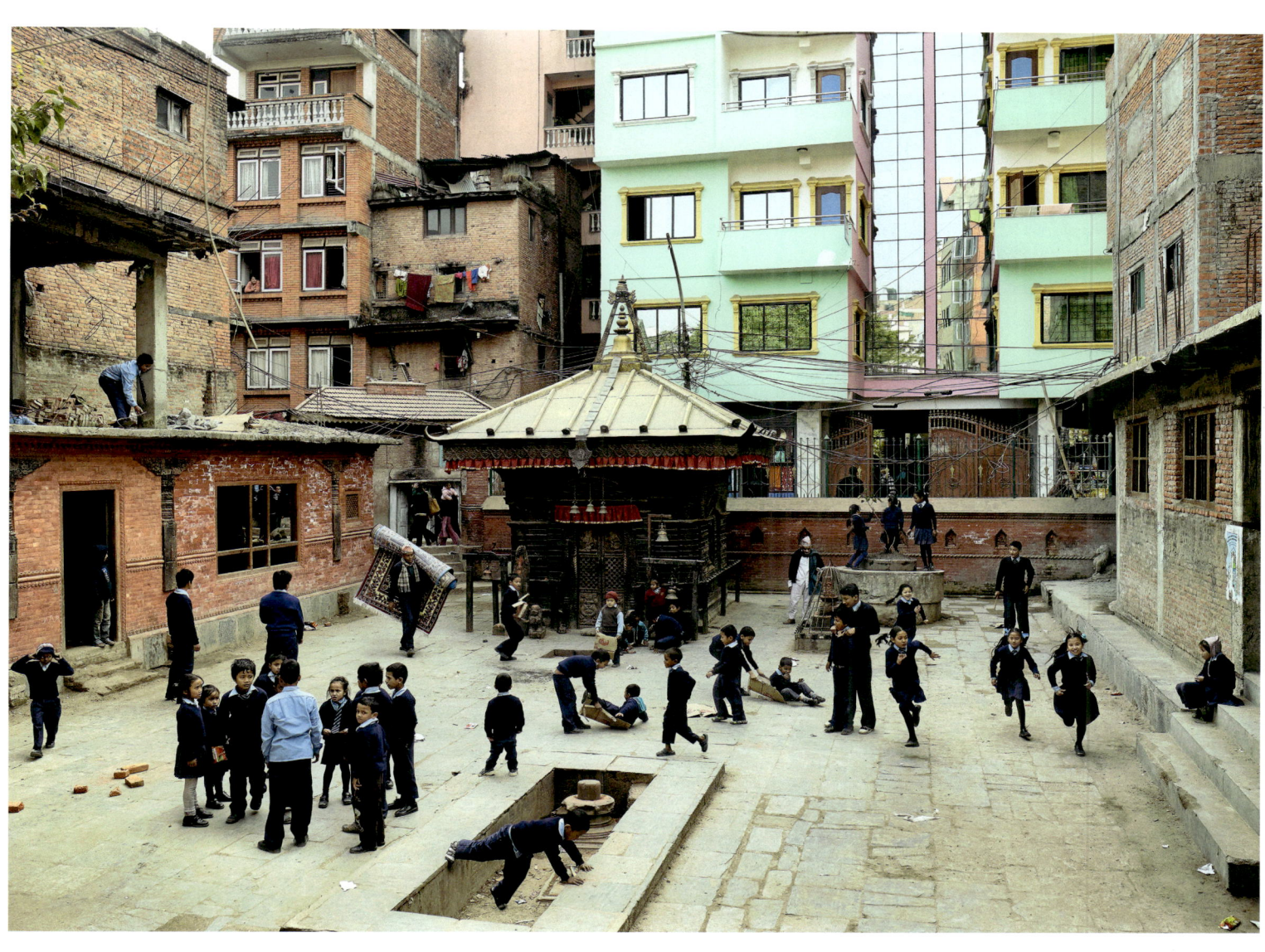

Bhakta Vidyashram,
Kathmandu, Nepal,
December 5, 2011

Kaloleni School, Nairobi, Kenya, January 20, 2011

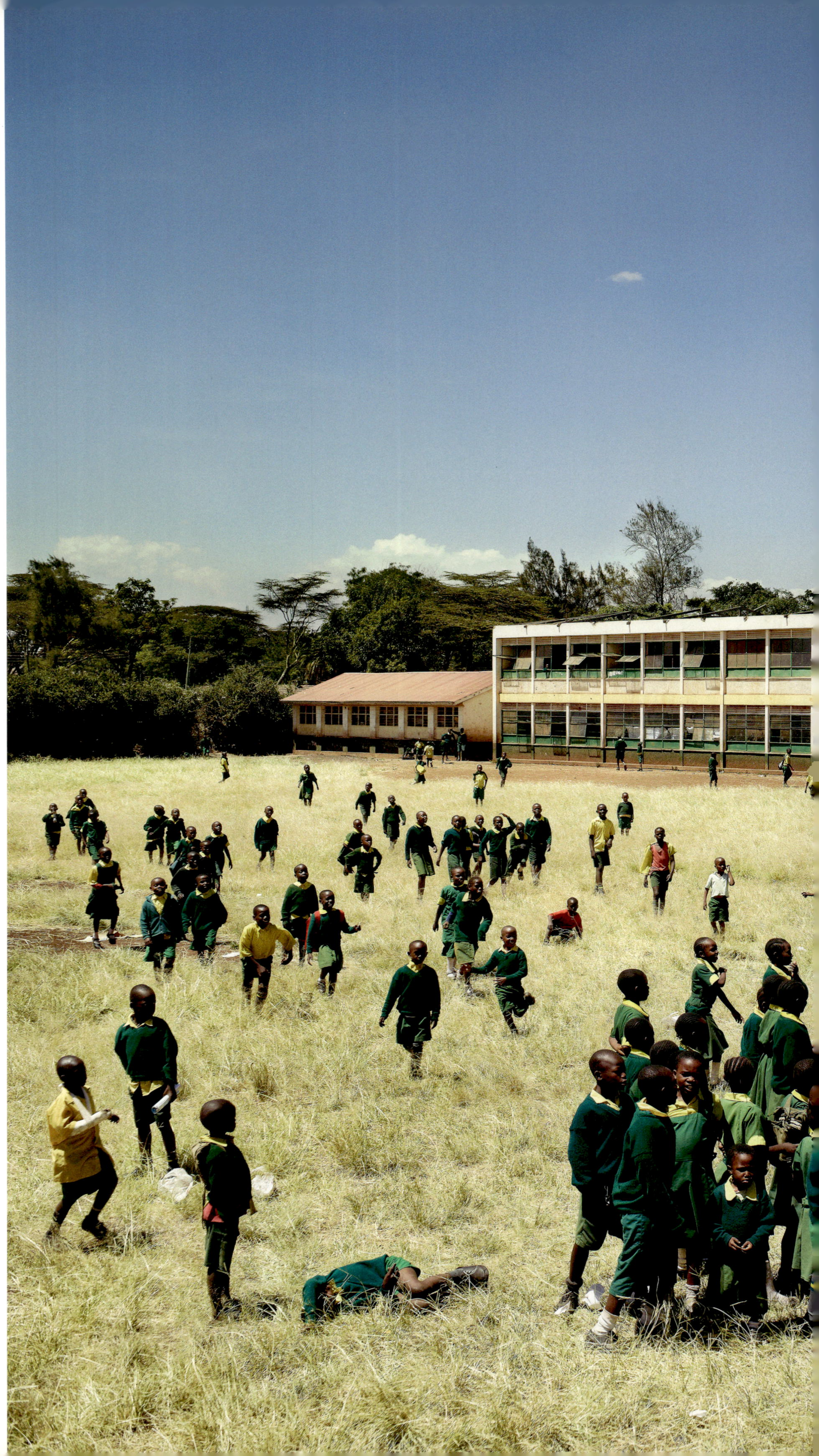

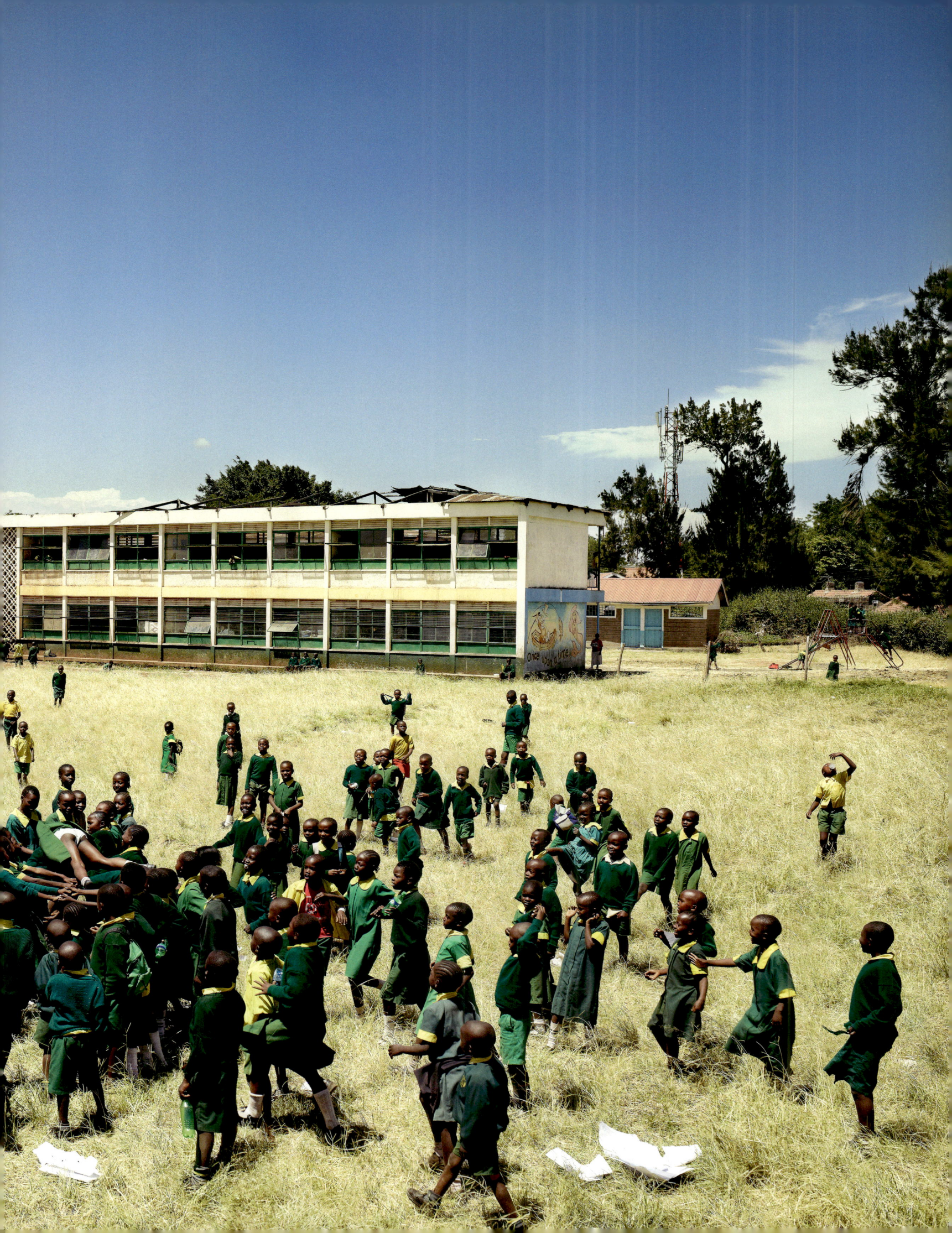

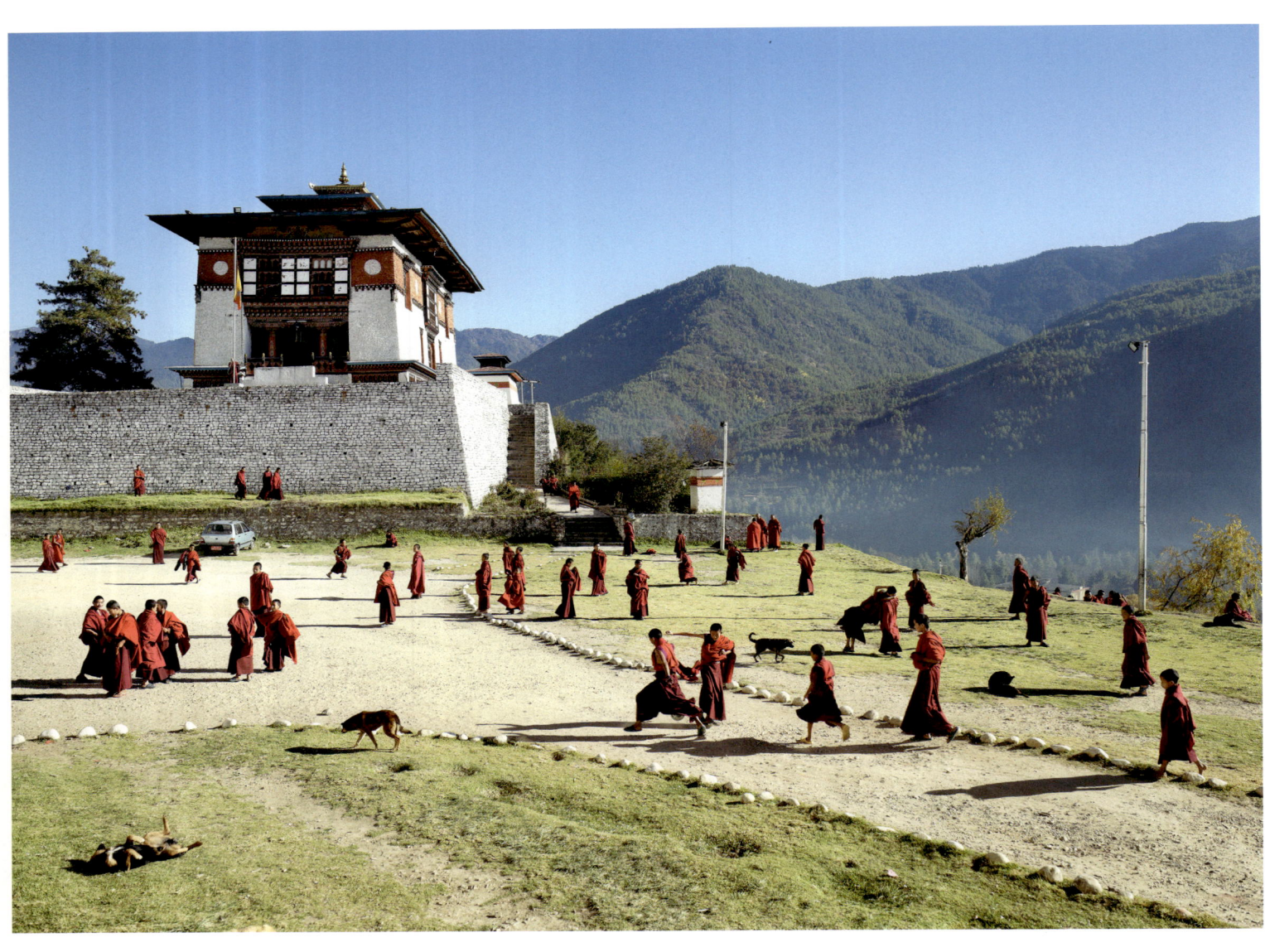

Dechen Phodrang,
Thimphu, Bhutan,
November 24, 2011

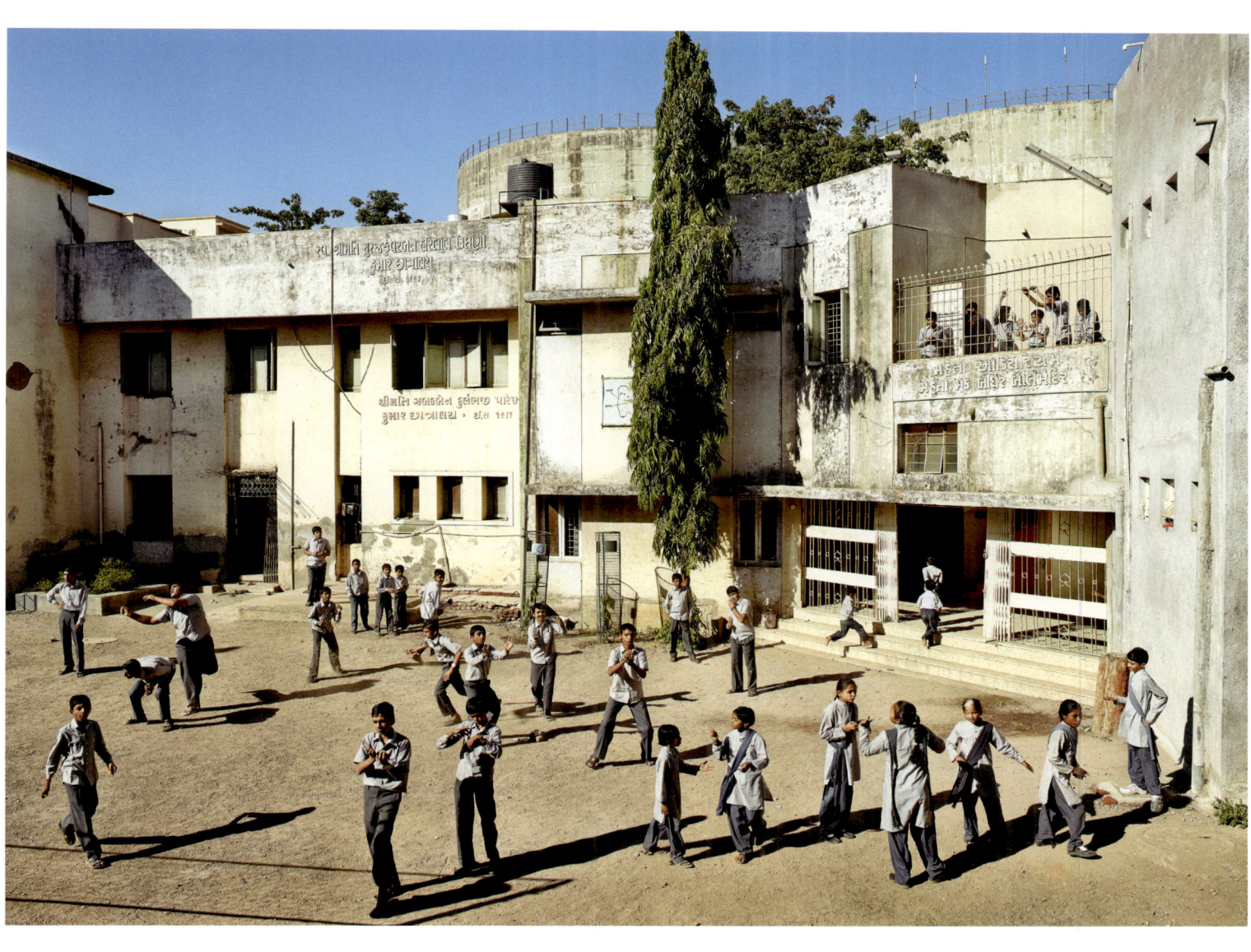

Virani Deaf & Dumb School, Rajkot,
India, November 27, 2012

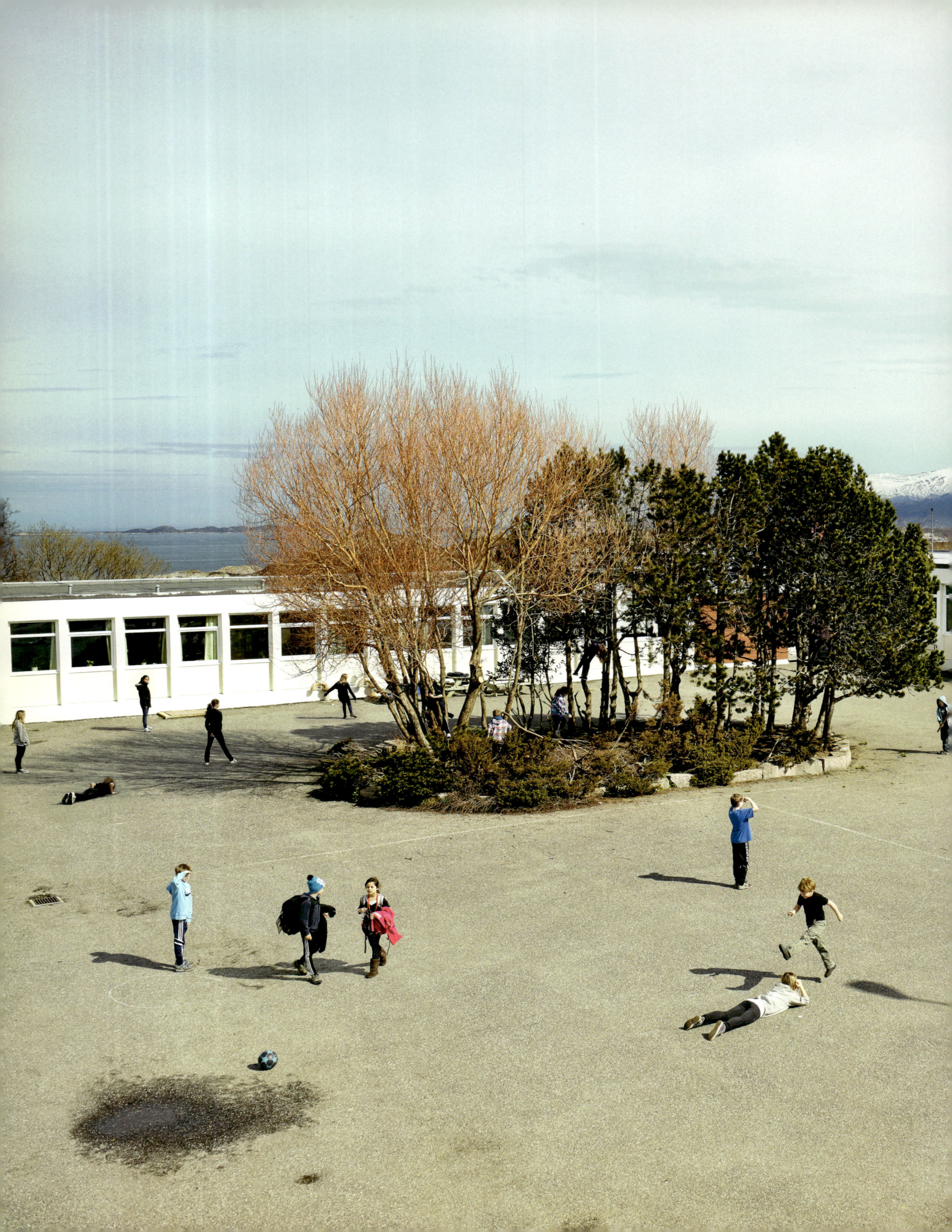

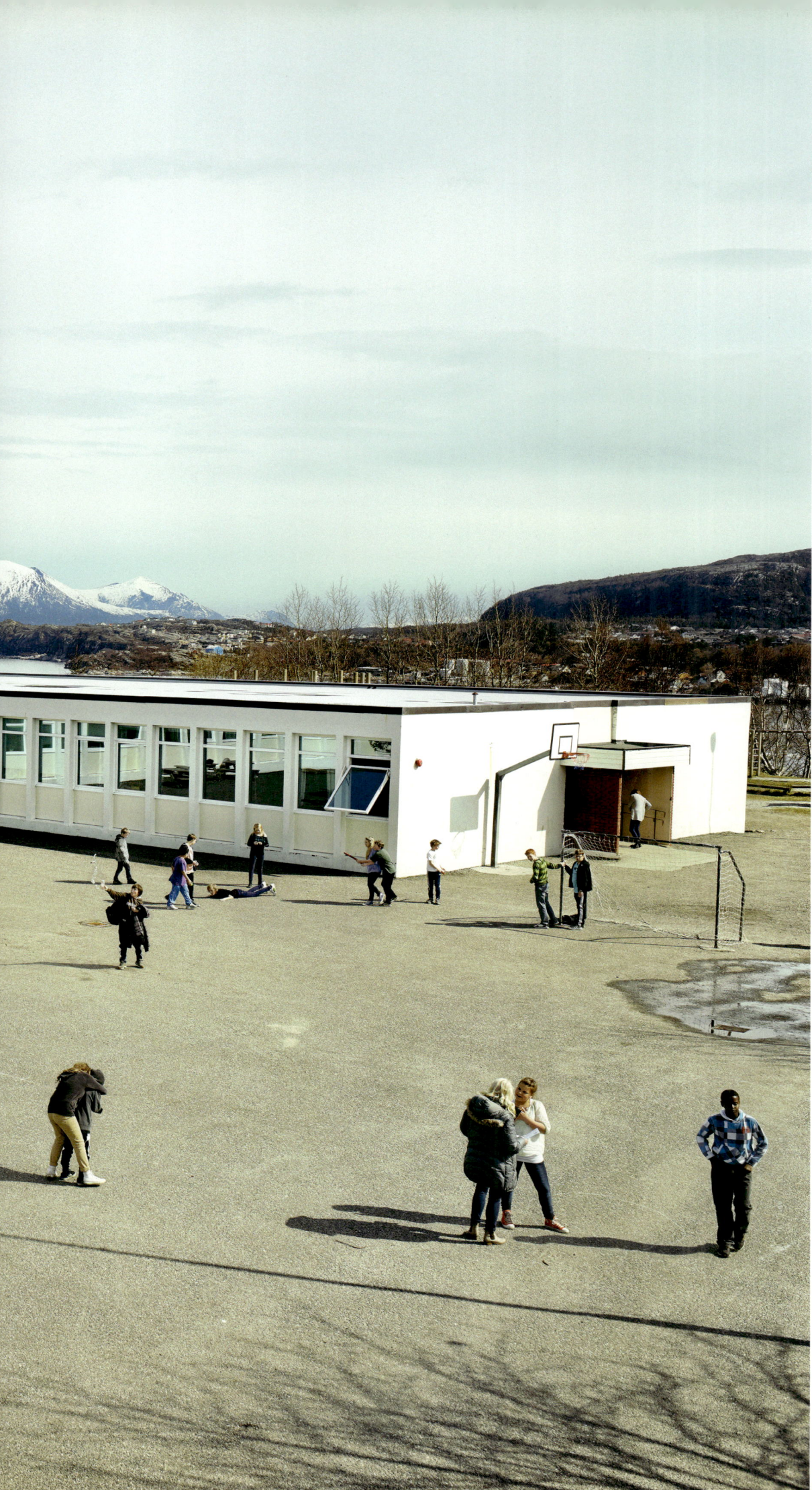

Bruno Ceschel considers a group
of photographers from Switzerland
driven to play.

Swiss Mess

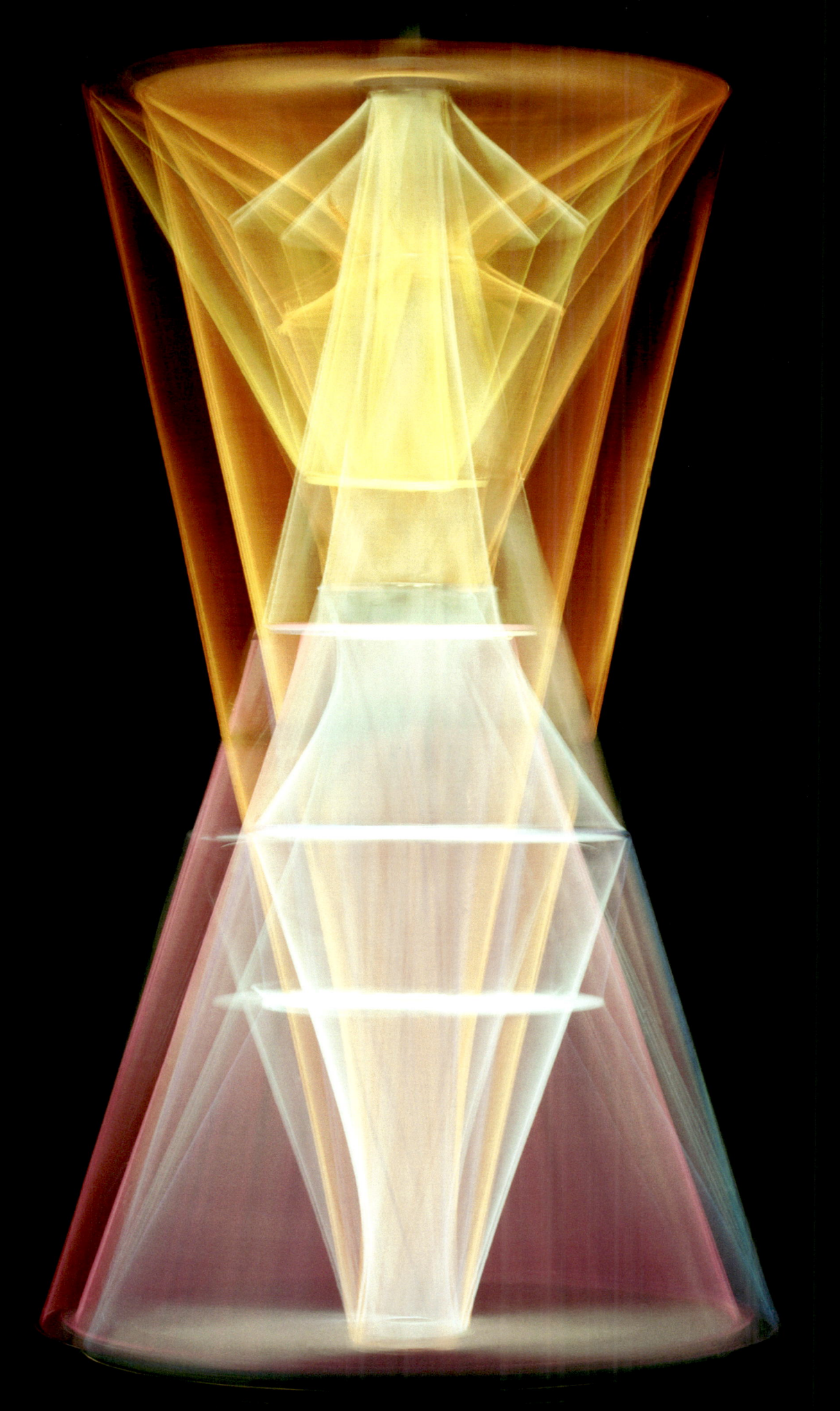

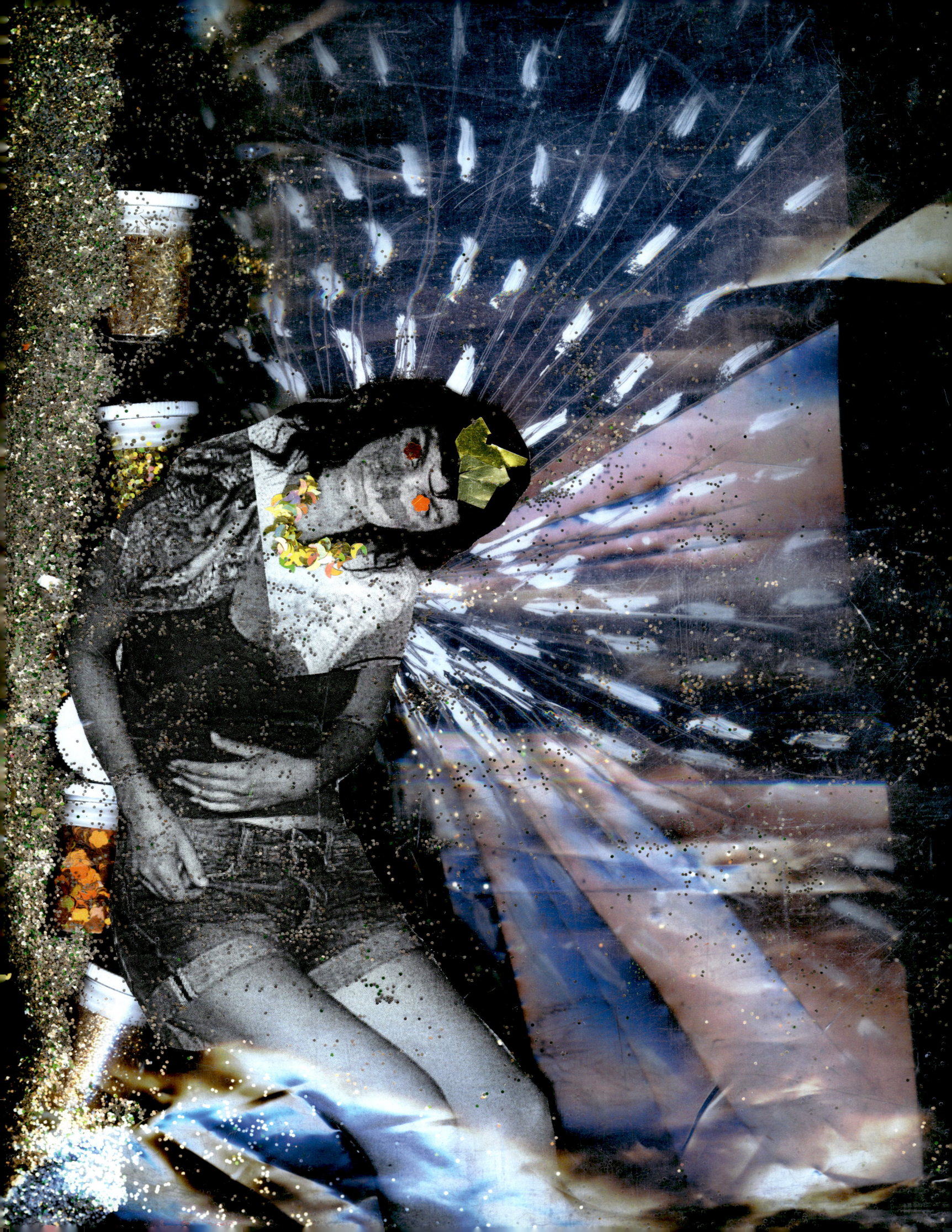

In a letter collected in his book *On the Aesthetic Education of Man*, philosopher Friedrich Schiller discussed the role of art in eighteenth-century society. To quickly summarize, Schiller suggested a mediation between Kant's breakdown of human nature into a sensuous drive (*der sinnliche Trieb/Sinnestrieb*) and a formal drive (*Formtrieb*) by introducing the notion of the play drive (*Spieltrieb*). The work of a gang of contemporary Swiss photographers that have emerged in the last decade can be characterized with this term. This *Spieltrieb* may be a methodology, a philosophical stance, an artistic statement in its own right— or perhaps all of the above. The drive isn't new, at any rate: it continues a tradition that extends back to Swiss artists like Dieter Roth and Jean Tinguely, and more recently to Peter Fischli, David Weiss, and Roman Signer. What all of them have in common is that their work reveals how play and playfulness can take the form of intellectual engagement.

The contemporary generation picks up on rich traditions of experimentation, invention, and freedom that united these earlier figures. They embrace, even celebrate, chance and failure. Taiyo Onorato and Nico Krebs, for example, have joyfully stretched and challenged the idea of the photographic process, the nature of photographs, how cameras operate (one body of work consists of cameras made from stacks of books, an animal horn, and other unexpected materials), and the role of the photographer. Their recent series *Spins* (2012)—long exposures of objects in rapid motion—offers a kinetic reinterpretation of the still life. Another duo, Matthieu Lavanchy and Jonas Marguet, with their 2013 series *I Want to Believe*, reveals a curiosity about the possibilities of the still life, playing with narrative and digital manipulation to create enigmatic riffs on form.

These artists are also brought together by a DIY aesthetic that counters the visual clichés of Switzerland—Helvetica, combed mountain pastures, sterile Zurich banks—with a rough and makeshift world, made by hand. Linus Bill's work takes the forms of abstract paintings, photographs, and screen prints, which exist both as exhibited objects and as photographic documentation of his studio processes. Stefan Burger's latest works are made from constellations of discarded objects—salad spinners, stockings, jeans—culled from thrift stores that are then installed on garish wallpaper, also made by the artist, featuring a second still life. Maya Rochat, who produces a series of post-feminist queer 'zines, proudly draws on a lo-fi aesthetic rooted in the punk and techno scenes that emerged in Zurich in the 1970s and '80s from a culture of squats, parties, drugs, and open rebellion against an opulently conservative and manicured Swiss society.

Many young Swiss artists orbit around two educational institutions, the Zürcher Hochschule der Künste and the École cantonale d'art de Lausanne (ECAL), both known for their uncompromising experimentation and marriage of art and graphic design. Although a common ethos connects the work in this portfolio, each artist inflects his or her version of play with a distinct flavor. A few, like Linus Bill, with his sometimes unsettling references to childhood, arrive at a place of confrontation, desecration, or even creepiness. Others toy with notions of aesthetics and absurdity. Walter Pfeiffer's naughty, diaristic photographs have titillated and amused fashion audiences since the 1980s. Nicolas Haeni likewise works in fashion and advertising, where his surreal and often performance-based photographs exist as agents of disturbance. Anarchic energy and humor underscore Olaf Breuning's diverse output across media as he has made odd and sometimes perverse visual pleasure a consistent strategy in his work, as in his recent photographs of piles of people costumed in dizzying patterns.

Not long ago, Maya Rochat wrote this in an e-mail: "I recently read about the musician Kim Gordon. I liked her idea that playing around and just doing stuff could be a critical position. I feel a similar need for a fragile and almost physical way of doing art. Non-seriousness as a refusal to fall asleep?" Can a refusal to succumb to dullness be understood as a critical position? Does a weird power exist in silliness and awkwardness? Perhaps. A laugh—theirs, the viewer's—might just help to keep us all awake.

Opposite:
Maya Rochat,
Glitter Orgy, from the series
A Plastic Tool, 2013
Courtesy the artist

Overleaf:
Stefan Burger, *Not Yet Titled*, 2013 (left);
Still Untitled, 2013 (right)
Courtesy the artist and
Freymond-Guth Fine Arts,
Zurich

Bruno Ceschel is a writer, curator, and lecturer on photography at the University of the Arts London. He is the founder of Self Publish, Be Happy, an organization that collects, promotes, and studies contemporary self-published photography books.

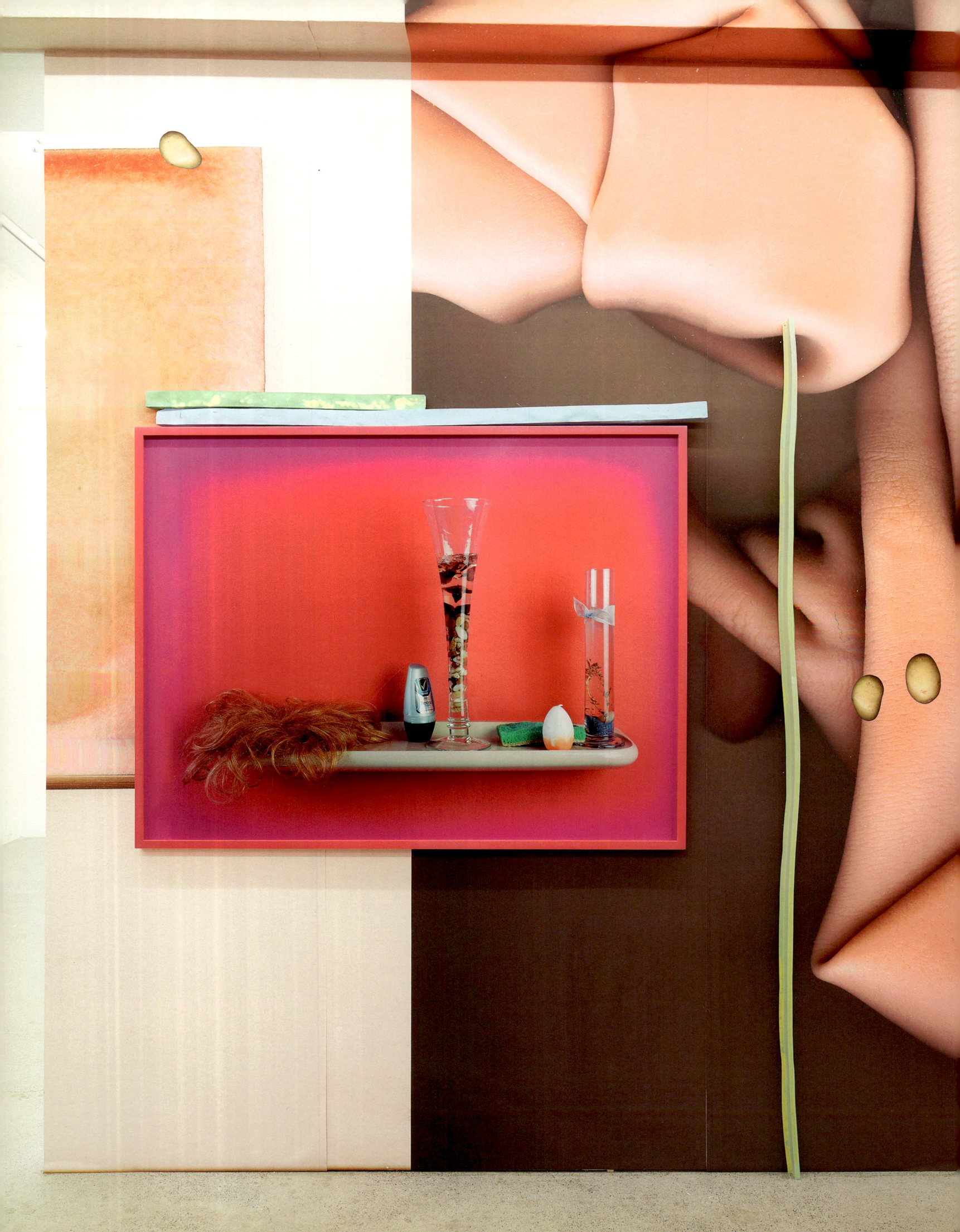

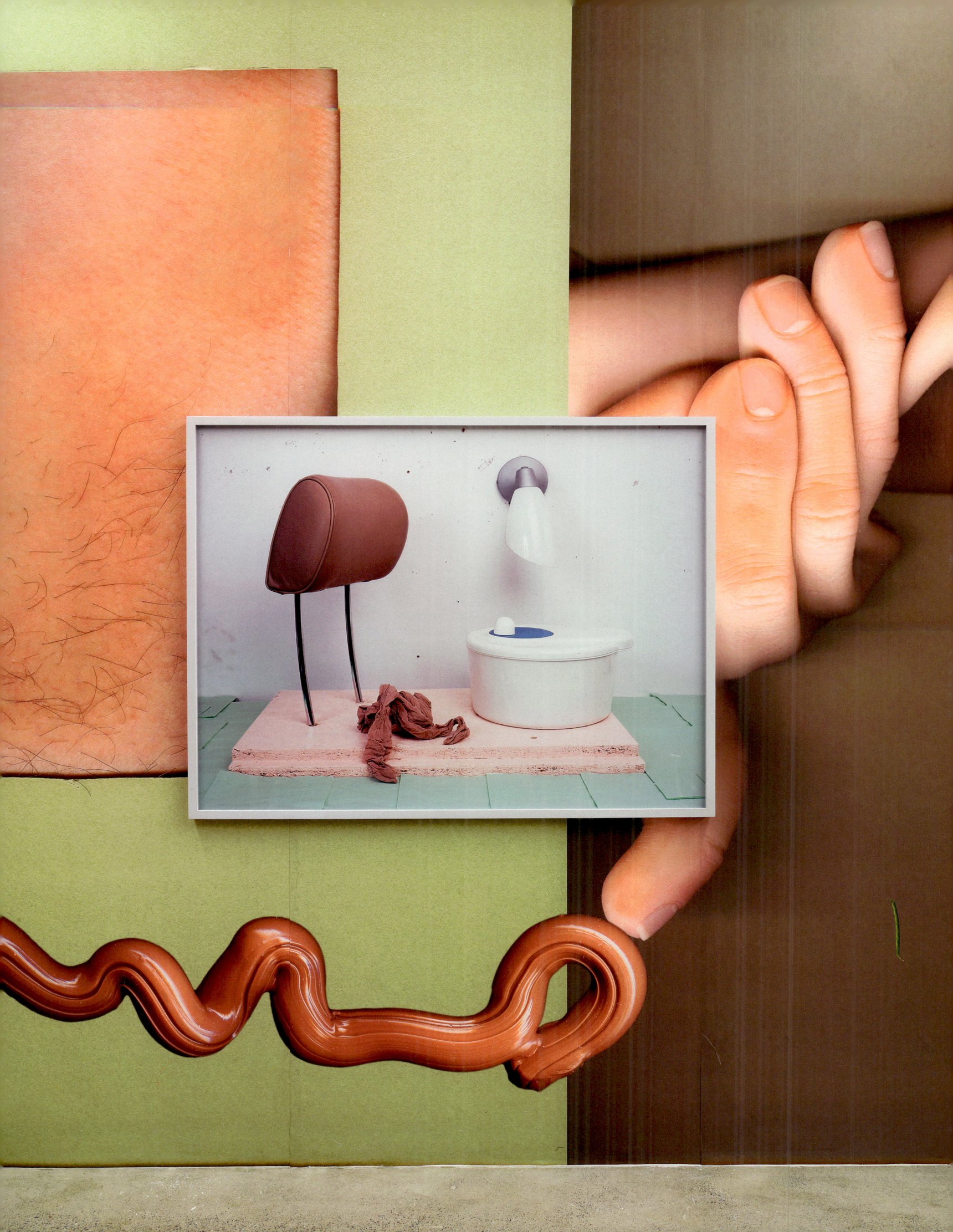

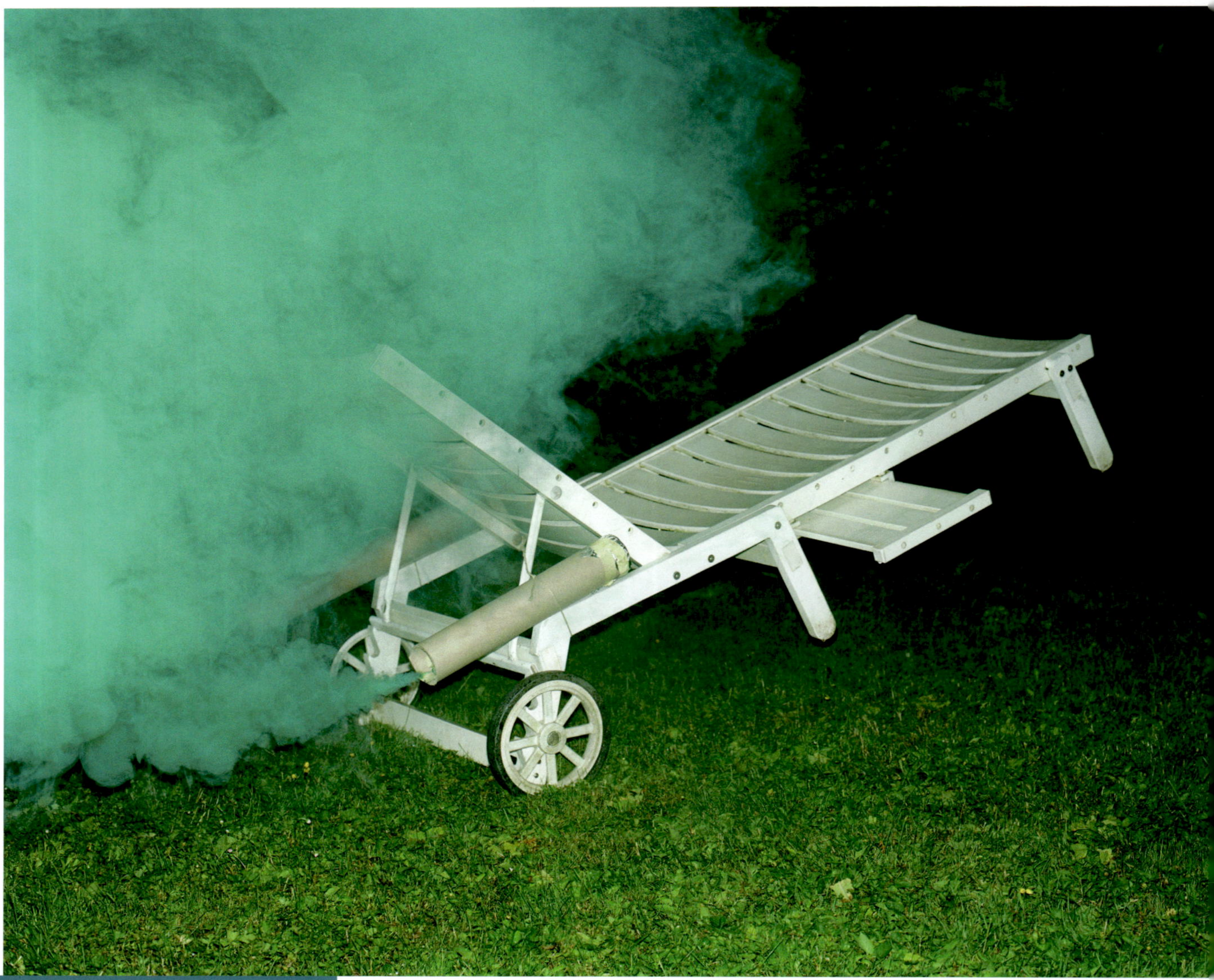

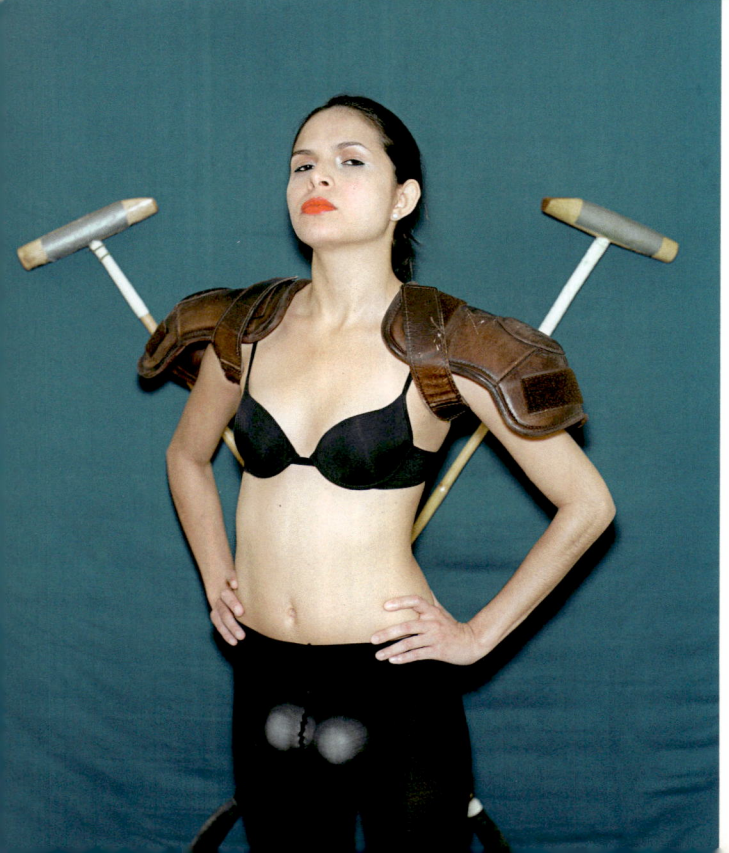

This page and opposite:
Nicolas Haeni,
And If We Dance?, 2009
All photographs courtesy
the artist

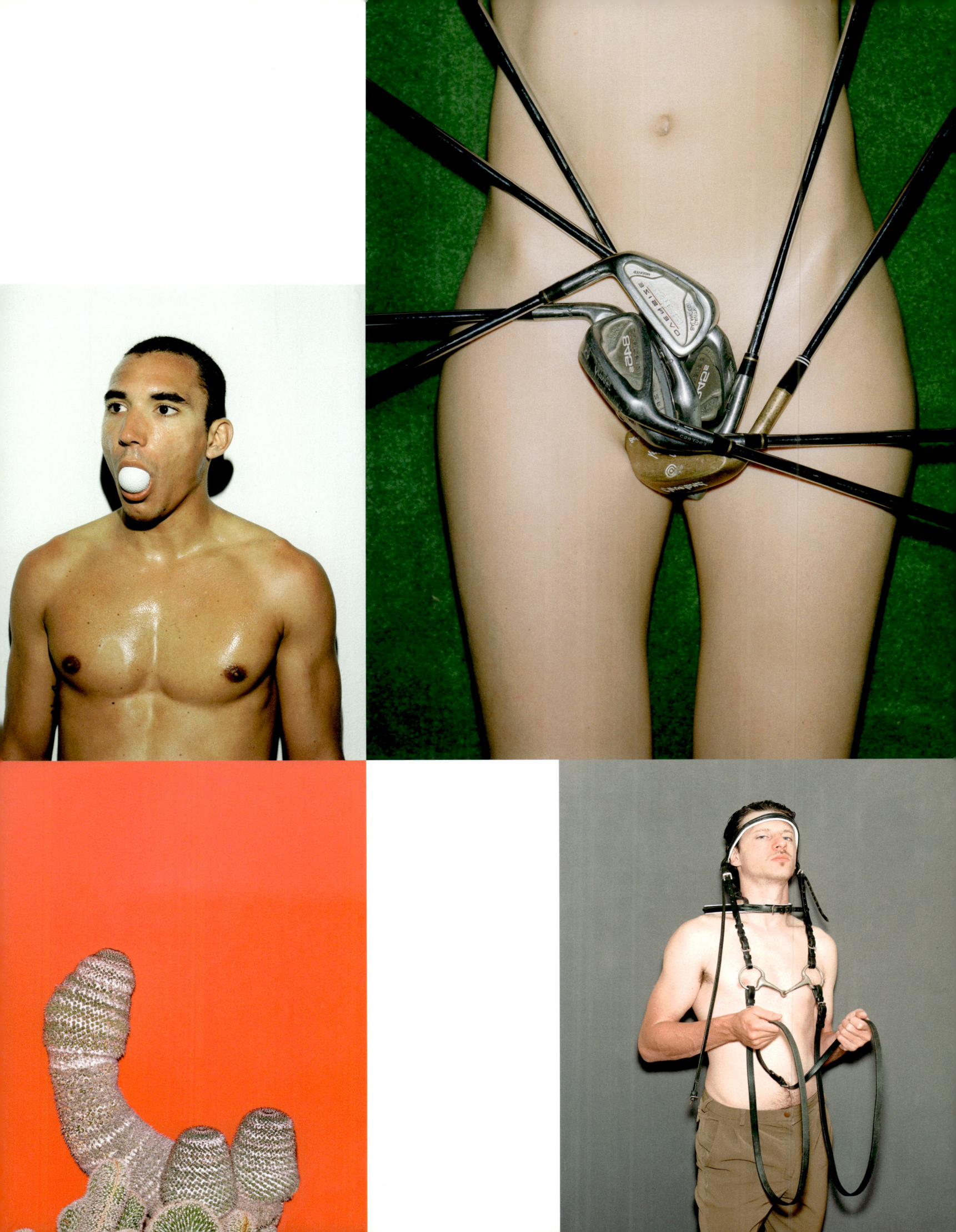

Walter Pfeiffer, *Untitled*, 2002 Courtesy Galerie Sultana, Paris

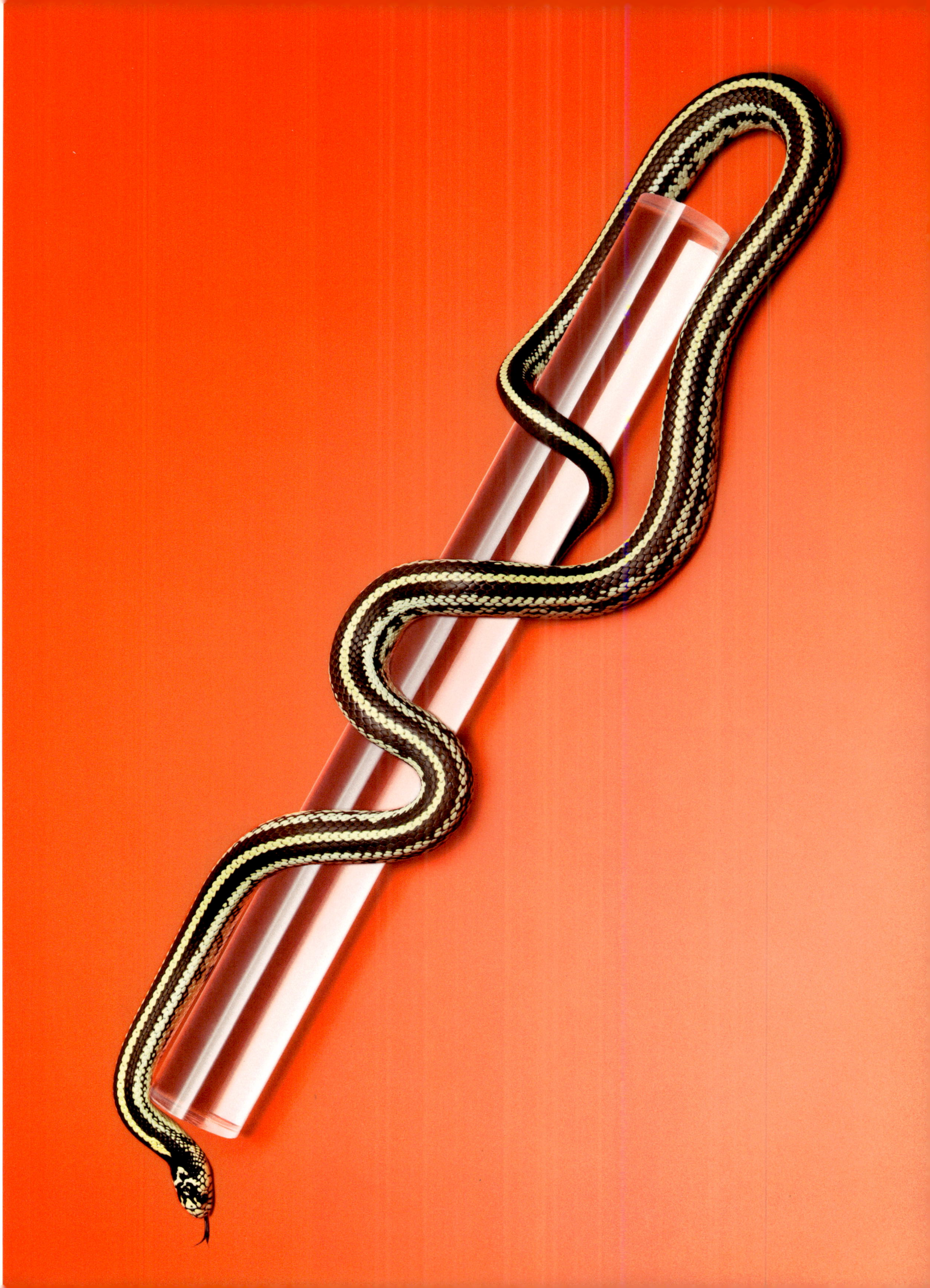

Matthieu Lavanchy and Jonas Marguet, *I Want to Believe*, 2013 © Matthieu Lavanchy and Jonas Marguet

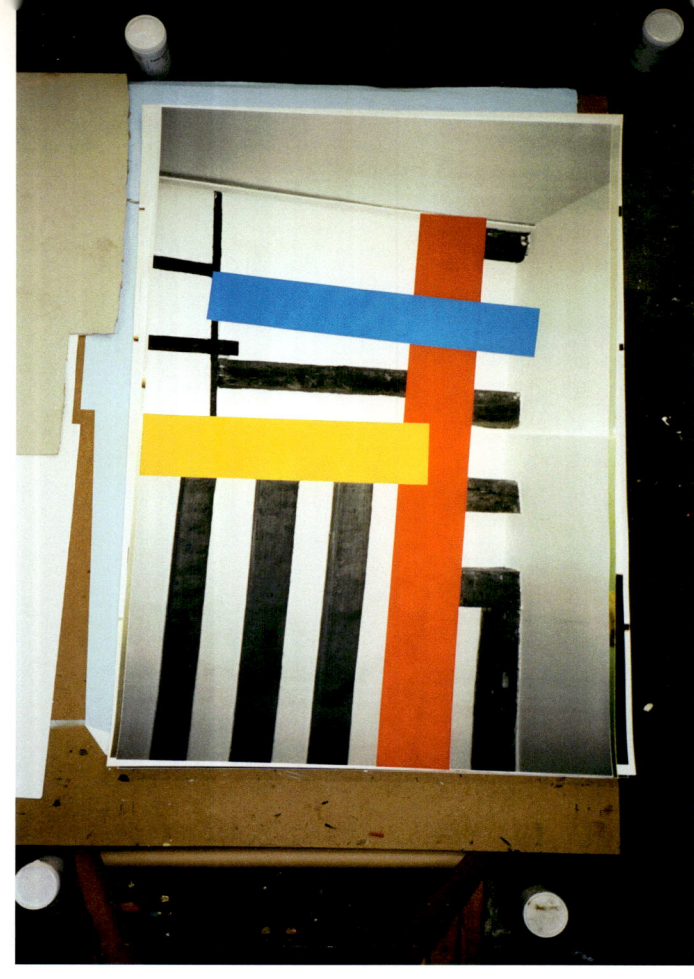

This page and opposite:
Linus Bill, from the
book *Topmotiviert*
(Highly motivated),
(Rollo, 2011)
All photographs courtesy
the artist

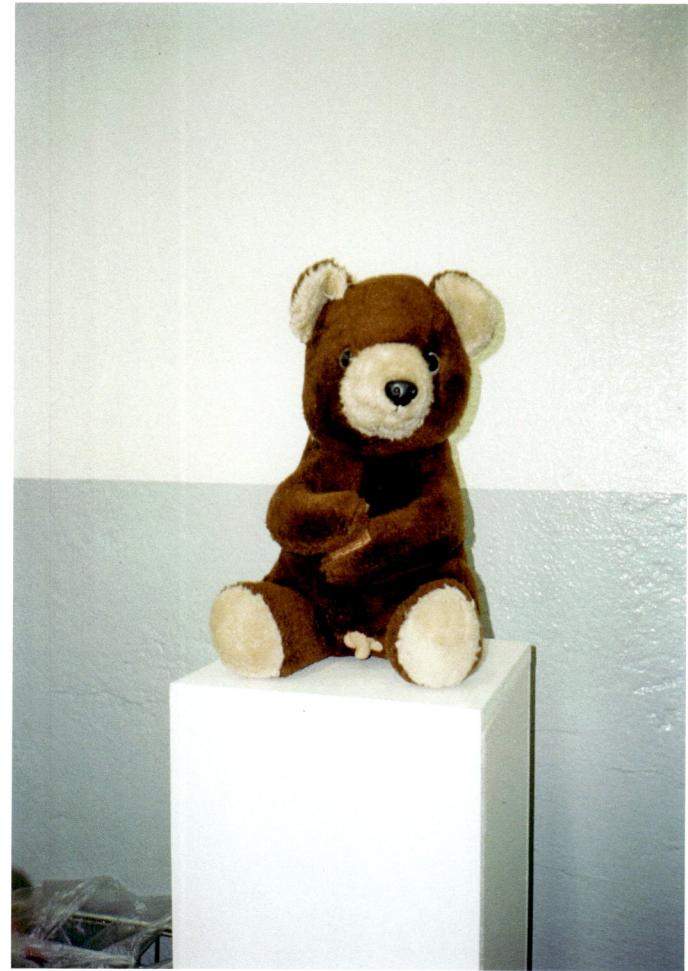

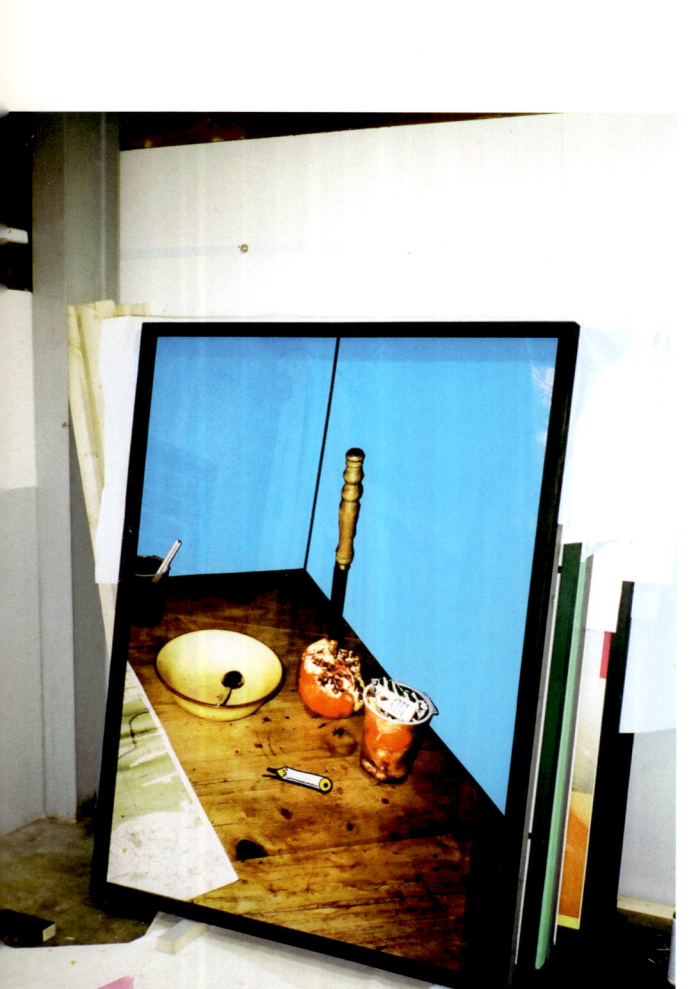

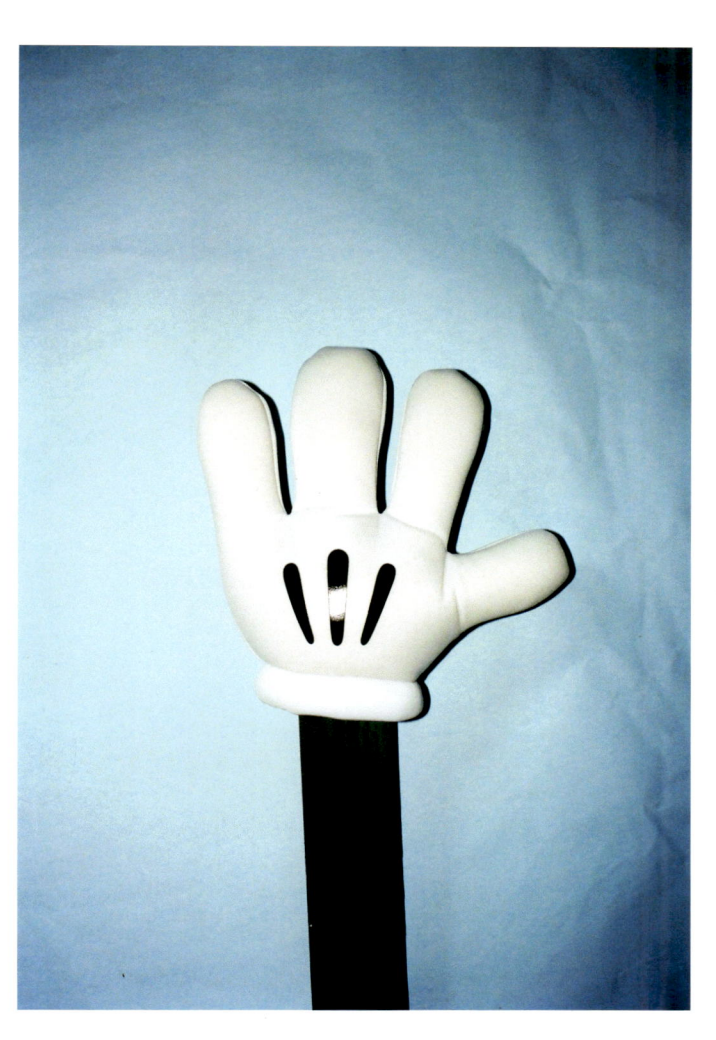
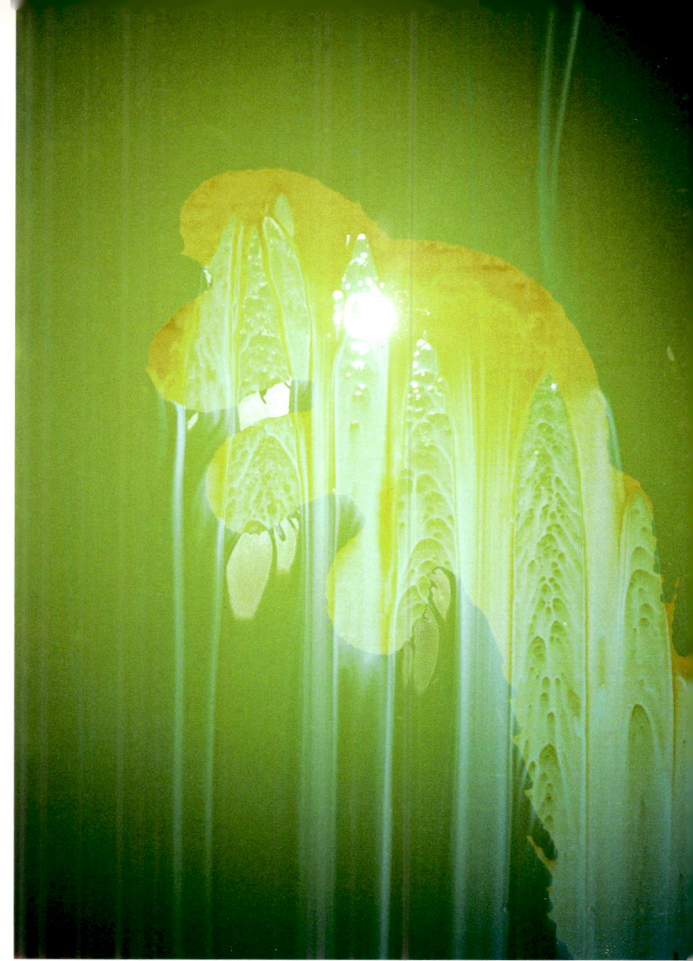
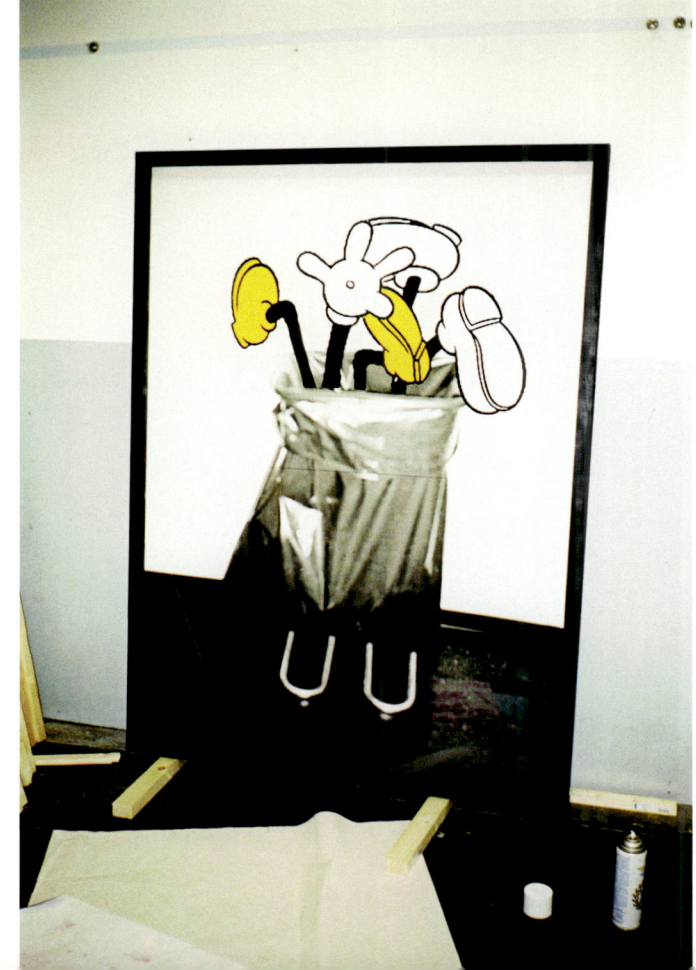

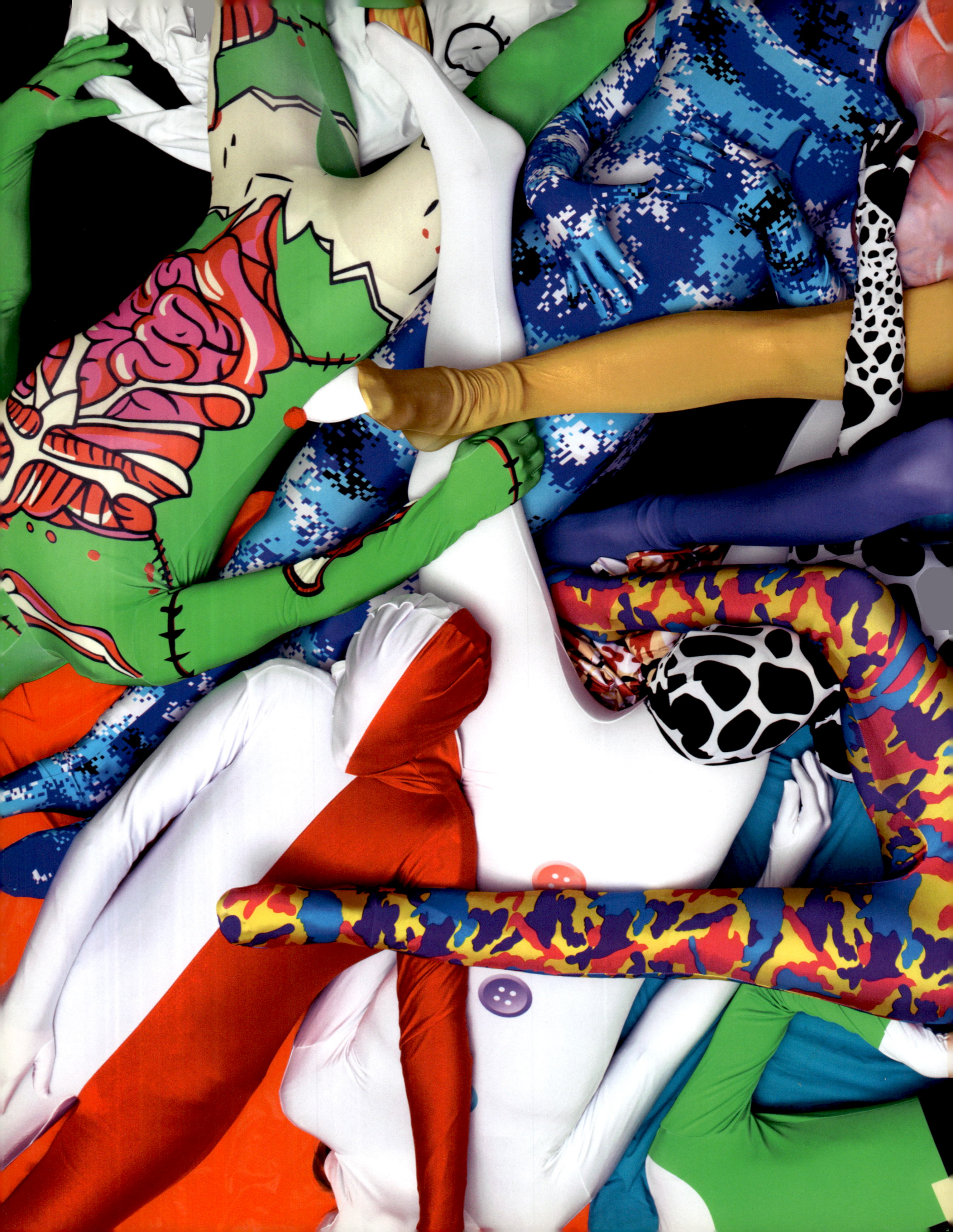

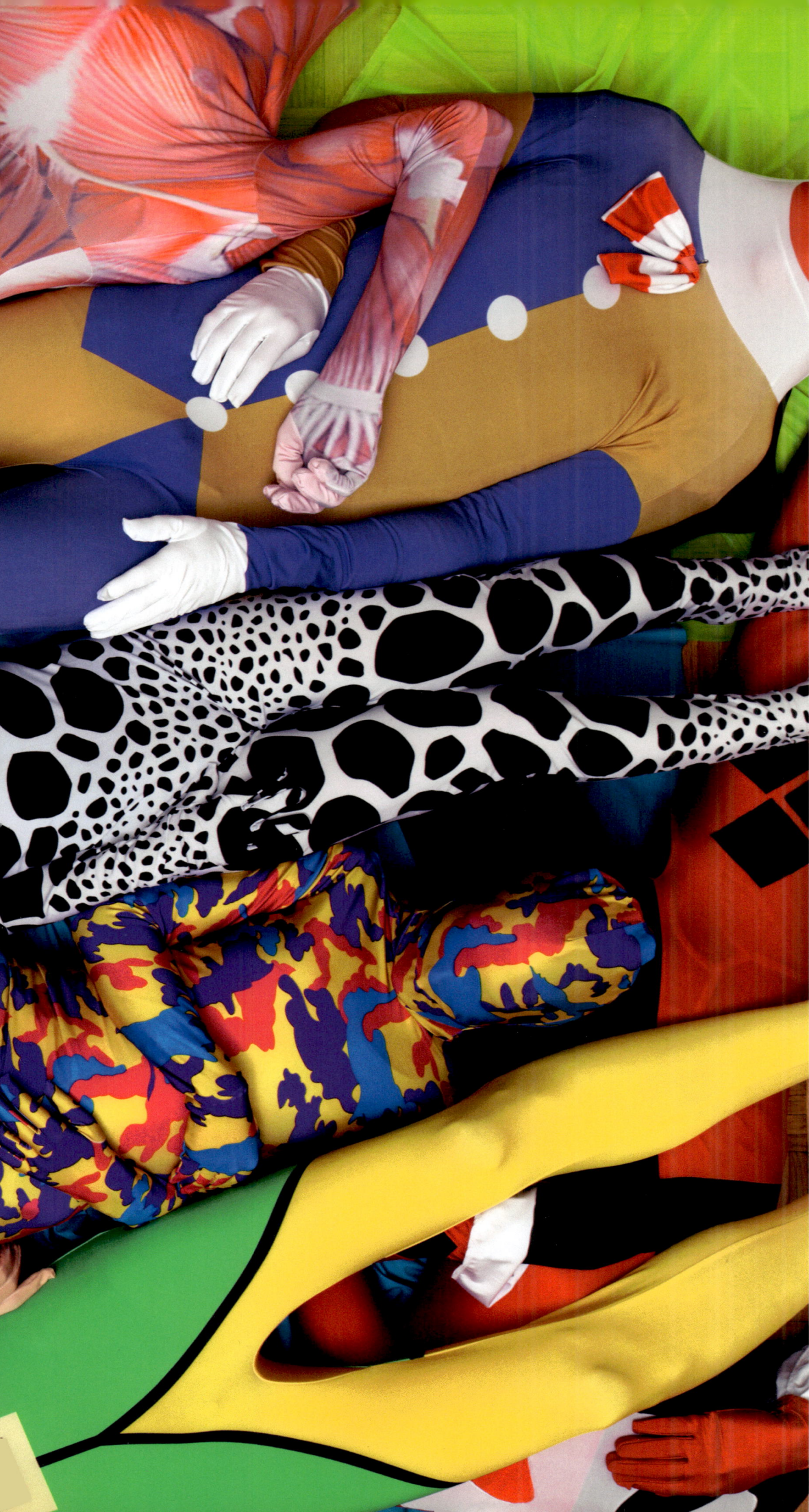

Olaf Breuning,
Pattern People, 2013
Courtesy the artist and Metro
Pictures, New York

In *Fotocronache: Photo-Reportage*, an amusing treatise on photography published in Italy in 1944, Bruno Munari staked out his position regarding the meaning of the picture-essay. Munari had been art director of the illustrated weekly *Tempo* from 1939 to 1943, and had mastered layouts for other Italian periodicals covering fashion, literature, and aviation; he was aware of the modern currency of photography and capable of engineering words and pictures on a page. "The camera," he noted, is "nothing but a very quick paintbrush." *Photo-Reportage* (published in English by Corraini in 2003) reveals Munari's understanding of photography as a playful game of pictures directed toward visual communication. Replacing the news with whimsical jokes, it includes a series of improbable picture-essays that poke fun at photojournalism and describe the life of a taxidermist, a nonexistent island of truffles, the fantastic world of toys, the endless academic definitions of art and *isms*, and a sequence of snapshots in a story titled "Due mani non bastano" ("Two Hands Are Not Enough")—about the frustrations of performing impossible tasks with two hands.

Photo-Reportage was Munari's statement about the exhilarating freedom of story-telling with photographs, proving that he could subvert the rules of the magazines he knew so well. Concurrently, he published another hilarious essay in the design magazine *Domus*, featuring a clumsy performance that mimicked a man trying to sit on an uncomfortable chair, a tongue-in-cheek comment about traditional petty-bourgeois values imposed on interior decoration versus what he championed as art that was serially produced. Munari was the kind of artist who wanted to transform codified visual language. "How can this be done differently?" he would ask, arriving at unexpected and inventive solutions that exploited the possibilities of any given instrument—the camera, the projector, the brush, even a piece of paper thrown in the air. His name became internationally recognized in industrial design and for his prolific output of children's books, but his art was much more eclectic and unpredictable than these projects suggest. One can argue that photography was the medium that fulfilled most effectively his pursuit of a democratic language, reaching out to people in ways that were both surprising and fun.

Munari's involvement with photography began early in his creative life. Initially an abstract painter based in Milan, he joined the Futurist movement in 1927, alert to the city's creative stimuli and artistic circles. At the Galleria del Milione, Munari was exposed to the work of Max Ernst, Wassily Kandinsky, and Lázsló Moholy-Nagy, among many others. In 1930 he opened a graphic design studio with a Futurist painter and friend, Riccardo "Ricas" Castagnedi, and this joint venture broadened his network across German, Russian, and Swiss graphic arts. These multiple threads converged into Munari's pivotal research on space and time, and into his multiform involvement with photography.

Bruno Munari's Light Games

Maria Antonella Pelizzari

Opposite:
Aldo Ballo,
***Bruno Munari,* 1956**
Courtesy Archivio
Aldo Ballo, Milan

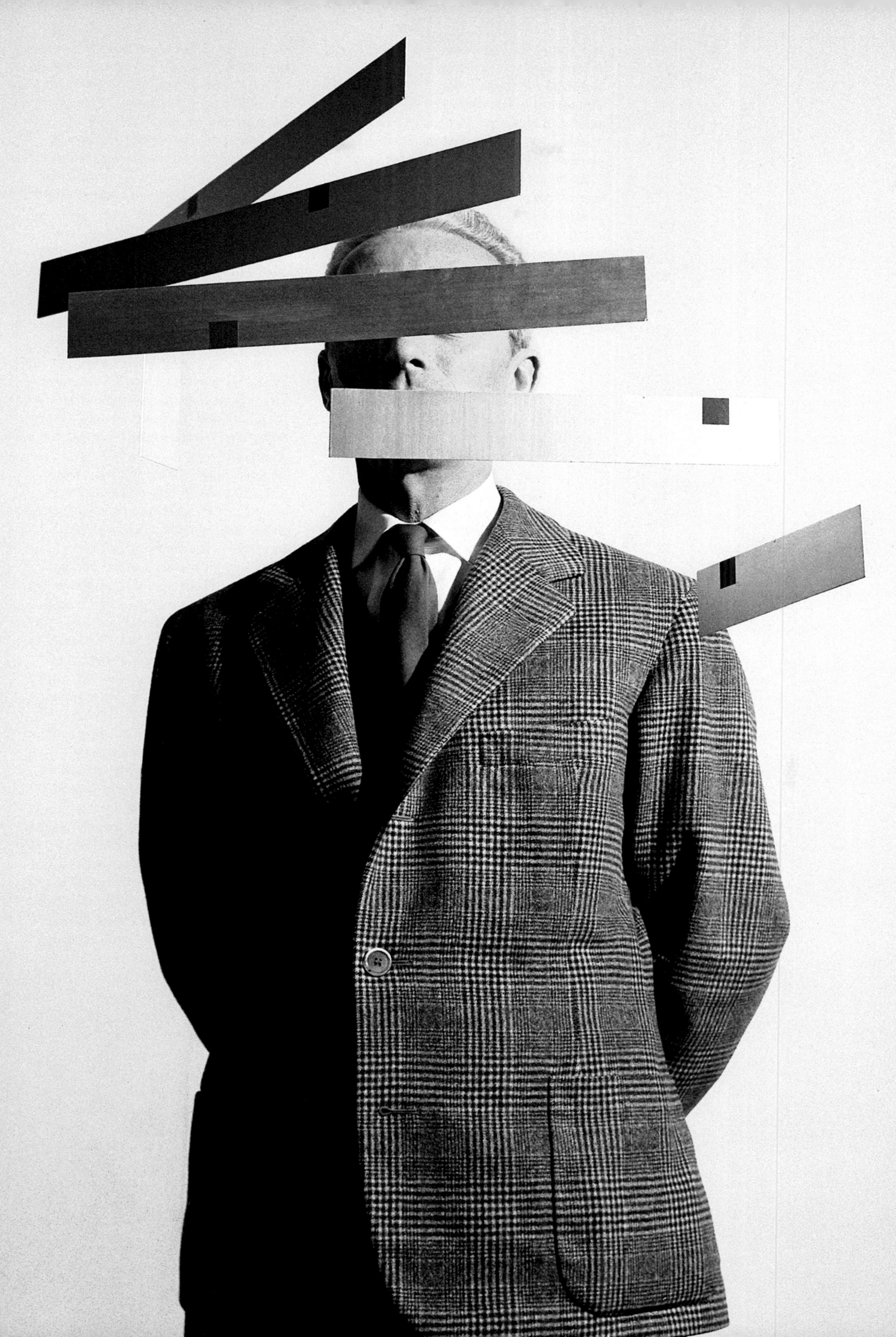

In 1934 Munari cosigned the "Manifesto tecnico della aeroplastica futurista" ("Technical Manifesto of Futurist Aeroplastics"), which proposed a new equivalence of machine and art. True to form, Munari contributed to this movement with "useless machines": minimal kinetic sculptures made of light-weight materials—cardboard, glass balls, fragile wooden sticks, silk thread—that changed configurations randomly, depending on environmental conditions. These machines were "useless" because they could not be assimilated into the chain of consumer goods; they functioned as art because they created unpredictable shapes and shadows. Munari channeled this research on the invisible and the imponderable into quirky and spectacular experiments with light and abstraction. Along with his kinetic explorations, he produced a wide range of photograms and conceived spatial installations with colorful optical projections. Aldo Ballo's portrait of Munari with his face deleted by his own creation, and Federico Patellani's montage of the artist in his studio, drawing a shimmering curve with a flashlight amid his design work and photographic mementos, hint at Munari's shaping of new worlds, working across media. Defined by one of his peers as "the magician of spaces," Munari envisioned a cosmic dimension where space defies logic, generating unforeseen patterns.

The exploration of photography as abstraction went alongside Munari's cut-and-paste work. Throughout the 1930s he contributed to periodicals several bizarre, at times subversive, photomontages that took on the politics of Fascism. One has to work through the artist's visual puns and incongruent shapes to discover the hidden meanings and veiled satire of these works— surrealist divertissements, ambiguous and nonsensical. For example, one of his montages of the modern "new woman" —half-woman, half-plane—hinted at the bombastic mythologies of aviation. A series of self-portraits in which Munari performs for the camera became another way for the artist to be lighthearted. He seems to make fun of Futurism in these clumsy masquerades, in which he wears a baggy poncho that could double as a tablecloth and a floppy airplane that hangs around his neck. The exaggerated size of his baseball gloves and the long barrel of the gun he holds—like some deranged Mexican bandit—signify the ludicrous pretense of power.

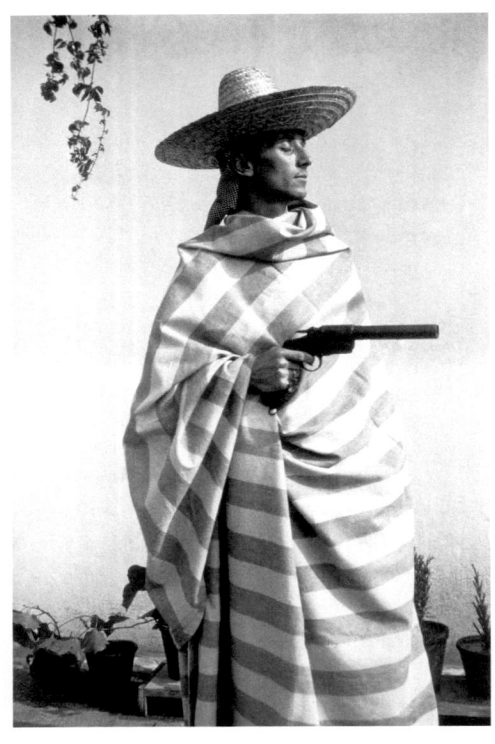 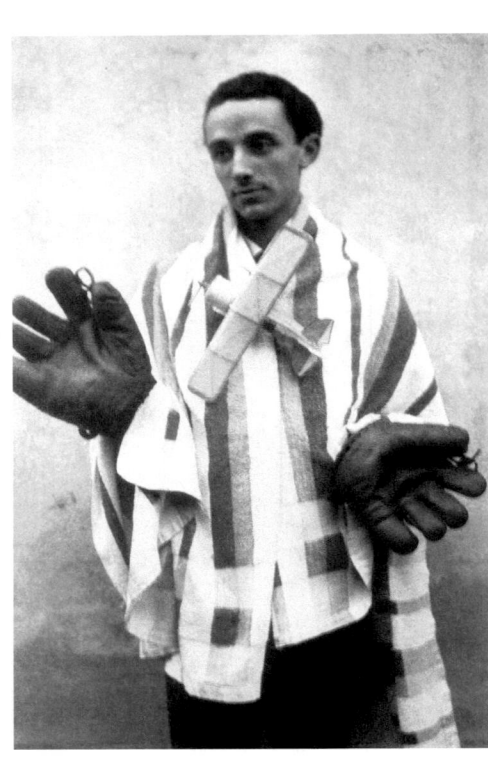

Left and right:
Bruno Munari,
Self-portrait, 1940
© Estate of Bruno Munari,
courtesy Archivio Fotografico,
Fondazione 3M, Milan

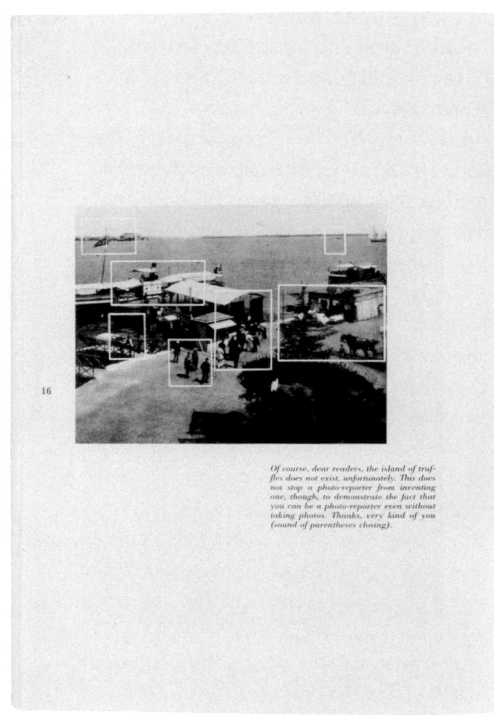

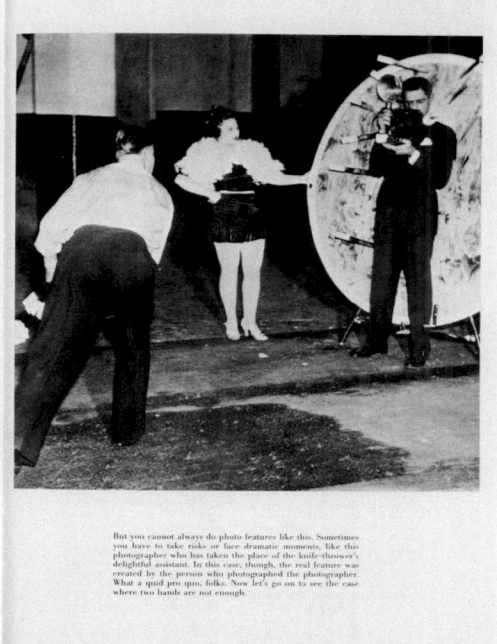

Munari's ultimate creative aim was to break the barrier between artist and world. Performances, interactive art, and work with new media were hallmarks of his practice—from these early experiments to work created decades later. In 1972 he published *Xerografia*, his first book on Xerox art. There he noted:

> *If you want to achieve an art by everyone […] you must find the tools that facilitate the artistic operation and at the same time give everyone the methods and the preparation necessary to operate. […] The technological possibilities of our era allow anyone to produce something with aesthetic value. They allow anyone to destroy his inferiority complex in the face of "art," to put into action his creativity, so long humbled.*

On October 24, 1967, his sixtieth birthday, Munari invited friends to a performance at Milan's Danese Galleria. Feeding a Xerox 914, he layered objects, surfaces, and lines on its scanning bed, demonstrating that the machine could generate fantastic, free, "original" images; hundreds of sheets of Xeroxed papers came out, demonstrating yet another form of writing with light. Munari's performance proved that a machine could produce unpredictable shapes, and it allowed his friends to participate, so that they might learn and marvel at their own discoveries; it was, in a sense, a summary of the reasons for his involvement with photography.

(*Special thanks to Luca Zaffarano for his assistance with this article.*)

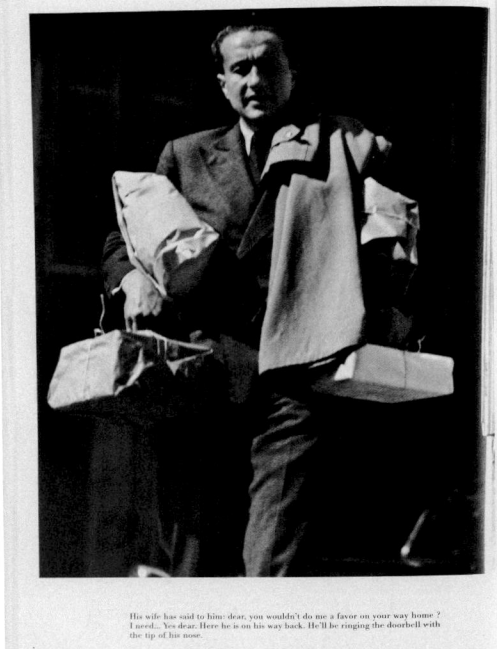

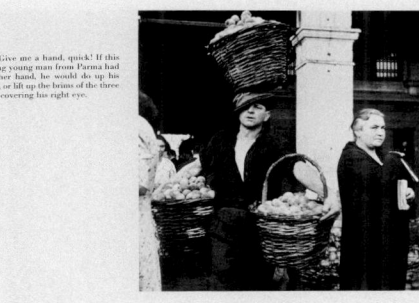

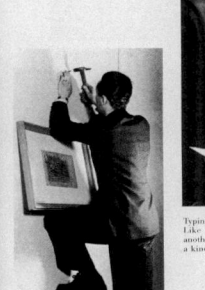

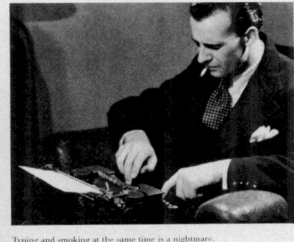

Pages from Bruno Munari, *Fotocronache Photo-Reportage: From the Island of Truffles to Quid Pro Quo*, Corraini Edizioni, Mantua, Italy, 2003 (first published as *Fotocronache di Munari: Dall'isola dei tartufi al qui pro quo*, by Gruppo Editoriale Domus, Milan, 1944)
Courtesy Corraini Edizioni

Maria Antonella Pelizzari, a professor of art history at Hunter College and the Graduate Center, City University of New York, is the author of *Photography and Italy* (Reaktion, 2011) and curated the 2012 exhibition *Peripheral Visions: Italian Photography in Context, 1950s–Present* at the Bertha and Karl Leubsdorf Art Gallery at Hunter College, New York.

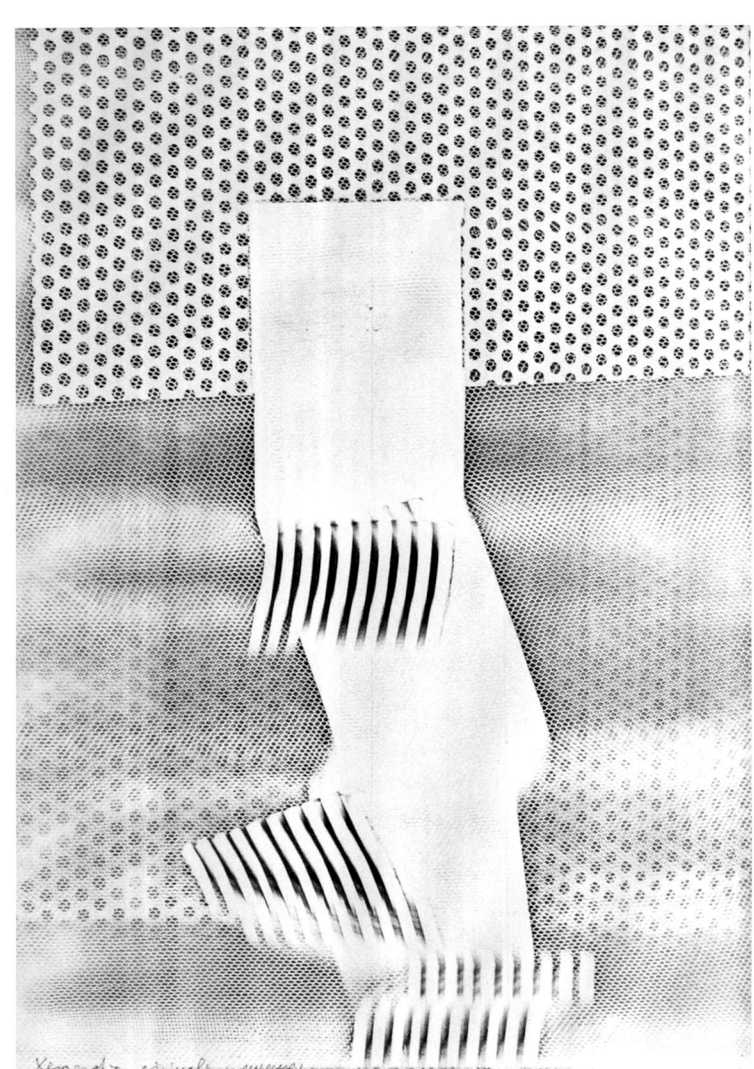

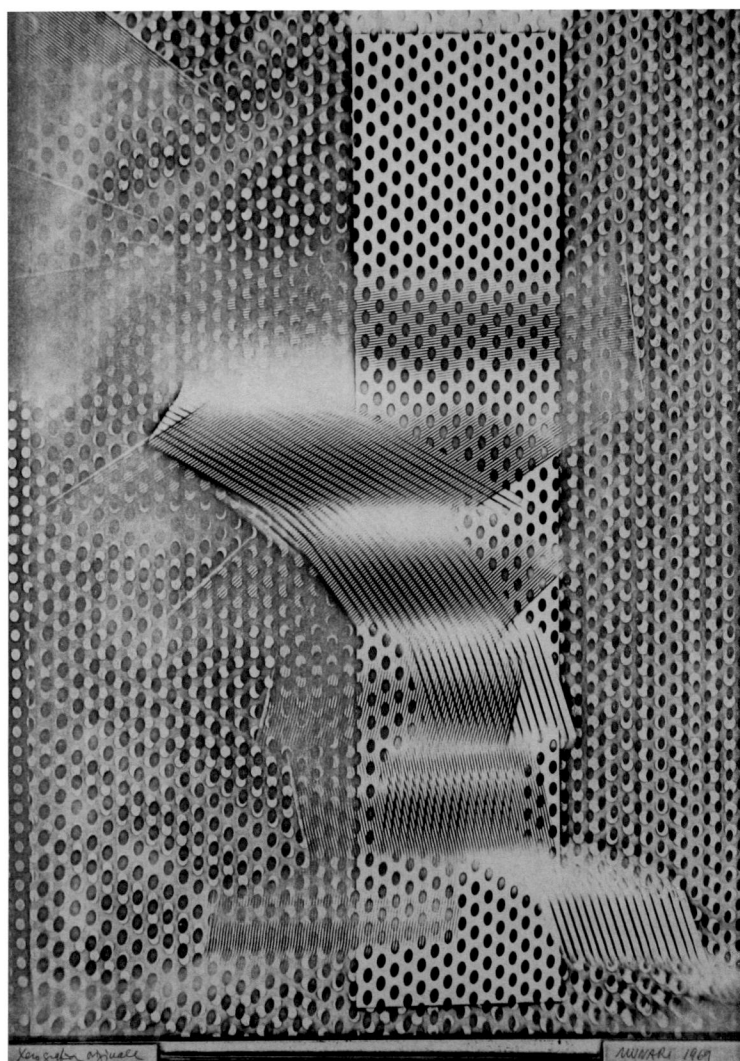

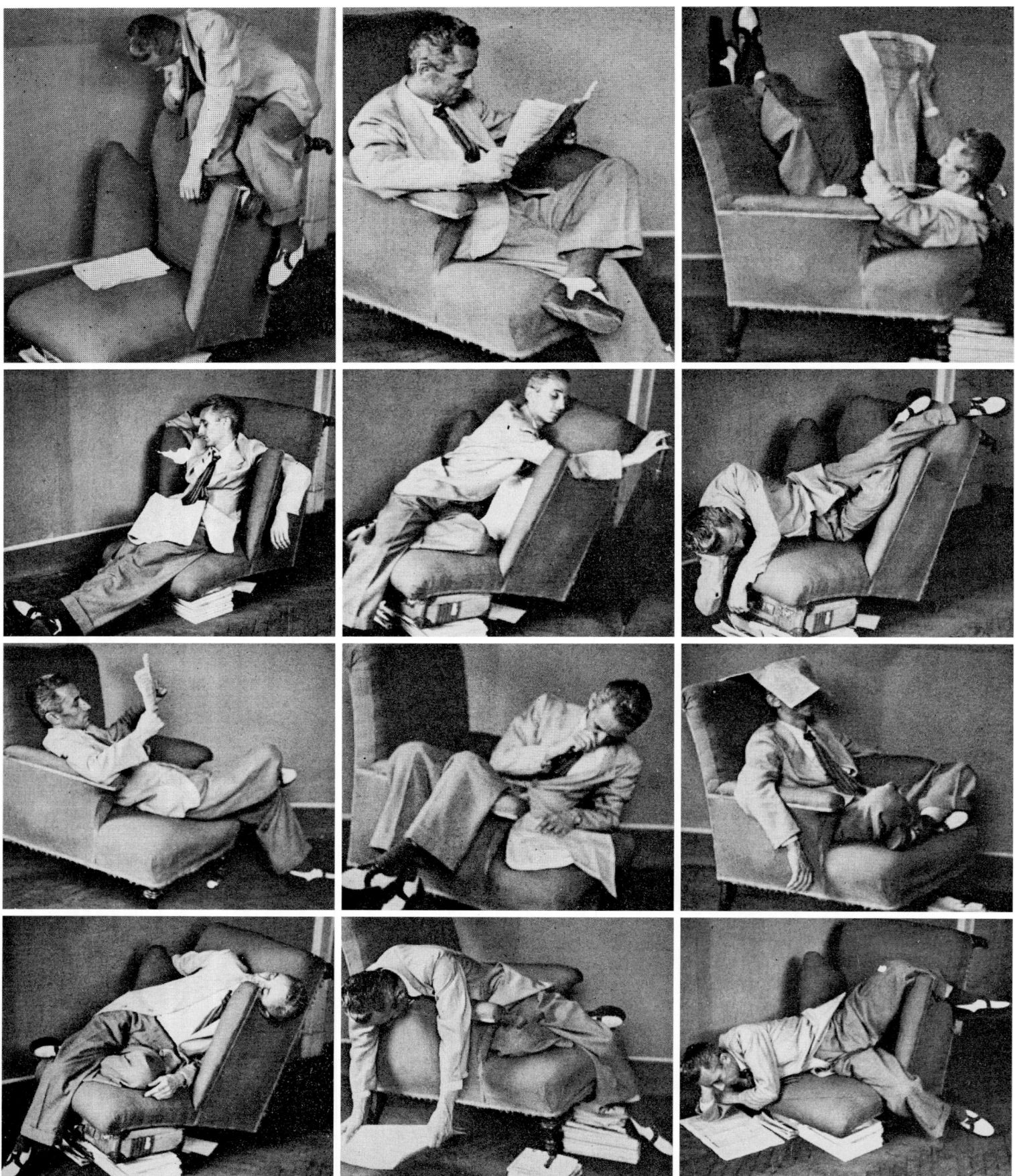

Bruno Munari, *Ricerca della comodità in una poltrona scomoda* (Seeking comfort in an uncomfortable chair), Corraini Edizioni, Mantua, Italy, 2012. Photographs first published in *Domus* magazine, no. 202, October 1944
Courtesy Corraini Edizioni

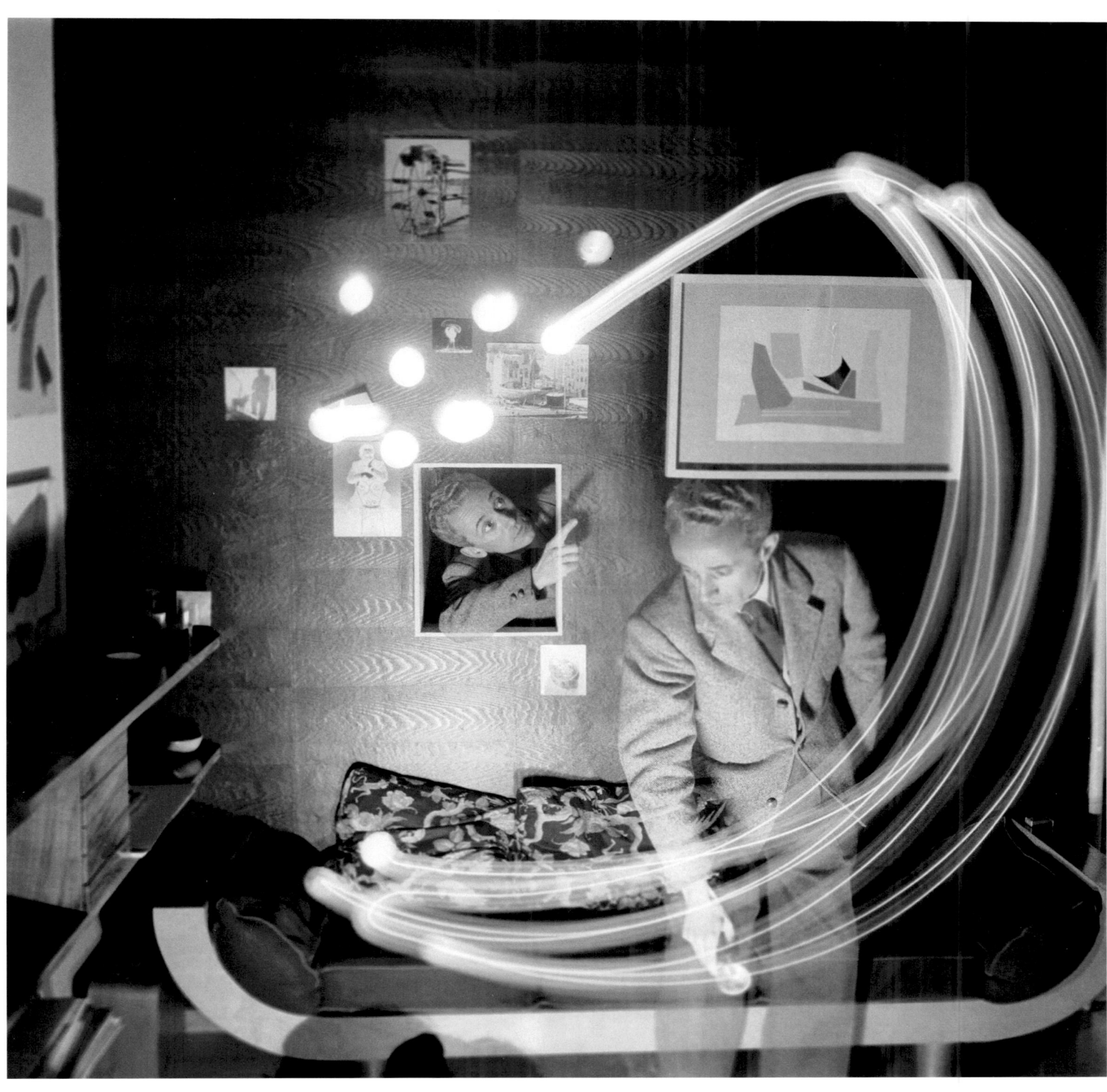

Federico Patellani,
Bruno Munari, Milan, **1950**
© Federico Patellani—
Regione Lombardia/Museo
di Fotografia Contemporanea,
Milan

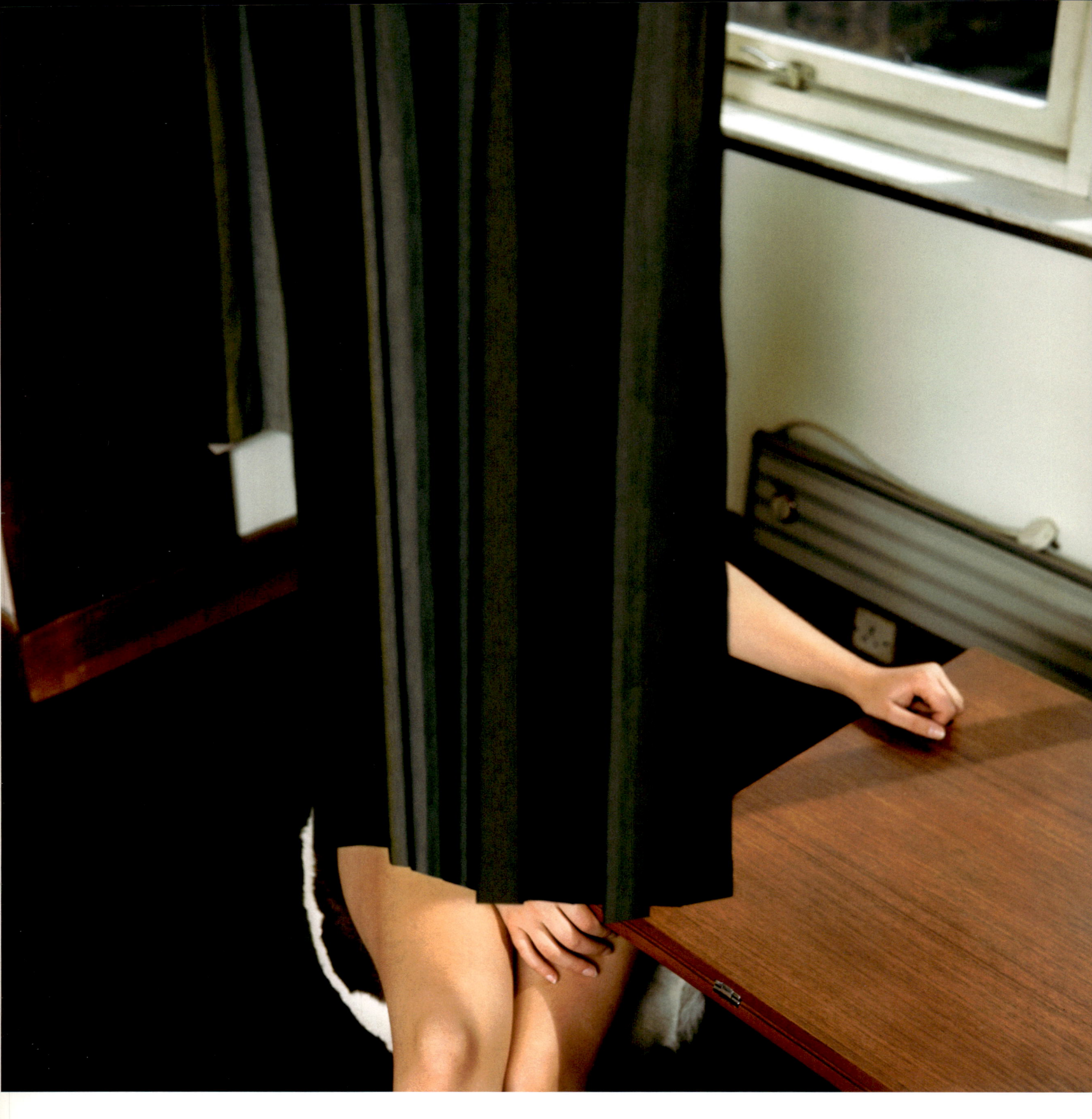

Drape (Colour I), 2011

In her *Drape* series, Eva Stenram plays with found images, pinups from the 1960s. The title refers to the curtains that are a pervasive element of studio pornography. This is digital montage with a particular set of rules. Although Photoshop allows images to be combined in infinite ways, Stenram works only with what is already found inside the original frame of the photograph. She copies and pastes sections of the image, extending the curtains to cover most of the figure. The bold pleats of fabric look familiar, strangely right even as they create a jarring effect. Images with a customary set of studio conventions become mysterious, both witty and slightly menacing.

As background usurps foreground the remaining bits of exposed flesh take on heightened importance. Some aspects of the women's poses—a pointed toe or a leg cocked out toward the lower-right corner—underline pinup clichés. In the absence of faces, breasts, or genitals, hand gestures take on added poignancy. We are redirected from the central figures to the superficial details of their surroundings, a fetishist's delight of tactile surfaces, from sheepskin to vinyl to velvet. It is hard to know where we are: the shallow spaces teeter between actual domestic environments and photographers' studios. Some of the curtains hang in front of real windows, while others appear to cover blank studio walls.

While Stenram interrupts the conventional staging of male desire, she embraces visual, and specifically photographic, pleasure. For this series she worked with pages from the 1960s U.S. men's magazine *Cavalcade*, and with anonymous black-and-white negatives of the same era. The images are classically composed and exposed, with formal satisfactions that carry over into Stenram's revised versions of them. The color magazine images retain the specific gritty hues of their period printing process. In exhibition, the pictures have been printed and framed to echo the scale and presence of 1960s art photography.

There is another level of visual pleasure in tracing this artist's intervention, especially noting the decisions she has made in finishing the jagged edges of the drapes. The digital manipulation is not meant to be illusionistic. The drapes have a stiff frontality that does not wrap around the figures, so they take on a fascination of their own. Stenram's gesture is almost puritanical; it imposes modesty on the female figures, shields them from a predatory gaze. Yet in obscuring the central action of the pictures, the artist draws us into a guessing game. Photography is so good at *showing* things that it is easy to forget how well it can activate the imagination. Hiding the main attractions of pornographic images, Stenram invites us to seek them in our minds. What are the models' expressions? Their hair and makeup? Their physiques?

Stenram has a history of working with loaded source imagery, ranging from family photographs to famous hoax pictures to NASA images of Mars. In each case her extensions and erasures reveal unexpected aspects of the originals and open up new spaces for exploring the imaginary.

Eva Stenram: Drape

Lucy Soutter

Lucy Soutter is an artist, critic, and art historian. She teaches at the Royal College of Art in London and is the author of *Why Art Photography?* (Routledge, 2013).

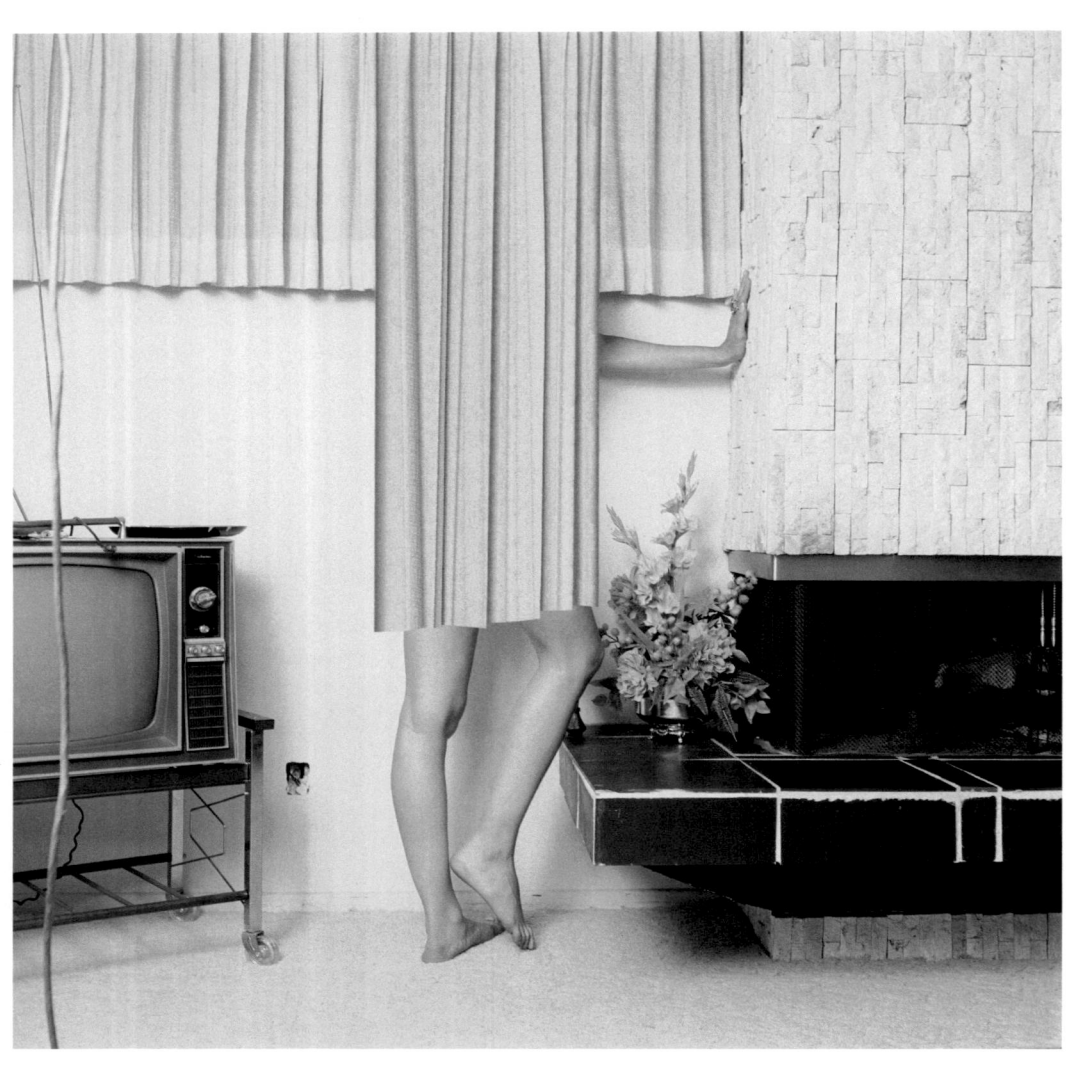

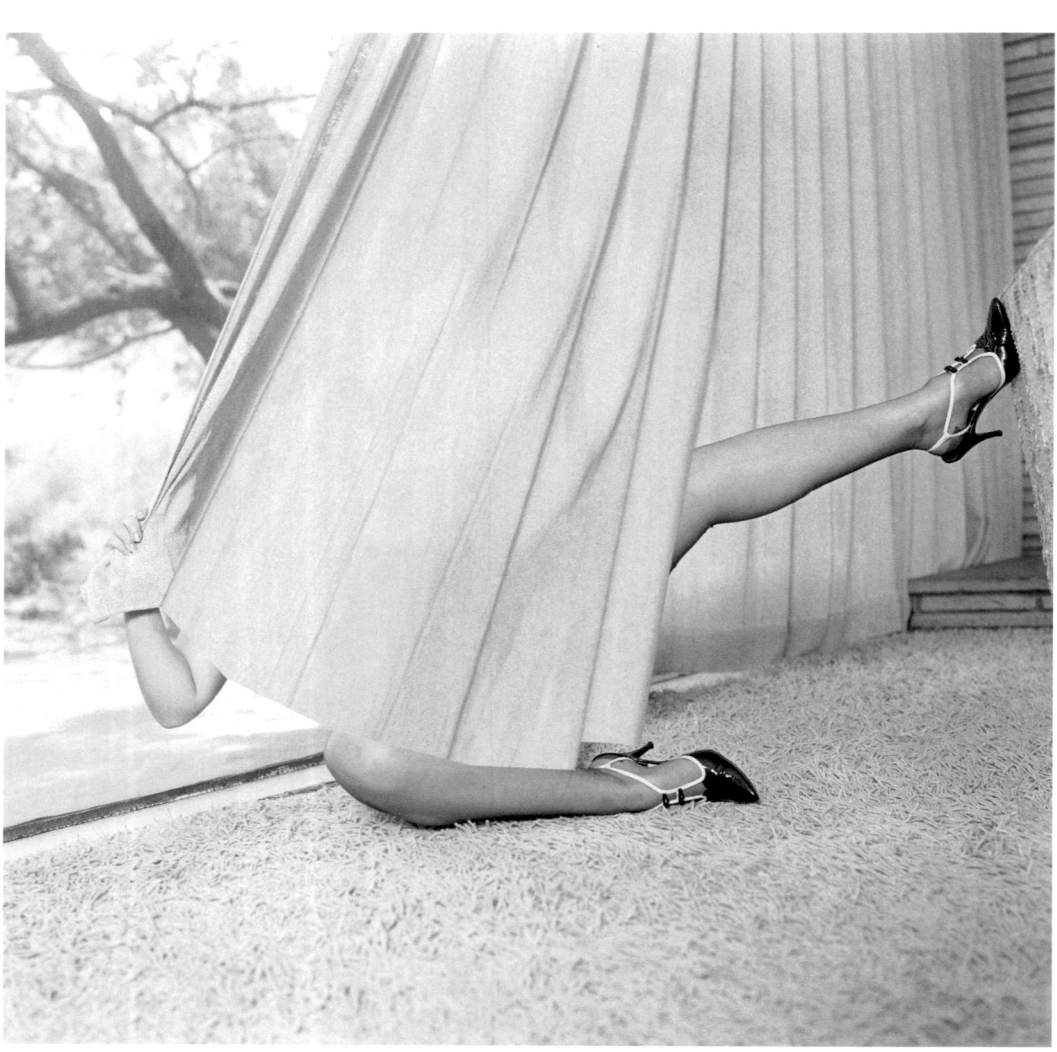

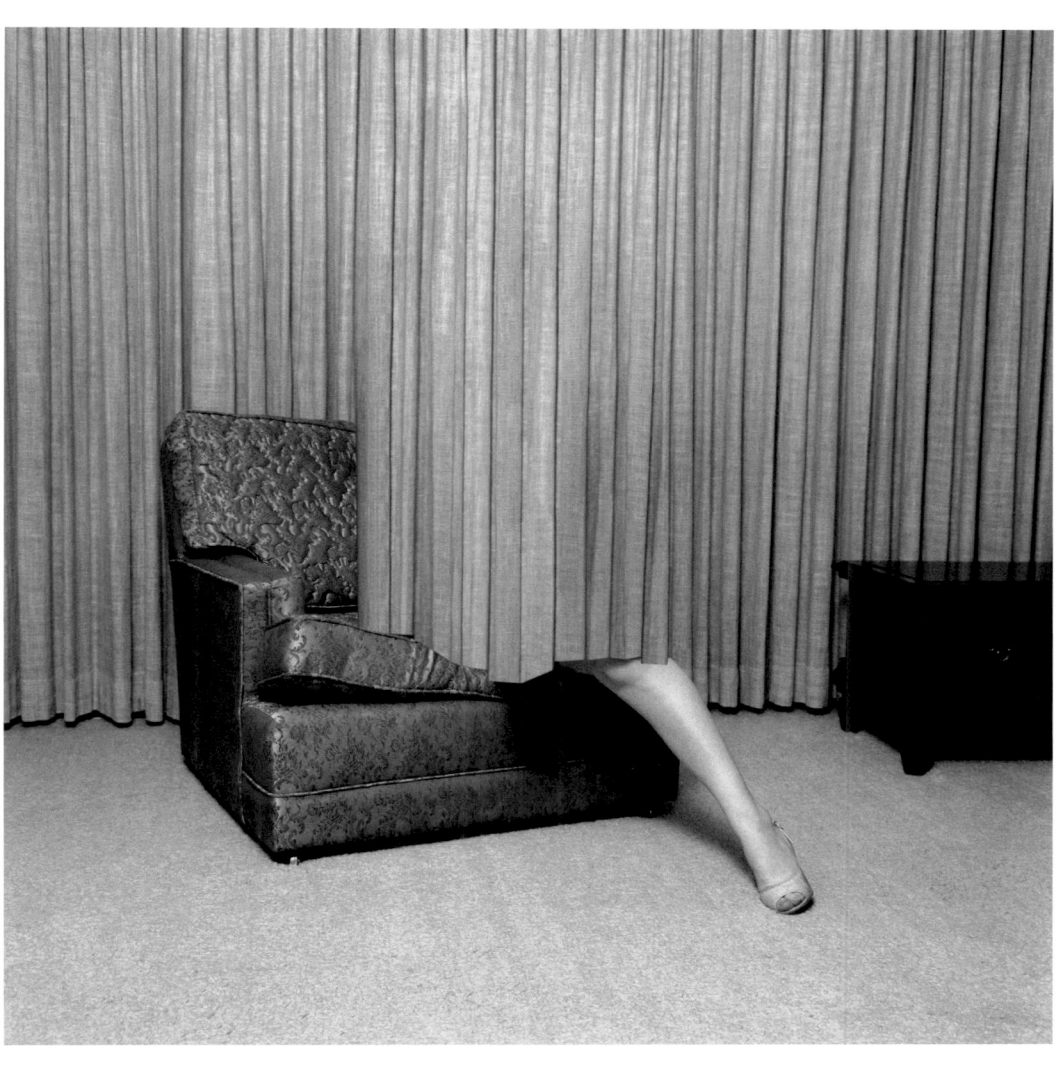

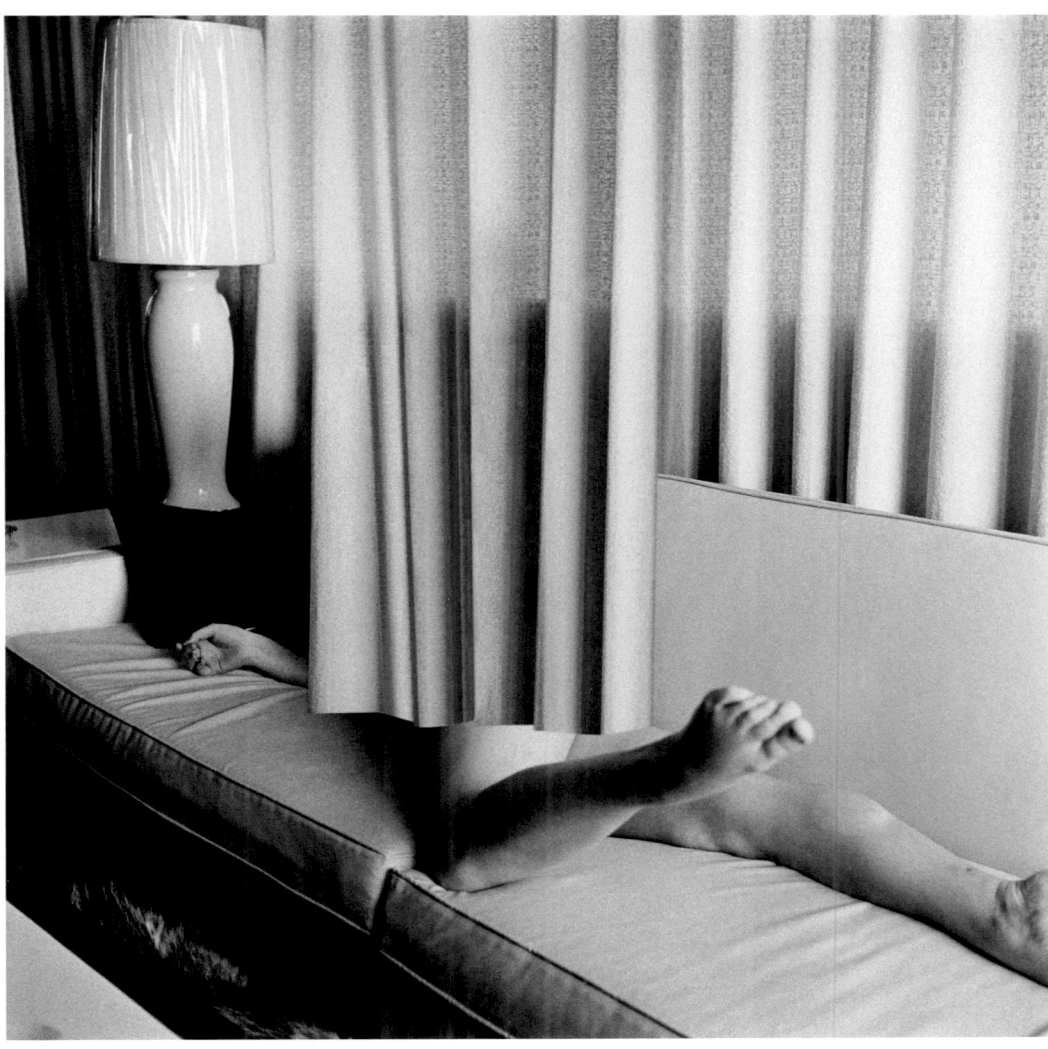

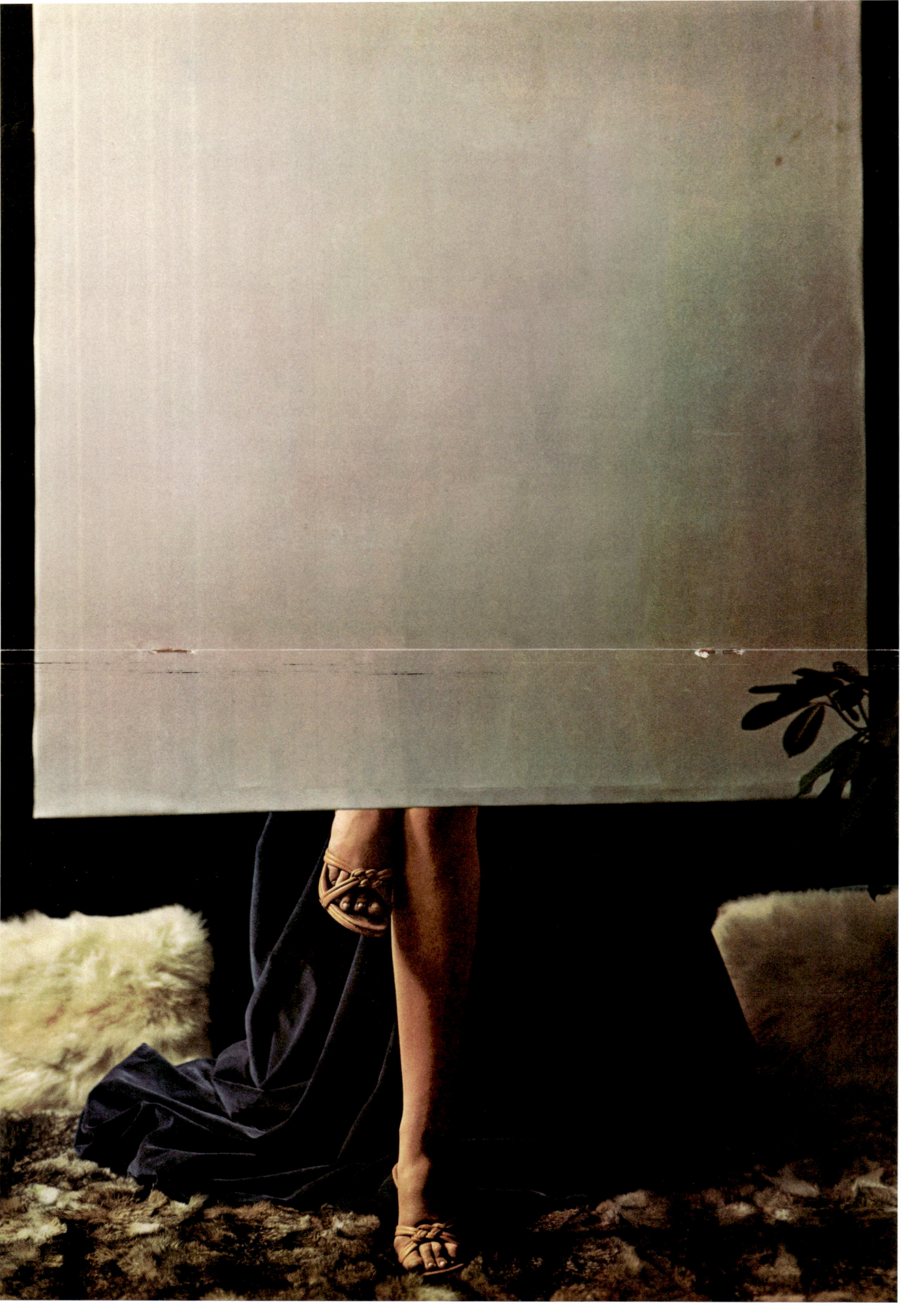

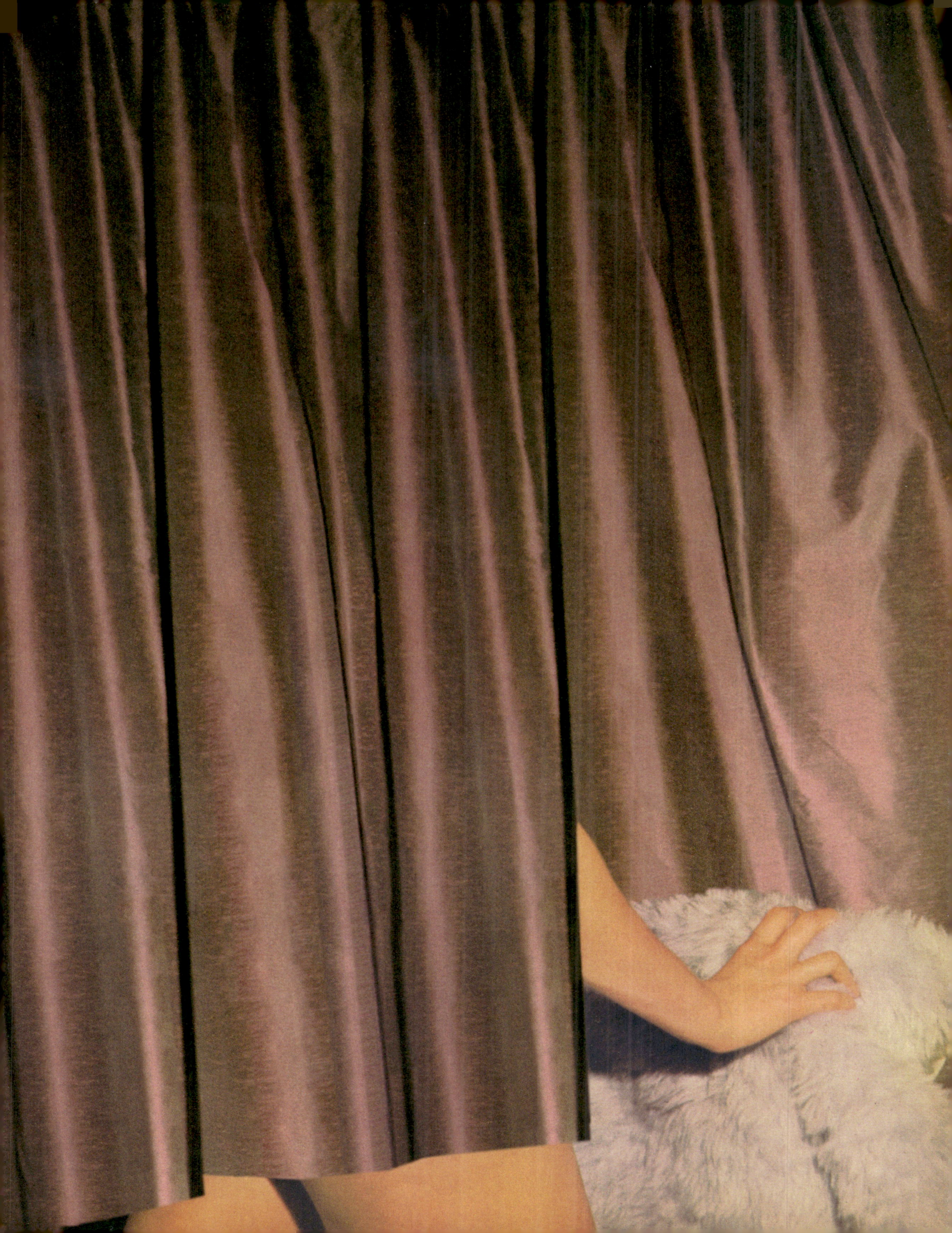

Object Lessons
Dr. Julius Neubronner's Miniature Pigeon Camera
1903

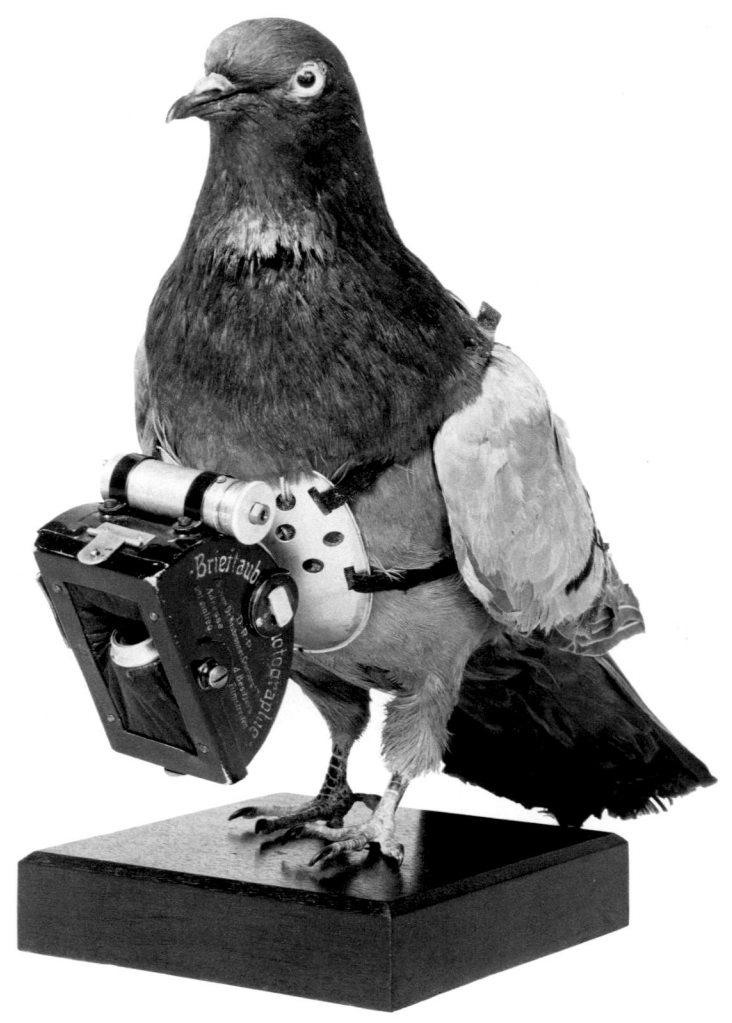

Courtesy Deutsches Museum, Munich

Nadar famously produced the first aerial photographs in 1858, when he floated above Paris in a hot-air balloon with camera in tow. Approximately fifty years later, German pharmacist Julius Neubronner devised a way to literalize the term for such pictures: "Vogelauge Ansicht," or *bird's-eye view*. After inventing a lightweight, miniature camera with a time-release shutter, Neubronner affixed to it a pair of tiny straps and slipped them around the wings of homing pigeons he had already trained to deliver medicines. The pigeons would be released from up to sixty miles' distance and fly directly home, automatically snapping pictures along the way.

The birds' aerial-reconnaissance images were popular among photography and aviation enthusiasts, in particular an early shot of the Schlosshotel Kronberg in which the photographer's wingtips can be seen. Governments were quick to spot the technique's potential. Pigeons had long been used for delivering written communications such as telegrams; even without control over a bird's exact location, speed, or direction, World War I battlefield tests using pigeon photography were encouraging. Yet their tactical usefulness was outrun by rapidly advancing aviation technology. Because of this, today we're inclined to see Neubronner's invention as a precursor not of surveillance drones but of *Winged Migration*, the NYU "Hawk Cam," and countless YouTube videos. The memory of this photographic enterprise has been domesticated—like the birds Neubronner so carefully trained.

— The Editors